Earls of Paradise

Wetland: Life in the Somerset Levels
Restoration: The Rebuilding of Windsor Castle
Perch Hill: A New Life
Sea Room
Power and Glory
Atlantic Britain
Men of Honour: Trafalgar and the Making of the English Hero

Earls
of Paradise

ADAM NICOLSON

HarperPress
An Imprint of HarperCollins*Publishers*

HarperCollins*Publishers*
77–85 Fulham Palace Road,
Hammersmith, London W6 8JB

www.harpercollins.co.uk

Published by HarperCollins*Publishers* in 2008

1

A catalogue record for this book
is available from the British Library

ISBN 978 0 00 724052 4

Maps by John Gilkes

Set in PostScript Linotype Minion
with Janson and Castellar display by
Rowland Phototypesetting Ltd, Bury St Edmunds, Suffolk

Printed and bound in Great Britain by Clays Ltd, St Ives plc

For Susan Watt,
with many thanks for so many years
of guidance, support and wisdom

Contents

Illustrations

View of Chalke Downland. *David Reed/Alamy*

Bluebells and Oak Trees in Grovely Wood Wiltshire. *Paul Glendell Photography/Photographer's Direct*

Ebble at Alvediston. © *Warren A Stallard/Photographer's Direct*

Wilton Estate map of the 17th Century showing Grovely wood. *Reproduced by permission of the 18th Earl of Pembroke and Montgomery and the Trustees of the Wilton House Trust, Wilton House/Photo: (WSRO 2057/S/3) Steve Hobbs, Wiltshire Record Office.*

A Wiltshire sheepfold, *c.* 1950's. *Eagle Photos (Cheltenham). Ltd 1951*

'Haymaking'. *The Museum of English Rural Life, University of Reading.*

Map of Wylye Village , 1742. *(WSRO 628/7/1) Wiltshire & Swindon Archives/ Wiltshire and Swindon Record Office.*

William Herbert, 1st Earl of Pembroke. *Netherlandish, 16th Century, oil on panel. National Museum of Wales.*

Portrait of lady, unknown, thought to be Anne Parr by Hans Holbein the Younger. *C.* 1540, *chalk on paper. The Royal Collection* © *2007 Her Majesty Queen Elizabeth II.*

Silver medal of William Herbert, 1st Earl of Pembroke by Stephen Van Hanwyck, *c.* 1562. © *The Trustees of the British Museum.*

The Front of Wilton House, detail from the 'Survey of Lands for the 1st Earl of Pembroke', 1566, *pen and ink on vellum. Reproduced by permission of the 18th Earl of Pembroke and Montgomery and the Trustees of the Wilton House Trust, Wilton House/Photo: (WLN 275900) Steve Hobbs, Wiltshire Record Office.*

Henry Herbert, 2nd Earl of Pembroke *c.* 1590, *oil on canvas.* © *National Museum and Gallery of Wales, Cardiff/The Bridgeman Art Library.*

Mary Sydney nee Herbert, Countess of Pembroke by Nicholas Hilliard. *C.* 1590, *watercolour on vellum.* © *National Portrait Gallery, London.*

The funeral cortege of Sir Philip Sidney on its way to St Paul's Cathedral, 1587, engraved by Theodor de Bry. *The Stapleton Collection/The Bridgeman Art Library.*

William Herbert, 3rd Earl of Pembroke, by Daniel Mytens, *c.* 1626, *oil on canvas. Courtesy of The Weiss Gallery.*

Philip Herbert, 4th Earl of Pembroke, attributed to William Larkin, *c.* 1615, *oil on canvas. Audley End, Essex, UK/The Bridgeman Art Library.*

Portrait of Lady Anne Clifford, 3rd Countess of Dorset by William Larkin, *c.* 1700. *The National Trust Photo Library/Private Collection.*

Shepherd's Paradise: Proscenium and Standing Scene O & S 245) *pen and black ink, Inigo Jones. © Devonshire Collection, Chatsworth. Reproduced by permission of Chatsworth Settlement Trustees.*

Garden design from 'The Gardens of Wilton' by Isaac de Caus, *c.* 1645, *engraving. The Stapleton Collection/The Bridgeman Art Library.*

Philip, 4th Earl of Pembroke and his family by Anthony van Dyck, *c.* 1634, *oil on canvas. Reproduced by permission of the 18th Earl of Pembroke and Montgomery and the Trustees of the Wilton House Trust, Wilton House*

Philip, 4th Earl of Pembroke and his wife Lady Anne Clifford.

Philip and Charles Herbert.

Lady Mary Villiers.

Anna Sophia Herbert and her husband Robert Dormer, Earl of Carnarvon.

Portrait of Charles Dormer, 2nd Earl of Carnarvon by Sir Peter Lely, *c.* 1700. *Sotheby's Images, London.*

Endpapers: Philip, 4th Earl of Pembroke and his family by Anthony van Dyck, *c.* 1634, *oil on canvas. Reproduced by permission of the 18th Earl of Pembroke and Montgomery and the Trustees of the Wilton House Trust, Wilton House.*

Acknowledgements

First, I want to thank Steven Hobbs, the Wiltshire County Archivist, for the immense amount of time, expertise and patience he has given me when researching this book. His enthusiasm and ability to discover key documents in the enormous and marvellously rich collections he has under his care has never flagged. It has been the greatest of pleasures working with him.

The staff of Cambridge University Library, the National Archives, the House of Lords Journal Office, the British Library, Hatfield House and Sheffield Archives have all been equally generous and professional with the documents in their care.

In Wiltshire, Alison J. Maddock and John Chandler both steered me towards important changes of view and Rosalind Conklin Hays, the co-editor of the Wiltshire collection in the Records of Early English Drama series, generously made available her preliminary transcriptions from the Wiltshire Quarter Sessions Rolls, in particular the libel sung by Jane Norrice of Stoke Verdon (A1/110/1631E no 151), which appears here on pages 161–2.

The volumes published each year by the Wiltshire Record Society, including the key document for this book, *Surveys of the Manors of Philip, earl of Pembroke and Montgomery 1631–2*, edited by Eric Kerridge in 1953, have been invaluable, none more than the brilliant act of research and editorship performed by Dr Joseph Bettey in his *Wiltshire Farming in the Seventeenth Century*, published by the Record Society in 2005. There is no more remarkable account of rural England on the cusp of the medieval and the modern. For membership details and past volumes, please contact The Honorary

Secretary, Wiltshire Record Society, c/o Wiltshire and Swindon History Centre, Cocklebury Road, Chippenham SN15 3QN

At Wilton House itself, William Herbert, the Earl of Pembroke and Montgomery, Chris Rolfe, Ros Liddington, Nigel Bailey and Charlotte Spender have all gone well out of their way to help me and I am very grateful to them all.

Katherine Duncan-Jones, Paula Henderson, Susan Koslow, the late Sir Oliver Millar, Barbara Ravelhofer, Robert Sackville-West, Alexandra Samarine and Kim Wilkie have all in their different ways set me on better and truer paths.

I am grateful, as ever, to Caroline Dawnay, Zoe Pagnamenta, Hugh van Dusen, Vera Brice, Jane Beirn, Helen Ellis and above all Susan Watt for making the complex and drawn-out task of writing books like this into the pleasure it has always been.

MAPS

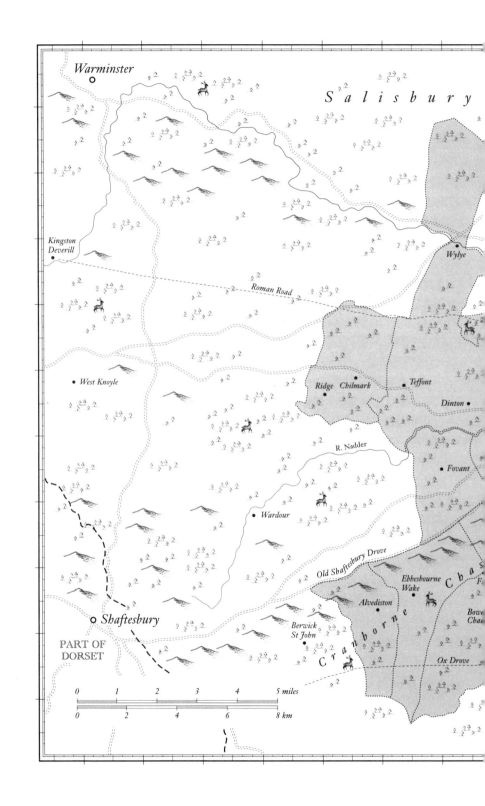

Warminster

Salisbury

Kingston
Deverill

Wylye

Roman Road

West Knoyle

Ridge Chilmark Teffont

Dinton

R. Nadder

Fovant

Wardour

Old Shaftesbury Drove

Ebbesbourne
Wake

Alvediston

Cranborne Chas

Shaftesbury

Berwick
St John

Bow
Cha

PART OF
DORSET

Ox Drove

0   1   2   3   4   5 miles

0   2   4   6   8 km

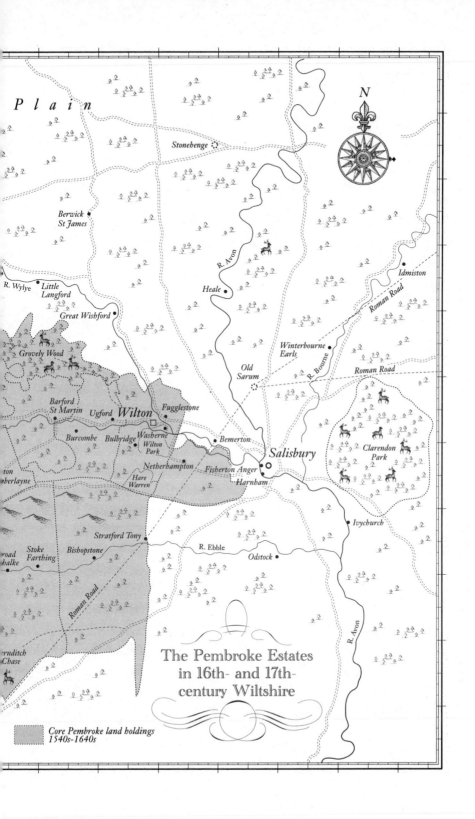

_P l a i n_

Stonehenge

N

Berwick
St James

R. Wylye • Little
Langford

R. Avon

Idmiston

Great Wishford

Heale

Roman Road

Grovely Wood

Winterbourne
Earls

R. Bourne

Barford
St Martin   Ugford _Wilton_   Fugglestone

Old
Sarum

Roman Road

Burcombe   Bulbridge Washerne
Wilton
Park

Bemerton

Salisbury

ton
berlayne

Netherhampton   Fisherton Anger

Clarendon
Park

Hare
Warren

Harnham

Stratford Tony

Ivychurch

R. Ebble

Stoke
Farthing   Bishopstone

Odstock •

road
halke

R. Avon

Roman Road

rnditch
Chase

The Pembroke Estates
in 16th- and 17th-
century Wiltshire

Core Pembroke land holdings
1540s-1640s

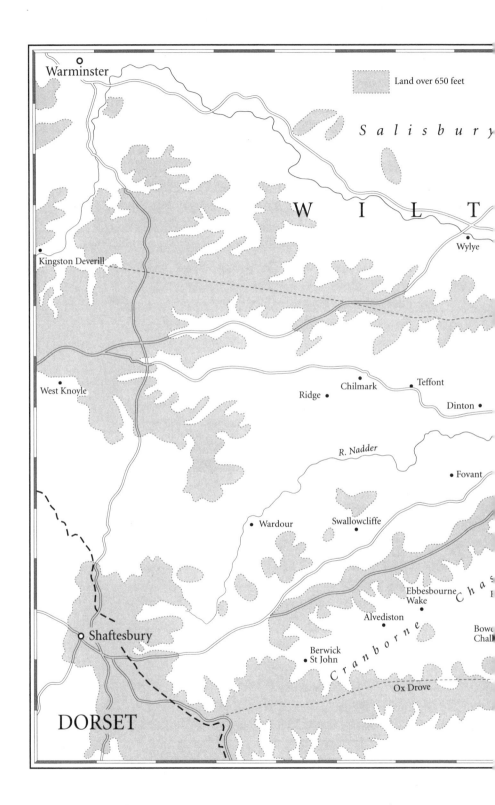

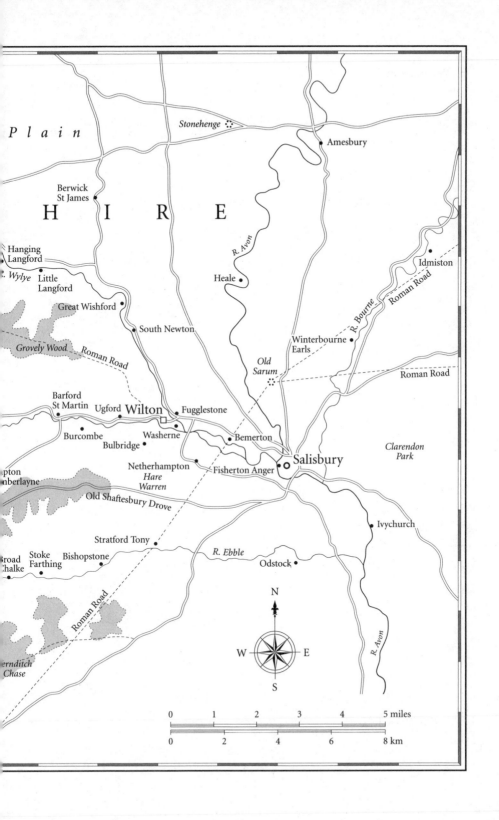

1

The Dream of Perfection

Arcadianism in Renaissance England
1520–1650

ENGLAND IN the sixteenth and seventeenth centuries dreamed of a lost world, an ideal and unapproachable realm of bliss and beauty. That realm had a name – Arcadia – and this book approaches the Arcadian ideal in three connected dimensions: across a long century – the arc of the English Renaissance from its birth in the 1520s to its death in the 1640s; through a family – the Earls of Pembroke, their wives and children, who were in the grip of that ideal over three generations, and whose standing, influence, wealth and appetite for beauty set them at the heart of English culture; and in a place – the great Pembroke estates at Wilton, spreading over 50,000 acres of the Wiltshire downs, a great house, its garden, many manors, villages, parks and hunting grounds in which something of the theatre of Arcadia could be played out. It is the story of a forgotten idealism flowering and then collapsing into the pain and brutality of civil war on the banks of a trout-filled Wiltshire chalkstream.

Looked at in a critical light, the world of the Pembrokes was one which none of us could tolerate now: it put the claims of social order far above any individual rights; it considered privacy, except for the highly privileged, a form of subversion; it was profoundly hierarchical and did not consider either people or the sexes equal; it tolerated vast excess and devastating poverty; it distrusted the idea of the market and would have loathed any suggestion, if anyone had made it, that market forces would somehow create social goods; it thought the poor worthy of pity if they remained within bounds and of punishment should they stray outside them; it distrusted the crown, not because the crown would erode individual freedoms but because it was intent on destroying older aristocratic privileges.

Anti-change, anti-state, anti-market, anti-equality and anti-individual: this first English Arcadia, in other words, set its face against the forces of modernity. It was driven by a hunger for the past and a fear of the future. If the last four hundred years have been shaped by a growth in government, the elevation of individual rights, the erosion of community, the dominance of the market and the destructive exploitation of nature, Arcadianism, the Pembrokes and the world of their estates said no to all of them.

The virtues this Arcadia cherished were the mirror image of all that: an overriding belief in the power and understanding of local community; a trust in the past and its customs; a love of nature not as a commodity to exploit but as a place in which to find rest and comfort; an independence from the power of central government; and a rejection of commercial values, relying instead on the mutuality of communal relationships. It was an organic ideal, a belief not in mutual exploitation but in the balance of different parts of society. To some extent, ever since, these have been the values of the counter-culture, an underlying thread of idealism which has run throughout the history of the modern world.

This form of Renaissance Arcadianism was the fusion of two streams which had been separate in the Middle Ages. They came together for the century this book describes, and diverged again afterwards. The period was a unique moment in English culture, a coming together of high classical ideals with a sense of the good society that was deeply rooted in England's medieval experience.

The old English stream was one of the lingering afterglows of feudalism. The country, in this view, was less a state than a gathering of individual communities or manors. Within each manor, the lord held sway not as a tyrant but as a father. The wellbeing of the manor depended on an understanding between the lord and his tenants. The lord would offer hospitality, protection and stability. The tenants would offer their labour and part of their goods. The sense of security which came from this rooted hierarchy was communal and depended on obedience and submission to the general good. The good society of the manor was an organism founded on the acceptance by all parties of power on one side and powerlessness on the other. But custom involved an acceptance of rights on all sides and power was to be exercised with justice and grace, just as the defence of the 'little common wealth' of the manor was to be conducted with courage and vigour. This social arrangement of mutual but unequal good was the great medieval legacy. Its belief in honour, nobility and duty, beyond mere financial relations, lay at the heart of the idea of the chivalric knight which would play such a part in the aristocracy's view of themselves in the sixteenth and seventeenth centuries.

The classical idea of Arcadia had disappeared in the Middle Ages. Bliss for medieval man was a heavenly not a worldly condition. No picture appears in the Middle Ages of a deliciously heavenly place on earth. When medieval poetry or painting looked at rural life, it was for something charming and simple, not a dream of perfection. Medieval man had to die to be happy.

Throughout Europe, that changed with the rediscovery of the classics in the fifteenth century. As Europe itself began to urbanise, the urban fantasies of classical Rome began to resonate with the cultural elite and Arcadia, a place of rural bliss conceived as an escape from the stresses of the city and the court, could once again take up the role it had played in antiquity. Its particular atmosphere had been, in essence, the invention of Virgil. The Greeks had celebrated two kinds of primitivism: the soft version of the Golden Age, often set in Sicily, where there was plenty and happiness and none of the vices of modernity; and the harder kind, often found in the harsh Greek province of Arcadia in the Peloponnese, a tough, wild mountain country, where there were no comforts and none of the sweetness of groves and purling brooks, but whose shepherds were admirably virtuous and honest and comforted themselves in their primitive lives with their songs and their pipes.

3

Virgil, in the *Eclogues* he wrote in the mid-30s BC for his rich Roman audience, fused these two realms. In his hands, Sicily, with the jewelled flowers of its everlasting spring, and the ease of a perfect existence where no work was ever needed and all time could be filled with talk of love, was joined to the Arcadian virtues of plain speaking and honesty, a sense of goodness removed from the slick brutalities of court. Sweetness and virtue became one and that combination is one of the reasons Arcadia could appeal to the great of Renaissance Europe: it held out the possibilities of happiness to the most sophisticated of men and women, a vision of release generated by the very urban, competitive world of which they were a part.

To that imaginary realm of virtuous sweetness, Virgil added another element. Arcadia was not part of heaven. It was an earthly condition and subject to mortality. Even in Arcadia death was there: *Et in Arcadia ego.* The beauty and perfection was tinged with sadness, and the sadness worked not as a destroyer of the beauty, but as a poignancy, an addition to it, a melancholy sense of the transience of earthly things which served, paradoxically, to enhance them. Virgil's Arcadia recognised that beauty on the point of disappearance had the added beauty of evening light, of impending loss as a glow on the untouched cheek.

This was the rich and suggestive classical inheritance which the Renaissance took up: perfect, sweet virtue made more perfect in a dropping light. In England, and nowhere more than at Wilton, it became allied to the other vision of perfection, the ideal of wholeness and social calm to be found – at least notionally – in the medieval manor, a world at ease with itself, where custom could govern next year as it had the last.

Subsequently, from the late seventeenth century onwards, this amalgam of classical and medieval inheritance bifurcated again. Arcadianism in the eighteenth century lost its social dimension. In the making of the great parks, and in the taste for the refined Meissen figures or Fragonard prettinesses, the pink-cheeked shepherdess and her satin-suited swain, set in the smoothed contours of the English landscape school, the slick of suavity around a Palladian house and the most expensive wallpaper ever devised, there was no political or social freight, beyond at least the expression of gentlemanly ease. Arcadia in the eighteenth century became décor, not a hope for society. Its money-cushioned languor became a commodity, to be bought, an accessory to market-success, not a criticism of individualism, market or state. This eviscerated Arcadianism became effete, the symbol of everything against which the hunger of the Romantics for a vivid reality would react. Eighteenth-century Arcadia had lost its soul and become the country in a Savile Row suit, decorated with hermitages and tree clumps which were no more than pale, polite ghosts of their great Renaissance forebears.

Before that sleek compendium of good taste conquered the world, there was another Arcadia, a knobblier, more complex, more troubled and more vital thing, amalgamating those classical and medieval inheritances and as a result having a life across an extraordinarily wide range. Everything from land and estate management to hunting, the way you stood, the way you dressed, the way you loved and married, architecture, garden design, poetry, drama, painting, court politics, attitudes to the common law, royal authority and the constitution were caught in its coils. The idea of the perfect world was far more than an aesthetic category in the sixteenth and seventeenth centuries.

This amalgamated English Arcadia, which is the subject of this book, was the elite dream of happiness. It is an ideology that has appealed ever since to those who have not subscribed to the mainstream: political conservatives, the Romantics, the young Karl Marx, William Morris, early conservationists and modern Greens. It came to play a central part in the shaping of America and in America's own inherited idea that it was the Arcadian dreamland of the European subconscious: the place of abundance and liberty, of an easy civility between its agrarian citizens, a country which bore the duty which came with those benefits, to be a beacon and model to the world.

You need look no further than Jefferson's 1782 *Notes on the State of Virginia* to recognise the central place which the Arcadian ideal had taken up in the American mind. 'Those who labor in the earth are the chosen people of God,' Jefferson wrote, 'whose breasts He has made His peculiar deposit for substantial and genuine virtue.' The hard-working, soil-engaged rural farmer, the descendant of the yeoman who worked the Pembroke manors in the Wiltshire chalklands, is for Jefferson the purest man who ever lived.

> Corruption of morals in the mass of cultivators is a phenomenon which no age nor nation has furnished an example. It is the mark set upon those, who, not looking up to heaven, to their own soil and industry, as does the husbandman, for their subsistence, depend for it on casualties and caprice of customers. Dependence begets subservience and venality, suffocates the germ of virtue, and prepares fit tools for the designs of ambition.

Expressed through something of a fog of Enlightenment latinity, this is nevertheless a heartland statement for American Arcadianism: the market corrupts; nothing is more nauseating than a customer; only the soil and air, the intimate connection with the realities of growth and subsistence, can provide the pure moral environment which America – and Arcadia – requires.

This was the tradition which aimed to shape the American West. Lincoln's Homestead Act of 1862 gave full title to 160 acres of America to anyone who lived on and worked the land for five years. Hundreds of thousands of square miles of the continent became the greatest experiment in Arcadianism the world had ever seen. It was not, at least in theory, a question of freehold, but the establishment of a moral community. The land handed out in this way was not to be considered a marketable property. It could not be sold to satisfy any debts and it could not be worked on behalf of anyone else. Guided by the idealism of the federal government, the idea of the English yeoman, self-sustaining on his hard-worked acres, more attuned to the earth than to the market, was laid out in section after section across the plains and mountains of a new continent. The reality, needless to say, was very different: rapid accumulation of vast estates by a variety of subletting agreements, which were in effect sales; a far more business-like approach to farming than any yeoman model might have envisaged; a scale of enterprise made necessary by the harsh environments which the inherited yeoman ideal simply didn't fit: all of this inevitably steered American land and farming towards a more market-based model than Jefferson or Lincoln would ever have envisaged.

But the river of belief which this tradition represents needed an outlet, and it emerged in three of the greatest contributions America has made to the world: the national park, the leafy suburb and the environmental movement which emerged from them, all products of an American Arcadianism which took root and blossomed in the late nineteenth century and which from there spread to conquer the world. They were each other's siblings. The greening of the city, the emparking of the wilderness, and the belief that human enterprise needs to be part of an ecological community: all three represent the fusion of nature and culture on which the Arcadian ideal relies.

'The earth does not argue,' Walt Whitman wrote in 1881, 'is not pathetic, has no arrangements, does not scream, haste, persuade, threaten, promise, makes no discriminations, has no conceivable failures, closes nothing, refuses nothing, shuts none out.' Those famous, lolloping words are themselves the descendants of an English Arcadian ideal, of which for about a hundred years, from the 1540s until the disasters of the English Civil War a century later, Wilton was the headquarters. This was where the only known performance in Shakespeare's lifetime of *As You Like It* was staged for James I in December 1603. This was where 'tongues in trees, books in the running brooks, sermons in stones and good in everything' could seem, for a moment or two, like a reality. Here the good life, love and the good society could be found in rural seclusion; here you could 'fleet the time carelessly as they did in the golden world'; and from here the realm of business, city and the court could all, by comparison, be seen as the source of wickedness and corruption.

Arcadia, for a powerful interval, came to be identified with this house, this place and this landscape. Those who were drawn to the Arcadian balm that Wilton could offer were the very people who were striving and struggling to win and thrive in the royal court at Whitehall. Wilton, par excellence, was the power house which saw itself as the Shepherd's Paradise. This was the Palace in the Trees, the stage set where nothing was more expensive than simplicity. It was where 'old custom made this life more sweet / Than that of painted pomp,' and where only courtiers and their powerful friends were on hand to taste it.

Increasingly, in the seventeenth century this ancient dream of the perfect world, closely identified with the ancient aristocracy on its ancient estates, was under threat, consciously or not, from both sides: from an increasingly efficient, hungry and autocratic state; and from a rising surge of individualist appetite. Arcadia was a dam set against that double tide. It was, in many ways, an organised and deeply entrenched world but it was not to last. The civil war, which in part at least can be seen as a war between the royalist forces of that growing state and the parliamentary defenders of the ancient constitution, had broken this world. Even from the 1660s, after the monarchy had been restored, the time of the first English Arcadia was looked back on with regret and longing. A moment had passed.

2

A lovely campania

The Wiltshire Downs as a theatre for pastoral

EARLY ON a summer morning – and you should make it a Sunday when England stays in bed for hours after the sun has risen – the chalk downland to the west of Wilton slowly reveals itself in the growing light as an open and free-flowing stretch of country, long wide ridges, which have ripples and hollows within them, separated by river valleys, with an air of Tuscany transported to the north, perhaps even a Tuscany improved. Seventeenth-century scientists thought the smoothness of the chalk hills meant they were part of the sea-floor that had appeared after Noah's flood had at last receded. It was old, God-smoothed country and pure because of it.

This morning, you will have it to yourself. At first light, the larks are up and singing, but everything else is drenched in a golden quiet. Shadows hang in the woods and the sun casts low bars across the backs of the hills. You will see the deer, ever on the increase in southern England, moving silently and hesitantly in the half-distance. It is a place of slightness and subtlety, wide and long-limbed, drawn with a steady pencil. In the steeper coombes, on the slopes which the Wiltshiremen call 'cliffs', the grass is dotted with cowslips and early purple orchids. Gentians and meadow saxifrage can still be found on the open downland. Chalkhill Blue butterflies dance over the turf. Fritillaries and White Admirals are in the woods. The whole place, as Edward Thomas once described the shape of chalkland, is full of those 'long straight lines in which a curve is always latent . . .'

This feeling of length – slow changes, a sense of distance – is at the heart of the Wiltshire chalk. It is not a plain, because everywhere the ground surface shifts and modulates, but it is nowhere sharp. It is full of continuity and connectedness, a sense that if you set off in any direction you would have two or three days' journey before anything interrupted you. This, in other words, is a place that feels like its own middle, the deepest and richest of arrivals.

John Aubrey, the great seventeenth-century gossip and anti-quarian, whose family rented a farm in one of these valleys, called his treasured country 'a lovely *campania*', a perfect Champagne country. There is no marginality; instead, settlement, rootedness, stability, removal from strife and trouble. 'The turfe is of a short sweet grasse,' Aubrey wrote of the place he loved, 'good for the sheep, and delightfull to the eye, for its smoothnesse like a bowling green.' The most delicious things here were the rabbits, 'the best, sweetest, and fattest of any in England; a short, thick coney, and exceeding fatt. The grasse is very short, and burnt up in the hot weather. 'Tis a saying, that conies doe love rost-meat.' Their tastiness was a sign of his country's beneficence.

Aubrey remembered, or at least remembered being told, that a century before, at the peak of the Elizabethan love affair with the idea of an imagined, beautiful world, 'these romancy plaines and boscages did no doubt conduce to the hightening of Sir Philip Sydney's phansie. He lived much in these parts, and his most mas-terly touches of his *Arcadia* he wrote here upon the spott, where they were conceived.'

More than any other Englishman, Sidney, a failed Elizabethan courtier, distrusted by the queen, and an ineffectual soldier, who had turned to poetry and romance as a substitute for the manly life of politics and action, had in his enforced retirement, staying here with his sister Mary, Countess of Pembroke, shaped the pastoral vision for his countrymen. Sidney's ideal became the exemplar of English completeness. Charles I would quote his *Arcadia* on the scaffold as he knelt in January 1649 for the executioner's axe and these Wiltshire downs and valleys were its source. As Aubrey's 'great-uncle, Mr Thomas Browne, remembered him, [Sidney] was often wont, as he was hunting in our pleasant plaines, to take his table book [a re-usable notebook] out of his pocket, and write down his notions as they came into his head, while he was writing his *Arcadia* (which was never finished by him).'

'My sheep are thoughts,' Sidney had written in that notebook, and, in this dream landscape, poetry and the place became the same thing. 'Doth not the pleasauntnes of this place carry in it selfe sufficient reward for any time lost in it?' one of his travelling knights asked his friend and cousin as they wandered together over the sheep-nibbled grass. It is the central Arcadian suggestion, that life itself in a world of beauty is its own reward.

> Do you not see how all things conspire together to make this country a heauenly dwelling? Do you not see the grasse[s] how in colour they excell the Emeralds, euerie one striuing to passe his fellow, and yet they are all kept of an equall height? And see you not the rest of these beautifull flowers, each of which would require a mans wit to know, and his life to expresse? . . . Doth not the aire breath health, which the Birds (delightfull both to eare and eye) do dayly solemnize with the sweete consent of their voyces? Is not euery *Eccho* thereof a perfect Musicke?

Sidney himself had appeared in a Whitehall tournament as a Shepherd Knight, he and his horse dressed head to toe in Wiltshire wool, the image of sadness and poignant distance from sin and power. That vision, first set down in the 1580s, was reprinted again and again throughout the seventeenth century. It became the English idea of the Golden Age and this downland was its theatre. Additions were made to it and endless variations played on its themes of love, longing, song and sorrow. Constantly weaving through its soft and mellowed language and rhythms was a hint of something harder. That reference to the grasses, all striving but of equal height, is an undoubted if lightly coded signal of a social system in which a tyrant did not dominate but where equal striving members of the grasslands community, the gentlemen of this elegant world, each contributed to the general beauty and ease. The downland turf was Sidney's symbol of social happiness. It was also a recognition, 350 years before the word was invented, of the meaning of ecology.

These wonderful lands – the chalk downs and the lush watered valleys of the rivers that run between them – spread over eighty square miles, were the core of one of the great aristocratic estates of Renaissance England, the power-base, cash cow and pleasure grounds of the Earls of Pembroke, whose great palace was and is at Wilton, a few miles to the west of Salisbury. The house is the gateway to the world they owned and it is that world – of enormous riches, profound culture, extensive political and military control, an ever-present threat of violence, great luxury, constant self-interest and a high idealism, part platonic, part Protestant and part descended from the chivalric ideals of the Middle Ages – which this book will set out to explore.

Most visitors to Wilton now simply drive to the great house and consume it, as if eating the cherry off a cake. But that is to arrive at the end of the story first. 'After all,' the diarist John Evelyn wrote after visiting Wilton in 1654, 'that which to me renders the seat delightful, is its being so near the downs and noble plains about the country and contiguous to it.' For John Aubrey, 'This curious seate of Wilton and the adjacent countrey is an Arcadian place and a Paradise.' It is out there, in the lands which both paid for Wilton and were the foundation of its meaning, that you must begin.

Every element of the perfect life is here. High on the chalk ridge just to the west of Wilton is the great royal hunting ground of Grovely Wood, set up as a forest by the Saxon kings, so old that it forms no part of the system of parishes that were created around it before the Norman Conquest. It is one of the twenty-five hunting forests mentioned in the Domesday Book, the precious reserves in which the king alone had the right to kill the game. Grovely – its name perhaps a memory of the patches of rough woodland that were growing here when the Saxons first arrived – is still thick with bluebells and wood anemones in the early summer.

Furzy coppiced oaks, heavily burred, stand about in the flowery lawns: 'Do not these stately trees seeme to maintaine their florishing olde age, being clothed with a continuall spring, because no beautie here should euer fade?' Philip Sidney asked in *Arcadia*. In the sixteenth century it was the home of a herd of red deer, the most prestigious of all quarries, dominated by the old ten- and twelve-tined stags, the 'harts' which were the source of ultimate honour in the hunt. In the forest, glades were kept open to provide grass for the deer and other parts were from time to time fenced off so that the new shoots of the coppice wood could grow. There are oak coppice stools in Grovely today which are sixteen feet across and in the survey made for the first earl in 1566, the wood was already famous not for its tall straight stems but for lots of crooked oaks in the old coppices that were good for firewood.

These coppices and pieces of open ground, or 'copses' and 'lights' as they were called, were functional but were also part of the aesthetic to which the Arcadian mind responded. Sidney's idea of the perfect country was one 'diversified between hills and dales, woods and plain, one place more clear, another more darksome, [so that] it seems a pleasant picture of nature, with lovely lightsomeness and artificial shadows.'

The word 'artificial' – like 'curious' and 'ingenious' – was a word of praise in a culture which did not yet distrust its ability to make things more beautiful than they were in their natural state. Arcadia was a dream of nature; there was no suggestion it was the same as nature itself.

Beyond Grovely stretched the great open expanses of the downland. Days here were spent in the saddle, living a life coloured by the idea of grace and civility. This illusion of a heightened perfection was what the Wiltshire downs, as much as any other part of the country, could offer the educated men and women of Renaissance England. The shepherds here used to wear long white woollen cloaks, 'with a very deep cape', coming halfway down their backs. They looked exactly as the connoisseurs would seed them in the paintings of Claude and Poussin. They carried crooks to gather the lambs; slings to cast stones at wandering sheep or threatening foxes; a scrip or shoulder bag in which to keep their bread and cheese; tar boxes, with which to seal and cauterise any wound; a dog at their side; and even a pipe or flute with which to pipe away their hours of tedium.

The white-caped shepherds used to catch the larks up there 'by alluring them with a dareing-glasse [a dazzling-glass], which is whirled about in a sun-shining day, and the larkes are pleased at it, and strike at it, as at a sheepe's eye, and at that time the nett is drawn over them. While he playes with his glasse he whistles with his larke-call of silver, a tympanum of about the diameter of a threepence.' Some preferred to catch, if they could, the slightly rarer wheatears, 'a great delicacie, and they are little lumps of fatt.'

All of this was a life out of time, shepherds and shepherdesses appearing now just as they had in Virgil's *Eclogues* and the Greek pastorals of Theocritus, the foundation levels of the Arcadian dream. Nicolas Poussin could have walked across these Wiltshire downlands and simply painted what he saw.

From the top of the downs, long droves descend into the valleys of the rivers which cut through the chalk tableland. Tauntingly, as if Sidney had been describing a reality, honeysuckle and wild clematis drape themselves across the hedges. The sun breaks into the droves past the thorns that are thick with mayflower. Cow parsley is just sprouting in the verges, the wheat and barley still a dense green in the fields beside you.

It doesn't matter which river valley you choose: the Ebble; or the Nadder; or the Wylye. Each of them will still greet you like a vision of perfection, the perfect interfolding of the human and the natural which is at the heart of the Arcadian idea. The chalk streams (all three of them still have the Celtic names they had in pre-Roman Britain) emerge in bubbling springs all along the valley sides. The water that has percolated down through the chalk hits a layer of clay and comes to the surface. Along that springline, below the arable fields but above the floodable valley bottoms, are the villages. These emergences are beautiful, soft, weed-rimmed places where the water erupts in shallow mushrooms and riffles. It is as if the water is simmering in the pools, before making its easy way down to the main rivers that slope off to the east. Sidney had seen them, 'these fresh and delightfull brookes how slowly they slide away, as loth to leaue the company of so many thinges vnited in perfection . . . and with how sweete a murmur they lament their forced departure . . .'

So mudless is this spring water that the rivers remain entirely clear as they move over their pale beds. The banks are spotted with kingcups and there are islands of white-flowered water crowfoot in mid-stream. The hairy leaves of water mint grow on the gravel banks, coots and moorhens scoot between them, and if you wade out barefoot into the shockingly cold water of the river, the small wild brown trout flicker away in front of you, running from your Gulliver-in-Lilliput intrusion. Among the trout are the pale bodies of the graylings, called *Thymalus thymalus* because their flesh smells of the wild thyme that grows on the downland turf, and which in the seventeeth century were known here as 'umbers', shadow-fish, their silvery greyness scarcely to be distinguished from the most beautiful river-water in England.

Walk down your valley. If you have chosen the Ebble, you will come to the village of Broad Chalke, clustered among its riverside trees, where John Aubrey lived both as child and man. Both he and his father Richard were the tenants of Manor Farm and Aubrey, in love with the past and with the Arcadian idea of peace which the horrors of the seventeenth century had made so distant, was entranced by the poetry that seemed just beyond his grasp in these valleys. In his garden he grew his pear trees; he stocked the stream with crayfish but they died as the water he thought was too cold (improbable). He liked to listen on a Sunday morning to the bells of the Broad Chalke church, 'one of the tunablest ring of bells in

Wiltshire which hang advantageously, the river running near the churchyard, which meliorates the sound.'

Those church bells heard through the bubbling of the water over the stony bed of the Ebble recur in another phrase from these valleys, in a poem by George Herbert, cousin of the Pembrokes, the appointed vicar of the church at Bemerton in the 1630s, a mile or two from the house at Wilton. His great poem called *Prayer* pours forth a cataract of images of what prayer might be. No grammar links them; just a bubbling forth of riches like the water welling up in the riverside springs. Prayer, for Herbert, is

> Softnesse, and peace, and joy, and love, and blisse,
>   Exalted Manna, gladnesse of the best,
>   Heaven in ordinarie, man well drest,
> The Milkie way, the bird of Paradise,
>   Church-bels beyond the starres heard, the souls bloud,
>   The land of spices; something understood.

'Church-bels beyond the starres heard': that is a phrase which takes to another level Aubrey's auditory vision of the bells gurgling by the waters of the Ebble. But the perceptions are cousins to each other, and they both descend from the powerful idea, persisting here for decade after decade in the sixteenth and seventeenth centuries, that these valleys were in some ways heavenly.

Make your way further down the valley of the Ebble, from Broad Chalke, past the watercress beds and the small manor houses, past the broken leats and grassed-over ditches, where the river used to be led out over the watermeadows, past the swans and their cygnets in the rushes, and on to the place called by the Saxons Stratford Tony, because that was where the street, the old Roman Road from Old Salisbury to Dorchester, forded the Ebble. Only then climb up over the ridge of downland to the north, coming to the crest at Cowper's Cross on the old Shaftesbury Drove where the huge lime trees still mark the miles along the race track where the Pembrokes used to race their famous horses.

You are now within striking distance of the Pembrokes' house at Wilton. As you approach, their Arcadian world thickens around you. You meet first a 300-acre wood called the Hare Warren, which the sixteenth-century Pembrokes fenced off from the rest of the downland to preserve it for the hunting of the hare, and then the wall of the 600-acre park that surrounds the house.

Both warren and park were as much designed to exclude as to contain. The hares and the park's fallow deer were kept in by their fences and walls but the intention was to provide a heightened and privileged world from which others were shut out. The park was pocket pastoral. Arcadia has always been an act of luxury, an expensive and comfortable version of wildness, wildness somehow kept wild but made lovely. And because of its expense – the park is a place in which no useful crop is grown – it was also an act of authority and power. The village of Washern which had been within the park was removed and its common fields taken over. The essence of Arcadia is that it belongs to the winners. It is beyond all conflict but it is only beyond conflict because all others have been defeated. The underlying meaning of parkland is as a reward for victory.

That is its central paradox: its peace is achieved through a form of violence and imposition. It relies, at its heart, on acts of exclusion. Its belief in the beauties of ancient community also relies on that community accepting the imposition of authority. Anarchy and Arcadia, even democracy and Arcadia, cannot co-exist. It is, in a sense, a dream of authoritarian freedom which carries its own contradiction in its heart. Arcadia is the dream of power.

Only here, buffered and padded by these many insulating layers, do you come to the great house itself, in the centre of this stratified and highly theatricalised world. Much of the park around the house was remodelled in the eighteenth century. The rather rough old hunting ground, and the immensely elaborate and consciously artificial garden which provided a setting for the house in the 1630s, were both swept away and the rather bland eighteenth-century taste for a placid, settled landscape was substituted. Something of the original drama of Wilton has gone, but ignore that for a moment, re-imagine the seventeenth century and approach the house.

Immediately in front of the palace was the great garden, rectilinear, visibly expensive, a precisionist creation, 'very fine with many gravel walkes with grass squaires,' as Celia Fiennes described them in the 1690s, 'set with fine brass and stone statues – fish ponds and basons with Ffigures in ye middle spouting out water – dwarfe trees of all sorts and a fine flower garden – much wall fruite.' These two elements of the palace in the trees – a stark juxtaposition of nature and culture, the idea in effect that a great classical house might play a role in a Shepherd's Paradise – may seem difficult and inappropriate to us now. We no longer connect these categories, but that connection is the essential mechanism of the Arcadia. To become a shepherd was not to lose one's sense of dignity or even hauteur, but to enhance it. To define nature was not to erase it but to perfect it. A palace in the trees was not a palace somehow slumming it, but a palace reaching a kind of perfection. Restraint and orderliness were central parts of the pastoral idea.

The house was the climax of the experience. 'Every mans proper *Mansion* House and Home,' Sir Henry Wotton, the ambassador and connoisseur, friend of the Pembrokes, of Donne and Inigo Jones, had written in 1624,

> being the *Theater* of his *Hospitality*, the *Seate* of *Selfe-fruition*, the *Comfortablest part* of his *owne Life*, the *Noblest* of his Sonnes *Inheritance*, a kind of private *Princedome*; Nay, to the *Possessors* thereof, an *Epitomie* of the whole *World*, may well deserve by these *Attributes*, according to the degree of the *Master*, to be *decently* and *delightfully* adorned.

But not too much. There was to be dignity, particularly in outward show. Inigo Jones famously understood a building's need for seriousness in a façade: 'Outwardly every wise man carries a gravity,' he had written, 'yet inwardly has his imagination set on fire and sometimes licentiously flies out.' The south front of Wilton is in that way calm and visually reduced. Acres of unadorned wall are relieved by nine great windows on the *piano nobile*, with a low basement and a balancing attic floor above and below them. Only the central, Venetian window is decorated with a pair of reclining classical figures in high relief, their backs and elbows leaning on the architecture.

Go inside and the mood changes. There is not a hint of coldness or chill to the interiors. The rooms, although generous, are not vast. Their grandeur can be measured on a human scale. Human masks, in fact, punctuate every wall, in the caryatid supporters of the fireplaces, and in the swags and deeply carved baubles which orchestrate the rooms. Here, the imagination, the dream of richness, is set on fire, yet another ring in the onion-skin arrangement of Wilton: open down, hunting forest, hunting park, rectilinear garden, grave façade, enriched interiors.

The way through the house was deeply altered in the eighteenth and nineteenth centuries and so the procession through the rooms which the seventeenth-century Pembrokes would have known is no longer accessible. But at the core of the house, the key remains to the entire Arcadian story of Wilton. One room is entirely decorated with hunting scenes, taken from Italian originals, and painted on panels set into the wainscoting. Rough portraits of the seventeenth-century earl and his heir are incorporated into the pictures. Another room, now called the Single Cube, has stories from Philip Sidney's *Arcadia* painted in panels below the dado.

This series of comfortable and livable but highly dignified rooms comes to a climax in the richest and most beautiful apartment to survive from seventeenth-century England. It is now called the Double Cube (thirty feet wide, thirty high and sixty long) but was known in the seventeenth century as the 'great Dining-roome, or Roome of State'. The history of this room is complicated and still far from certain in detail, but it is at least probable that a room of this kind was made here in the 1630s. The decoration is so rich that the pure harmonics of its proportions, inherited by Jones from

Palladio, nearly disappear beneath the gilded encrustations. The rooms are thickened with carved swags and suspended gilded pom-poms. There is a vast fruitiness to the decoration, apples, peaches and pears dripping from the walls. Nothing is held back. It is as if the architecture is putting on the warmest and most inviting of shows. (The painters were those used by Jones for his masques in Whitehall.) A giant cove, painted with putti and Pan masks, the Pembroke arms and motto ('Ung Je Servirai' – I will serve One, meaning God) and still more bowls and swags of fruit, reaches up to the ceiling. Around the marble fireplace, mannerist motifs – broken pediments, swagged consoles – jostle with the gilded statues of Bacchus and Ceres, the god and goddess of country riches. The whole complex is a shrine to fertility, a space designed for enjoyment, an arrival.

On the west wall of this glamour-encrusted room is the still point at the centre of the whole 50,000-acre world: a great portrait of the earl and his children. Each of the ten figures it portrays is just larger than lifesize and they dominate, as they were meant to, the baubled, swagged and gilded space in front of them. The picture is by van Dyck, painted in the late winter of 1634 or the spring of 1635, and it shows the Pembroke family at the sunniest and most optimistic moment of its existence. The oldest surviving son, fifteen-year-old Charles, Lord Herbert, in scarlet, is to marry the young heiress in white before him, the twelve-year-old Mary Villiers. Even the three dead children of the family, with garlands of roses in their hands, attend as putti. The younger brothers to the left and the older sister with her husband to the right, the elegant, bronzed Cavalier Earl of Carnarvon, surround the great man and his wife, the Earl and Countess of Pembroke, who sit centrally, facing us, as if king and queen.

The painting is full of grace and aristocratic poise, of riches at ease with themselves, of what now would be called privilege and was then considered nobility. It exudes a distant and forgotten handsomeness, an abandoned world of elegance, beauty and power.

It is neither stiff nor louche. It is regal but familial, both real and ideal. It occupies the perfect middle ground, a moment of completeness at the centre of its own Arcadian world, but one which, as the story of this family will reveal, has brittleness and fragility at its heart.

And is not euery manor a little common wealth?

The inherited community of the Middle Ages

THE PEMBROKE LANDS in Wiltshire were ancient country, drenched in continuities. In common with the rest of southern England, it looked in the sixteenth and seventeenth centuries much as it had for at least a thousand and maybe two or three thousand years. There would have been differences in details: woods had grown up where fields had been before; fields had been cleared where trees had once clothed the landscape. There were more people, and more houses. But the villages, as ever, were made of the materials the land could provide. Wheat straw thatched the roofs, cut not with a scythe but more carefully and more slowly with a sickle, a smaller, neater tool, but justifiable in economic terms because a sickle would guarantee a good length in the roofing material: longer straw made dryer roofs. In the walls, the oak frames were infilled with hazel panels, made with exactly the same technique as the hurdles used to enclose the sheep in the folds, the young pliant wands woven between the uprights or 'sails' – the wattle – smeared with mud and straw – the 'daub' – and then painted with limewash. Occasionally, for the walls, a mixture of chalk or 'clunch' blocks would be used, quarried from the hill, and then mixed with flint and brick from the valley clays. All of this one can still see in the houses of these valleys. Nothing would have come from more than a mile or two away. This was an immutable pattern, the intimate folding of men, their farming and their habits of life on to the opportunities and constraints which the landscape offered them.

John Aubrey, ever alert to the possibilities of ancientness, recorded in the manuscript notes he submitted to the Royal Society in 1675 that his friends, the Gawens, had lived in the same place at Alvediston, a few miles west of Broad Chalke, for 'four hundred fifty and odd yeares'. More intriguingly than that, there was a little barrow up on the down stretching south from Broad Chalke which was called 'Gawen's-barrow, which,' Aubrey carefully noted, 'must bee before ecclesiastical lawes were established.' The real implications of that name were more exciting: Aubrey was wondering if his friends had also been here since the Bronze Age.

The high chalkland on which those remains persisted would have been nothing without the river valleys. Settlement needs water, and the dewponds on the downs – in fact enormous clay-lined dishes to catch the rain – provided water good enough for sheep but desiccating to human taste. Each sip seems to leave a residue of chalk in your mouth. The spring-fed valley water is different, as bubblingly restorative as any in England, marvellous to lie in on a hot summer afternoon, your back on the pebbles, the water dancing around your head and shoulders. The Arcadian world of the Pembrokes' Wiltshire valleys relied for its existence on the constant and mutually supportive relationship of these two environments, the high chalkland and the damp wet valleys, each providing what the other lacked.

The same system of land management, and the virtually immobile social structure which it created, had persisted across the centuries. It was, apart from some alterations at the margins, a profoundly conservative and unchanging world. Farming patterns and social relationships had lasted here essentially unchanged from before the ninth century. This extraordinary continuity, even as the world was revolutionised around them, became the dominant fact of the Pembroke estates. This was the old world. Its ancient methods looked like a version of Arcadia. And it was a world the Pembrokes were intent on protecting.

Its roots stretched back into the Dark Ages, perhaps to the

moment when the Viking armies were threatening the wellbeing of much of the Midlands, East Anglia and Wessex, perhaps before then, when violence was still endemic among the Saxon chieftains and their warbands. The documents are thin on the ground but it seems certain that the system of the manor emerged from a world of violence and the need for protection within it. A warlord offered land and defence, a villein – a man of the village – supplied in return labour and loyalty.

This was certainly how the landowning class of the sixteenth and seventeenth centuries understood the history of what they owned. John Norden, the pre-eminent surveyor of the early seventeenth century, a professional and a devout Christian, conservative in his ideals, first published his *Surveior's Dialogue* in 1607. It was a popular book which went through three large editions, and was the leading text on the meaning of land, its duties and rewards, in early modern England. Norden was voicing the accepted nostrums of the society he was addressing. After the departure of the Romans, Norden told his audience of gentlemen, the country was left as

> a very Desert and Wildernesse, full of woods, fels, moores, bogs, heathes, and all kind of forlorne places: and howsoeuer wee finde the state of this Island now, Records do witness vnto us, that it was for the most part a vniuersall wildernesse, until people finding it a place desolate and forlorne began to set footing here, and by degrees grew into multitudes; though for a time brutish and rude.

In that wild time, when life was lawless, there was mutual benefit to be had in community. The arrangement was originally voluntary on both sides. 'In the beginning of euery Mannor, there was a mutuall respect of assistance, betweene the Lord who gave parcels of land . . . and the tennants of euery nature, for ayding, strengthening and defending each other.'

But time passed and what had begun as a voluntary arrangement stiffened into the 'custom of the manor'. Both service to the lord and the rights of the tenants had become obligatory 'and either, in right of the custome due to the other, constraineth each other to do that which in the beginning was of either part voluntary.'

Central to the system was the idea of balance and mutuality in community. In Norden's pages, you can hear the discussions of the English ruling class before the civil war, the vision of what they still saw as the organic integrity of the manors they owned and controlled. Norden derived the word itself from the French verb 'mainer' – to keep a place in hand, or in check. Control was the essence of good management but in harness with control and discipline was the idea that the landlord's own life, that of his family, his 'posterity', the lands they held, the lives of those who lived on their lands, were all part of a single, organic whole.

It is, in this ideal and moralised world, a picture of a profoundly hierarchical community, deriving its security and wellbeing from the natural relationship of parts. 'And is not euery Mannor a little common wealth,' Norden asked, tapping big political issues in the use of that phrase, 'whereof the Tenants are the members, the Land the body, and the Lord the head?' That organic analogy worked in detail. Above all, the land's bodily nature needed to be attended to:

> If it be not fed with nutriture, and comforted and adorned with the most expedient commodities, it will pine away, and become forlorne, as the mind that hath no rest or recreation, waxeth lumpish and heauy. So that ground that wanteth due disposing & right manurance, waxeth out of kinde: euen the best meddowes will become ragged, and full of unprofitable weedes, if it be not cut and eaten.

This idea of organic health, and of balance as the source of that health, runs unbroken from the farming of the fields to the management of the country. It is an undivided conceptual ecology which can take in the workings of the physical body, the court at Whitehall, the family, the village, the land itself, the growing of crops, the transmission of wellbeing to the future, the inheritance of understanding from the past, and above all the interlocking roles of nobility, gentry and commonalty. It is the ideology of an establishment which is concerned to keep itself in the position of wealth and power. There is not a hint of democracy, let alone radicalism, about it, but it is a frame of mind which also sets itself against any form of authoritarianism. The workings of the medieval and post-medieval community depend at their heart on a balance of interests, contributions and rewards. It is what, in the sixteenth and seventeenth centuries, was called, quite consciously, a 'common wealth': wellbeing derived from a life lived and considered in common. The custom of the manor was not to do with the regulations of the state; nor with individual freedom. It was a deeply conservative, pre-modern and pre-market system, which recognised no overriding rights of the individual; nor of national interest. It believed, to an extent the modern world can scarcely grasp, in the rights of the community as a living organism.

Again and again in the *Surveior's Dialogue*, Norden emphasised the point. Good decisions in the management of land were 'the meanes to enable the Honourable to shelter the virtuous distressed'. Increasing revenues from a manor allowed the tenants to be treated well. This was a form of obligation, just as, in a family, duty was owed both ways:

> As children are bound to their parents by the bonds of obedience, so are the parents bound to their children by the bond of education; and as servants are bound to their masters in the bond of true service, so are the Masters bound to their servants in the bond of reward. In like manner, tenants being bound unto their Lords in the bond of duety, so are Lords bound vnto their Tennants in the bond of loue.

That last word recurs. Tenancy is not a matter of rent, or at least not only of rent; it is, Norden says, quite explicitly, a love structure. The relationships within a manor, he tells the landlords, must be 'in a mutual manner, you to be helpful vnto them, and they louing unto you. And by this meanes, should your strengths increase far more by their loue then by your lucre, & their comfort grow as much by your fauour as doth their groanes vnder your greediness.'

There was, Norden warned his gentlemen readers, 'no comforte in a discontented people' and discontent in them came from avarice and indifference in their landlord. His own wellbeing, as the head of the body, was utterly dependent on their wellbeing as its limbs. Extortionate rents and the application of raw market principles would destroy the lord as much as the people.

These questions, and their implications of bodily and moral balance, would, on a far larger scale, become the central concern of seventeenth-century England. How much was government a question of agreement? What status did customary rights have in a changing world? What were 'the ancient liberties' on which the people brought up within that system could rely? Did an emergency mean that those liberties could be ignored or overturned? Did the king owe the same duty of care to the kingdom as the earl owed to the inhabitants of these ridges and valleys? Was a government a question of agreement and respect? Or of authority and compulsion? These were the questions that would lead to civil war and in that civil war these Arcadian ideas were ranged on the side of parliament and the ancient constitution against a king and his ministers who had broken the age-old bonds of love and duty. Conservatism was at the heart of Arcadia as it was of the English revolution.

The whole system of the chalkland manors depended on people adapting the way they farmed to what the land could tolerate and what the land could offer. On that basis, the manors divided into three layers: at the top the wide grazing of the open downland; in the valley floor the lush damp meadows and marshes; and between the two, on the valley sides, the arable fields and woods. Throughout the Middle Ages and in the centuries that followed, sheep were grazed by day on the downs and in the evening led downhill along the droves to the arable fields to manure them, in effect using the sheep to transfer the nutrients from the chalk on to the arable land. They also served the purpose of fixing the seed corn into the tilth.

The lush valley meadows were the third part of the system. In the early spring, the grass started to grow there before there was any available on the down. There too in the summer, the big hay crops could be grown which would feed the animals in the winter, particularly the oxen of the manor's plough team. Good valley grazing allowed the village to keep a larger flock, which meant that more arable ground could be cultivated, which meant that more grain could be grown. Although wool and meat were produced from the flocks, their essential product was grain, the stuff of life, the food on which people depended for survival. All was connected: chalk turf and valley hay, down and meadow, the digestive system of the sheep and the wellbeing of men, women and children.

Ownership of this means of production was not shared. Each farmer owned his own beasts, his own seed corn, his own house, his own garden, barns and backyard. He also owned his own strips in the huge open arable fields. But this assemblage of private property was managed in common. Sheep were owned by individual farmers but were grazed in communal flocks, tended by those white-caped shepherds whose wages were paid in proportion by all those whose sheep he looked after. Flocks of several hundred sheep were usual on chalkland manors and in many ways they dictated the shared nature of the farming. It was only practical to graze them together and to fold them together on the same arable field. Villages, as elsewhere in the Midlands and in the chalk country, usually had three open fields (sometimes two, occasionally four or more) of which one lay fallow every year. It was usually laid down in the custom of the manor that the folding of the sheep on to the fields should begin one year at one end, the next at the other. Only that way would the fertility delivered by the sheep be spread evenly across the strips from year to year. Each farmer had to provide winter hay for the sheep, and contribute his few pence towards the employment of a cowherd, hogward, hayward, and even a mole catcher for the manor. Those who failed to meet their obligations to the community would be denied 'the fold' – that lifegiving manure from the sheep – without which their land would not grow the grains on which they relied for their existence. It was a brutal sanction, but as the manor records show, not one which the villagers were slow to impose.

This was the world through which Sidney had wandered, unable to distinguish sheep from thoughts. The two worlds co-existed in the same physical space but occupying different dimensions within it. The yeomen, husbandmen, labourers and shepherds of sixteenth- and seventeenth-century Wiltshire were pursuing a poor and highly regulated life in the very same places as the gentlemen from Wilton were in pursuit of an otherworldly dream existence. What might be called the conceptual geography of the Arcadians – a daily move-ment from the great house towards the high open spaces of the downland in search of spiritual wellbeing – was a curious mirror image of the economic reality of the poor: a daily movement of flocks up on to the downland grazing, gathering there, through the mouths, stomachs and bowels of their sheep, the necessary fertility for their survival.

Of course the two Arcadias inhabited different universes. For Queen Henrietta Maria's *Shrovetide Masque* in 1633, a haberdasher, a property man, a shoemaker and two tailors were required to fabricate a complete shepherd's costume for each of the courtiers taking part. The countesses and ladies who were dancing were all equipped with a shepherd's crook, a lambskin, a wig, a cap and a garland. No account of the money spent on these costumes survives, but they do for other masques and the average price for a dancing costume in the 1620s and 30s came to just over £62. There were probably twelve or fourteen dancers in the *Shrovetide Masque* and so something over £800 was spent on the shepherd's costumes. At least the same again would have been spent on the scenery. *The Triumph of Peace* performed at Whitehall over Christmas 1634, an admittedly massive fantasia of universal wellbeing, cost more than £3000.

One only need set those figures against the wages paid to shepherds in seventeenth-century Wiltshire – £1 a month for an experienced man even at the end of the century, less than half that,

9 shillings a month, for a boy, £5 8s for his year's work – to measure the gap between the two Arcadias. A Whitehall crook would have bought the services of a real shepherd for a year. But for all that, there were real bonds connecting the worlds of Sidney's sheep and Sidney's thoughts. He described the landscape of Arcadia:

> There were hilles which garnished their proud heights with stately trees: humble valleis, whose base estate seemed comforted with refreshing of siluer riuers: medowes, enameld with all sortes of eypleasing floures: thickets, which being lined with most pleasant shade, were witnessed so too by the cheerefull disposition of many wel-tuned birds: ech pasture stored with sheep feeding with sober security, while the prety lambes with bleting oratory craued the dams comfort: here a shepheards boy piping, as though he should neuer be olde: there a yong shepherdesse knitting, and withal singing, and it seemed that her voice comforted her hands to worke, and her hands kept time to her voices musick. As for the houses of the country (for many houses came vnder their eye) they were all scattered, no two being one by th'other, and yet not so far off as that it barred mutuall succour: a shew, as it were, of an accompanable solitarines, & of a ciuil wildnes.

That is a description of sixteenth-century Wiltshire but it is also more than that. Political code is made to ripple through its innocent descriptions: this is a world which isn't crowded but isn't lonely, neither urban, nor solitary, with a hidden but apparently benevolent authority hanging over it, a sociable world filled with a musical harmony to which even the birds are well-tuned. This, in its ideal light, might be a description of the working of the manor and of its hope for communal wellbeing. At that deep and important level, the two Arcadias connect.

Documents survive in the Wiltshire records which add some reality to these Arcadian dream pictures. The shepherd in sixteenth- and seventeenth-century Wiltshire, far from being the careless lover of the Arcadian imagination, was one of the best paid and most responsible men in the village. In his hands was the critical job of safeguarding the communal flock which was the basis of the entire village's survival. By the fifteenth century, he was earning ten or twelve shillings a year (for which one could rent thirty acres or more of arable ground) plus an allowance of grain, a lamb in the spring, a fleece at the summer shearing, a cheese, the milk of those ewes whose lambs had died and the milk of all ewes on Sundays. He was allowed to keep some of his sheep in the lord's own pasture and was absolved from all communal duties. The shepherd was not the poorest of the poor, but even something of a village grandee.

A fascinating document in the Wiltshire records called simply 'Concerning the Shepherd' describes the reality of life for a Wiltshire downland shepherd in September 1629. It consists of the requests laid down by the people of Heale, a small community in the valley of the Avon a few miles north of Wilton, his collective employer. They required of him 'That in person he diligently Attende and keepe his flocke. That he absent not himself from them, but upon urgent and necessary cause, and then put the same, to some sufficiente body, and not to Children either boyes or girles.'

There is a hint here, isn't there, of independence and even truculence in their employee. He also had to keep the sheep out of the corn. Any damage done by the sheep to the growing crops will be docked from his wages 'according as two other tenants not interested in the said damage shall value the same'. If a sheep died, he had to bring the carcass to the owner's house, in case he had sold the sheep and was cheating his employers. He had to look after the communal hay-rick on which the flock would depend in the winter. He was to prevent 'wool-pickers' – and this is a measure of the poverty and tightness in these valleys – from coming to pick the tiny scraps of wool that caught on the hurdles around the fold at night. He must 'mend the scabby', carefully cut and destroy the blackthorn furze that always threatens to take over downland grazing, must drive 'alien' sheep or pigs into the communal pound and not keep any except the community flock, a temptation to free enterprise he was to resist. If any of the community pay him in 'naughty corne, the shepherd upon complainte to be righted by the lord of the mannor on the party soe offendinge'.

This was scarcely the Arcadian picture of ease and contentment, the dream place which the critic Renato Poggioli called 'a breathing spell from the fever and anguish of being'. Its regulatory tightness was in fact a symptom of those very pressures. But at the same time, the existence of the regulations and the expectation that they would be obeyed, that there was communal management of a shared resource, that the shepherd should stay with his flock and not deputise except in emergency, that he should look after both animals and grazing – one can see in the presumptions behind those requests a version of the cooperative and even the authentic world of which the sophisticated would always dream.

The system operated hard up against its limits. Animal diseases could devastate flocks, with no understanding among the villagers of where the disease might have come from nor what to do about it. In the seventeenth century, the habit developed of feeding tobacco to sick sheep in half-magical attempts to cure them of the many disgusting diseases they are prone to. Up to a third of each year's crop had to be held back for the following year's seed corn. Fertility was always at a premium and any opportunity to receive the dung, or 'soil' as it was called, which should have gone to one's neighbour, was always welcome. If someone was found to have done wrong or strayed outside the limits laid down by custom, punishment would be swift. The manor can be seen either as a system of cooperative balance or, like a coral reef, a world of such intense internal competitiveness that its struggles and rivalries had been frozen into a set of symbiotic duties and obligations, the balance of wrestlers in a clinch, by which life alone was sustainable.

Those obligations were all pervading. Women and children were set to weeding the arable crops in the early summer. Their husbands and fathers lived under a fearsome burden of communal work, or work done for the good of the lord of the manor. Every year the villager had to thresh a bushel each (seventy or eighty pounds in weight) of wheat, rye, barley, beans, peas and two bushels of oats, mow two swaths of a meadow and reap, bind and carry half an acre of it. Agreement after agreement specified the amount of dung each man had to carry from his own yard to the arable fields, the number of hurdles he had to make for the fold (a practised man could make two and a half hurdles a day) and the regular amounts of money he had to contribute to the lord of the manor, in return for his right to farm the land: nutsilver at the time of nuts, a rental penny at Easter, lardersilver at 1d or 2d a head, the substantial tax of tallage at 6s 8d each, the 3d per head for the compulsory and customary drinking sessions called scotales and the cock and three hens at Martinmas in November.

This system of obligation and dominance, even as early as the twelfth century, had started to evolve. The work duties of the villeins had often been changed into money payments, 3d or 6d for 'all autumn work'. These villages were not designed to be self-sufficient but to produce, in the grain, a crop which could be sold for cash. Cash played a part in a complex picture of partly 'customary' labour – the obligations entered into in the far distant past – and wage-based labour. Some men were paid particular rates for particular jobs, others were taken on for a year or half a year, some simply had rent-free holdings in return for work.

The Black Death in 1348–9, which killed between a third and a half of the population of England, changed the balance of this world. Entire villages died. In some, single men were found still alive among houses full of the dead. The relationship between lord and villein shifted. Too much land and a shortage of labour meant vacant holdings, decayed tenements and collapsing rental values. The bargain on which the ancient communities had worked – land in return for duties – was no longer worth making. After 1350, those with labour to offer found themselves in a suppliers' market and the age of compulsory labour on the lord's land was largely, although not entirely, over. From now onwards people occupied their houses and lands by what became known as 'copyhold' – literally a written copy of what they had agreed with the lord, or in fact with his steward, as written down in the manor records. Until the end of the seventeenth century, this was the dominant form of tenure on the Wilton estate.

The 'manor based on copyhold tenure' sounds such a dry and legalistic term, but is in fact the label for an intriguing social experiment, lasting two hundred years or so, in the villages of rural England. It occupies a middle ground, which we would hardly recognise today, between the tight and oppressive lordly control of the early Middle Ages, which came to an end with the Black Death; and the almost equally oppressive regime of the eighteenth and nineteenth centuries, against which Cobbett and others would rail, where the sheer financial dominance of the landlords had erased any rights of the ordinary people. The sense of mutuality in community relationships, which was the dominant note in the copyhold manor, was never stronger than from about 1450 to about 1650. It is at least an interesting coincidence that the second half of that period was almost precisely the time when the fashion for pastoral, for the Arcadian vision, was most central to English culture. Was pastoralism – like the modern environmental movement – the expression of a world realising that something real and valuable, which previously had been taken for granted, was now under threat and disappearing from under its nose? If imagination is the cousin of memory, then are the dream worlds of Renaissance England in fact the reassembled fragments of a remembered existence which their fathers and grandfathers might have considered normal?

The copyhold system was, of course, both good and bad. The tenancy was usually given for three lives, sometimes to a man, his wife and a son; a man, his sister and her husband; a man and two sons; or a widow, her son and daughter. It gave security to the farmers and allowed them to invest in improvements which a short lease could not allow. Land and buildings were only rarely let to single individuals; the agreement for three lives, if to a man, his wife, his sons, meant that its terms would extend to whichever of these was the last to die. No one, in other words, would be ejected from their house and farm on the death of a husband or a father. Copyhold agreements for three lives meant that the maintenance of the social fabric was built into the economic structure of the place.

But its conservatism was also a brake. The entire system was presided over by the memory of how things had always been done. Wisdom was essentially proverbial; what was known was good, what was strange was bad. Anything inherited was to be held on to; anything innovatory to be looked at with suspicion. The real story of this ancient form of life was not freedom but imposition, the restrictions on the individual which the workings of the community required. No modern surveillance society could match the reality of a chalkland village in which work patterns, sexual habits, the ability to sell and trade, forms of inheritance and friendship were all closely supervised, not by the distant lord of the manor but by the other villagers themselves. The all-seeing eyes of neighbours, deeply familiar with 'the custom of the manor', that inherited habit, monitored every inch and second.

Whether and where you could collect sticks for firewood, the thickness of the hedge around your garden, the suitability of your chimney for fires, the state of your roof, the dirtiness of the path up to your door, the ringlessness of your pigs' noses, the size of your back room, the clothes you wore, the way you talked in public, the amount you could drink, your behaviour in church: on every conceivable issue, the village could police the habits and trangres-sions of its inhabitants, and having 'presented' the offenders could sentence and punish them. Village stocks and ducking stools were both the symbols and instruments of control. Right up until the seventeenth century, villagers guilty of theft or adultery were beaten in English villages 'until their backs were bloody'. Wilton had its own 'cage, pillory and stocks'. The tumbrel and 'cucckingstool' – 'a chair in which scolds were sat down to be dunked (*demergebantur*) in the river' – were kept in the little 'parrock' – an enclosure fenced in with hurdles – belonging to a townsman called Richard Hatchett.

The village was never more vigilant than on the question of land, its boundaries, uses, and access. Common land was not common to anyone: it was common to the few villagers who had rights over it. Others were excluded. The great open fields were not open in any democratic sense: their individual strips, even if re-allocated each year among the villagers, were individually named and individually owned, marked and policed. You could be had up for trespassing on them just as much as on any enclosed land. Acres of parchment were devoted to precise and enforceable rights to and exclusions from wood, marsh and moor.

Why so tight? Because most of rural England, from the Middle Ages onwards, spent most of the time under stress. There was a desperate shortage of fertility: farming systems could only just sustain the human populations that depended on them. If for every grain sown, the average return was between three and four grains, one of which had to be kept as seed corn for the next year, the land was an asset to be cosseted. Nothing could be allowed to disrupt the habits which, so far at least, had allowed the village to feed its people. Poverty bred fear, fear conservatism and conservatism shut out strangers.

This, in many ways, was the reality of Arcadia, a reliance on rules inherited from 'a time beyond which the memory of man runneth not to the contrary', not because those rules stemmed from a Golden Age but because of the risk that changing them would dissolve the system on which survival depended. Communal memory was the arbiter of life. The 'custom of the manor' from 'time out of mind' was both a moral duty and a set of practical requirements. There was to be no private dealing of which the court and village did not know the details. The manor courts, which in their different forms could deal with petty crimes and with all property transactions and transfers, were to be the places in which grievances were to be aired and arrangements made because only in the openness of those courts, which all copyholders could attend, was communal wellbeing – common wealth – to be found.

The closed-circuit supervision of one's neighbours' prying eyes ensured that people would not cut down their timber trees, sublet their land for longer than a year nor sell any part of it except in open court. They had to maintain their buildings. If they did not, they would be warned three times, at six-monthly intervals. On the third time, a stake would be driven into the ground by the front door (said to be the origin of an asset being 'at stake'). If nothing had been done by the fourth time, the property would be forfeit. Then the 'customary tenant' – the expression means 'the holder of the land by the custom of the manor' – would be driven out of his 'tenement', the held thing. Although there were freeholders in these villages, they were only free of the labour and money dues which the copyholders owed to the manor. They were not free of the custom of the manor itself. And if they failed to observe the rules of the village, or committed treason or a felony, they too could be deprived of their freehold. In that sense, no one, except the lord of the manor, owned anything here. They, as tenants, merely held their tenements. Survival was conditional on obedience. It was a system about as far from the modern conception of the individual and his rights, let alone a welfare state, as it was possible to get.

Estate management, health and safety issues, anti-social be-haviour, the highways, property law, animal health and welfare, environmental health, planning permissions, local taxation, police issues, rights of way, agricultural practices, land rights and infringe-ments, supervision of property held in common: every one was dealt with by the lord's steward and a jury, or 'homage' as it was significantly called, of twelve of the copyholders. The village was not merely an economic unit; it embodied and enacted almost every conceivable dimension of social and political life. This, not England, was a man's country and political consciousness penetrated to the very depths of village England, a constant and constantly honed practising of a set of political rules which felt like the frame of life. Economic management, a deal between the members of a community and moral policing all came together in an arrangement that was essentially corporate. Privacy in such a world was not only scarcely available; it would also have seemed wrong.

That 'custom of the manor' represented an equilibrium of interests between tenant and landlord. The landlord, in fact, could only impose what the tenants would agree to. The way, for example, in which the area of each holding was measured was more responsive to the reality on the ground than to some abstract, imposed rule. Rent was dependent on acreage but an acre in the 1630s was not the precisely defined unit it is today. An acre was simply the area of ground which a plough could cover in a single day. If the ground was heavy, the acre would shrink to match the conditions; and if the soil was light, the acre would expand. Everyone knew that, no one would think of altering it and the conditions of the agreement were all deeply familiar.

Detail was all. No one manor had rules identical to any other. Even neighbouring villages in the same valley, or on other sides of the same chalk ridge, would have quite various habits and requirements. The customs of Great Wishford in the Wylye valley and Barford St Martin in the valley of the Nadder were 'set down in writing' in 1597. A copy of them survives among the Pembroke papers. They were set down jointly because both villages 'ever had an old Ancient Custome' which gave them rights in the great old royal forest of Grovely on the chalk ridge that lay between them. They could both pasture 'all manner of Beasts and cattle throughout all Grovely for all the year' (except 'cattle of two Tooth and Goates, and pigs above a yeare old'.) 'Ever out of mind,' they could collect fallen boughs twice a day, once in the morning, once in the evening. By 'an ancient custom & time out of mind' on Holy Thursday every year, the men of Wishford could collect 'One load of Trees'; on Whitsunday the men of Barford could do the same but only 'upon a Cart to be Drawn home with Men's Strengthe'. In addition, Lord Pembroke's ranger had to bring them, every year also on Whitsunday, 'One fatt Buck, the one half to Wishford, and the other to Barford to make merry withal amongst the neighbours & the ranger is to have from each of the manors of Wishford & Barford one white loaf, one gallon of beer & a pair of gloves or 12d in money for the Whole.'

In Burcombe, on the Nadder just east of Barford, 'the Custom of this Manor' constituted in effect a memory and inheritance of the duties required of the medieval villeins. A sixteenth-century copy of the customs laid down exactly what work had to be done for the earl by each of the copyholders. Each small tenant (with a house and fifteen acres) had to plough and hedge half an acre of barley land for the farmer who had rented the lord's own demesne land; the larger tenants (with a house and thirty acres) had to perform twice that amount of work, with 'the same Farmer giving to them their Breakfast'. At harvest time, the small tenants had to provide 'one sufficient Reaper for one day' or 3½d, the large tenants 'one man and one woman for one day or 7d at the choice of the said farmer'.

Together, the tenants of Burcombe had to 'mow and cut down' the hay in the seven acres of the meadow called Westmead (for which more breakfast was to be provided by the farmer) and then, when it had dried in the sun for a day or two, make it into stooks for which the farmer would provide bread and cheese. Another four and a half acres of hay of Burcombe, which was still in the earl's hands for the horses at Wilton, had to be made by the tenants, for which the lord's bailiff would provide 4s 4½d 'for and toward the provision of their drink'. These were the customs which were 'writ and Remember'd'.

Inevitably, it didn't always go well. Individual ambition would constantly break through the carefully woven fabric. At Heale, a tiny place in the valley of the Avon, north of Salisbury, the villagers were clearly having a difficult time with a recalcitrant member of the community. John Harford was a freeholder who was not playing by the rules. He was asked to turn up at the court that was held by the steward there on 4 April 1607. Harford didn't arrive and so they fined him 6d (which he could have spent on having two fat pigs butchered and dressed, or a sow spayed). Then the homage got on to the main business. 'The homage doe also presente John Harford for tyinge of his horses upon the Lynchards [the banks between the arable strips] in the Corne feildes before the Corne was rydd contrarye to an ancient order made here in this Courte and therefore he is merced [fined] 3s 4d', a sum for which he could have had three dozen sheep hurdles or seventy yards of new hawthorn hedge planted.

There was a great deal of other business. Christopher Whytehorne, another non-appearer, hadn't scoured his ditches and was required to do so 'between this and Allhallowtyde nexte' (1 November). A copyholder had died since the last court and the 'heriot' or death duty – almost invariably the best beast they had, or its value – was payable to the lord. No one was to fish with nets in the river except the lord. The entire village had to agree to remake the pound with strong hooks and locks in which any stray animals could be securely shut up. There were also problems with people living in the village who didn't belong there. No one who wasn't part of the system was allowed to stay, a sign in itself of the tightness of the food supply, but the judgement was relatively calm. The strangers had to be gone by the end of the summer. 'The homage doe also presente that Roger Dawkyns is an ynmate and liveth in the widdowe Youngs howse, and tyme is given her to rydd him therhence on this side the feaste of St Michaell the Archangel next cominge [29 September] upon paine of loasing 5 shillings.'

John Harford was the one figure who was failing to support the system. He had not delivered to the communal shepherds the nine hurdles he owed the community. If he didn't provide the hurdles 'the daye before the lambes goe afeilde' he would be fined 3s 4d and 'the fouled shall skypp over the said John Harford's lande', the ultimate sanction of no fertility, no corn, no money, no future.

The court met again in September and Harford was still behaving disrespectfully to the community. His pigs were going 'unringed contrarie to an Anciente order made here in this courte and therefore he is amerced 3s 4d'. His fines for the year amounted to a poor man's wages for two months. One can perhaps see in this behaviour the stirring of another world, of a man longing to escape the petty and irritating bonds which the village imposed. The court made another judgement on a form of individualistic behaviour of which Harford may or may not have been the guilty party. 'Yt is also ordered att this Courte by the Lord of this mannor by the Consente of the tenants and homage,' they began, in a formula which laid the foundations of a carefully agreed point of view,

> that noe tennent or Commoner of this mannor at any tyme hereafter shall keepe any manner of Sheepe or lambes, teggs, hoggs or ewes upon or in any parte or parcell of the Common downes or feildes of the mannor, but shall keepe them in the Common fould there to be foulded, and to be kepte in the only keepinge of the Sheapeard of the Common flocke of sheepe of this mannor accordinge to an anciente ordinaunce heretofore made in this Courte uppon paine of 6s 8d for everye such offence.

The elaborate and legalistic language, the sheer saloon bar pomposity of this, and the enormous fine to be imposed – the price of over four pounds of pepper, two dozen bars of soap, or four leather-bound writing books – is a measure of the importance attached to keeping the system whole. Harford and his kind looked like a threat from the future.

These old remembered rights, sanctions and duties were the living inheritance of the Middle Ages. When the castle at Wardour, a Wiltshire manor belonging to the Pembrokes' neighbours the Arundells, was blown up after a savage siege in the civil war, all its records were destroyed. After the war was over, both tenants and the steward of the manor went to inspect the records of Shaftesbury Abbey, to which the manor had belonged in the Middle Ages, and copied out the medieval rules. There was no sense of incongruity in this. These were the rules and their age was more a guarantee of their excellence than otherwise. Fifteenth- or fourteenth-century codes were to regulate the lives of the people of Wardour in the 1660s. That was normal. Nothing changed.

Everywhere you look in these customary regulations, the memory of the Middle Ages is there. Even in mid-seventeenth-century records, in a country where the worship of the saints and all the practices of the Roman Catholic church were meant to have been abolished for 120 years, the pattern of the year continued to be measured out according to the ancient saints' days. At Chilmark, a few miles west of Barford St Martin, the common was to be closed off to the copyholders' animals from 'Ladyday [25 March, New Year's Day in the seventeenth century, the Feast of the Annunciation of the Blessed Virgin Mary] to the Feast of the Invocation of the Holy Cross [3 May]', when the tenants from both ends of Chilmark Common were allowed the use of it until 'the Feast of St Martin the Bishop [11 November]' when it was again closed to them and opened to the animals of the neighbouring village, until the following spring.

This Christian calendar calibrated the year, its ceremonies and associations miraculously twinned to the seasons. Candlemas or the Feast of the Purification, on 2 February, marked both the point that was halfway between the winter solstice and the spring equinox, the day on which winter was half over, and the day, forty days after the birth of Christ, on which Mary was presented at the temple, the moment at which she also re-emerged into the world. It was the time of transition, and the opportunity for bitter peasant prognostication:

> If Candlemas Day be fair and bright,
> Winter will have another flight
> But if it be dark with clouds and rain,
> Winter is gone, and will not come again.

Lady Day on 25 March, the Feast of the Annunciation, the moment at which Christ was conceived, was also the beginning of the farming year, the first hint of spring, nine months before Christmas, the seeding of the future. Easter, in April, marked the fullness of spring, and the culmination of the Christian story, the fertility of things finally defeating the darkness of winter. On through the year, as custom after custom makes clear, the people of the chalklands lived in an environment where ancient and inherited signals provided the landmarks for their lives. At Rogationtide in early May, as the arable crops were just sprouting, the whole village would offer prayers (*rogationes*) for those crops and their animals, beating the bounds of the village, of individual fields and even individual strips within them, to establish in the minds of this and future generations exactly where those boundaries were. These weren't always certain, and besides, there was always suspicion that one or two leaseholders might try to encroach on the land of the customary tenants. In 1618, the tenants in the manor court at Heale, in the valley of the Avon, decided to lay down the law:

> Yt is also ordered by the Lord of this Mannor by the Consente of the tenants of this mannor that the homage shall between this and Witsuntyde next stake out all the Tenants' lands of the Mannor, and that they shall then viewe what wronge the Leasehoulders have done to the Coppyhoulders in the feilde, and sett out and stake out the bounds, and shall presente the wrongs att the nexte Courte and by whom the same have been soe donne.

Beating the bounds wasn't some folksy, antiquarian community festival; it was defining the means of survival. But it was also more than that. The land itself was the central mnemonic of their lives, the map of who they were, the method by which the place and the social relationships within it were known. To plough an acre strip – each 'a furrow long' and four rods, 16½ feet, wide – would take a day. That was an arrangement which folded together land, body, property and time. The body itself would have known immediately and by utter familiarity what an acre meant. The eye could estimate a furlong at a glance. Each strip had a name: Bere furlong, Peashill, Saltacre, Bracelet, probably after 'bercelet' meaning a sheep dog,

Hatchet acre, Elbow acre, Pyked furlong, after the sometimes strange crooked outline of the strips. Inherited meaning was folded into the copyhold land like sugar stirred into a cake. No signs or signals were needed; it was simply known, part of what was, time out of mind.

The Pembrokes' cousin, the poet George Herbert, who in the early 1630s was the vicar of Bemerton, in the valley of the Nadder between Wilton and Salisbury, gave many overlapping reasons for beating the bounds in May: it was a blessing of God for the fruits of the field; it established 'Justice in the preservation of the bounds'; it was a moment for 'Mercie, in relieving the poor by a liberal distribution of largess which at that time is or ought be made'; and it was an act of charity and neighbourliness, 'in living, walking and neighbourlily accompanying one another, with reconciling of differences at that time, if they be any'. For Herbert, these were the four dimensions of a village's existence: metaphysical, legislative, personal and social. The melding of communal action with communal need and communal belief which beating the bounds represented is the clearest of all demonstrations of the depth and multiplicity of meanings that were soaked into these places. Seen from an era of individual rights, the manor system may look like a nightmare of restriction and denial; from its own perspective, it was a deliberate and effective mechanism for a multi-dimensional life, in which land was not a commodity but the matrix for existence.

The year rolled inexorably onwards: Midsummer Night was celebrated on 24 June, six months from Christmas and holding up a mirror to it. Huge bonfires were lit, boys picked flowers which they gave to girls and the girls threw them into the flames to keep them free all year of agues and afflictions. The following day was the Feast of St John the Baptist, the figure who represented not the redemption of the world but the heralding of a new version of it. The first of August was Lammas, or Loaf Mass, Day when the first wheat harvest of the year, baked into a loaf, was brought into church and tenants were bound to present a sheaf of the new harvest to their landlords. By 24 August, Bartlemas or St Bartholomew's Day (Bartholomew had been flayed alive and was the patron saint of butchers), all pigs' noses were to be ringed; by Michaelmas, the Feast of St Michael and All Angels, on 29 September, all animals were to leave the common fields; at St Luke's Day, 18 October, all lambs were to be counted as sheep; and by Martinmas, the Feast of St Martin, on 11 November, the commons were to be cleared of grazing beasts. Of all this complex mapping of life on to land, history and inherited meaning, only Christmas, the Feast of the Nativity, 25 December, is now remembered, a sign in itself of the destruction and disappearance of this Arcadian world.

4

A countrey of lands and Mannours

The Pembrokes impose their vision on Wilton
1542–1570

WILTON HAD ONCE been the capital of England and Wiltshire was named after it. It had been the royal capital of Wessex, destroyed by the Vikings in 871 after they had come rampaging down the Roman road through Grovely Wood, and rebuilt afterwards by Alfred. But here Wilton's history took a decisive turn. Alfred moved his capital to Winchester, which was more easily defended, and Wilton was left as a place of ancient significance but no present power. Alfred gave the site of his palace for an abbey.

In the mind of medieval England, Wilton combined grandeur and sanctity. It was no rural backwater. In 890 Alfred laid a foundation stone for the religious house where aristocratic women could take the veil. There were to be thirteen new nuns, joined by thirteen others from an old priory which had been established earlier in the town. From the beginning it was high and holy. Saint Edith, the daughter of King Edgar and Queen Wulfthryth, became a nun here, but relinquished none of her status or her royalty. When the unwashed hermit Saint Adelwold, Bishop of Lindisfarne, a man seeking holiness not in the ease and comfort of Wiltshire but on a seabird-encrusted rock in the North Sea, visited the nunnery and reproached her for her luxuries, Edith told him that 'she in her garments of gold thread could be as virtuous as he in his filthy skins'. That is the voice of Wilton: hauteur allied to purity.

The status of the place remained high throughout the Middle Ages. King Canute and William the Conqueror both endowed the nunnery. Miracles were performed at the shrine of St Edith and pilgrims flocked to the place where the blessings of a royal saint could be bestowed on them. The young girls who took the veil here were of the highest birth: earls' daughters, the sisters of kings. Property flowed towards them. Lands, many of which belonged to the Pembrokes in the seventeenth century and some of which remain at the heart of the Pembroke estate today, were granted to the nunnery more than a thousand years ago. In 934 Athelstan gave Wilton the manor of North Newnton in the forest of Savernake. In 955 King Edwy gave the abbey the vast acreages at Chalke, Broad Chalke and Bower Chalke, on which Philip Sidney and John Aubrey would later dream of Arcadia. More lands and mills followed from King Edgar and King Ethelred. King Harold's daughter became a nun there. After the Norman Conquest, his sister Edith, widow of Edward the Confessor, came to join her.

By the time of the Domesday Book in 1086, the abbess at Wilton was as much of a magnate as any earl, controlling just over 29,000 acres, the vast majority of it on the downs and the valleys of the chalk streams to the west of Wilton. From it, the nunnery received an income of £246 15s a year, the highest of any in England.

Royal daughters and royal gifts continued to pour into Wilton throughout the centuries. Little of the glory which appeared at Wilton in the sixteenth and seventeenth centuries outdid what had been done here in the Middle Ages. Feasts were held in which swans and peacocks were stuffed and roasted. The nuns failed to pay their taxes and were held up for inspection. Edward I sent his daughter to be a nun here, Henry III sent oaks for rebuilding the abbey, 'gold tinselled silk' and a barrel of French wine. They were corrupt: the nuns refused to spend the night enclosed in the abbey walls; some had children. The abbess lived in luxury, with her own pantry and her own 'abbessebred' which was baked only for her. A special kind of better quality ale was brewed for her and her guests alone.

By the 1520s, any rigour there had ever been in the ancient abbey had gone. The nuns were in dispute with the Bishop of Salisbury.

Few of them ever wanted to stay the night inside the abbey walls, unsurprisingly, as they had a business and an estate to run. Cardinal Wolsey, the great factotum of royal government, sent his henchman Thomas Benet to impose some discipline but the headstrong women were impossible to keep shut up. Benet wrote pathetically to his master that 'in no wise any of them by gentle means nor by rigorous – and I have put three or four of the captains of them in ward – will agree and consent.' Further attempts were made to get them to conform but to no effect. As a signal of the way the Tudor world worked, when the election of a new abbess came up in 1528, a man called John Carey, Anne Boleyn's brother-in-law, wanted his own sister Elinor to be chosen. Cardinal Wolsey tried to persuade the king to have her elected. Anne Boleyn got involved. Money was offered to the king but in the end he wrote to Anne: 'I wolde not for all the gold in the worlde clog your conscience nor mine to make her a ruler of a house, which is of so ungodly a demeanour.' A terminal state of affairs: not that the king was averse to a bribe; just that Wilton was so dreadful a place even he would feel tainted by it.

The world was changing around the nuns. The election of a new prioress in 1533 was as crooked as any Protestant reformer could have required. Two candidates, both called Cecily, attempted to bribe their way into the position. Cecily Lambert, using Thomas Cromwell, Wolsey's successor at the centre of government, as her agent, offered the king £100 if she were elected. Cecily Bodenham borrowed large amounts to scatter among the nuns. Bodenham won and immediately rented out some of the key lands at Fovant, a small village above the Nadder (its name has the word 'fount' buried inside it) as well as others in the Elysian fields of Broad Chalke and at Washern (just across the Nadder from Wilton) to her friends and relations, on highly favourable terms. They had probably contributed to her election campaign funds.

As the net revenues of the abbey in the late 1530s were just over £700 a year, this was clearly a prize worth bargaining for. It would not be long before Thomas Cromwell, rapidly acquiring for the crown the assets of over 800 monasteries, a nationalisation of the most important properties in private hands in England and Wales, got this one too. On 25 March 1539, New Year's Day, the abbey surrendered to the crown, just over 700 years after Alfred had laid its foundations. The nuns were treated perfectly well. Cecily Bodenham was given a pension of £100 a year and a nice house at Fovant. There she was to have orchards, gardens and meadows and a cartload of fuel every week from the large wood down in the valley. Her friends and relations were inevitably ejected from the farms she had procured for them. The prioress was given a pension of £10 and thirty-one other nuns varying sums down to £2 a year. The entire giant property entered royal ownership and the long sequence of grand abbesses, their names a litany of high-born medieval Englishness – Isabel de Warenne, Maud de la Mare, Juliana Gifford, Emma Blount, Lucy Loveny, Sibyl Aucher, Maud de Bokeland, Felise Lavington, Joan Beauchamp, Christine Codford, Isabel Lambard, Edith Barough, Alice Comelonde, Cecily Willoughby, Isabel Jordayne and Cecily Bodenham – came to an end.

Just over a year later, it would be in the hands of the man who would become the first Earl of Pembroke. He was as tough, powerful and cynical, and his wife as serious and high-minded, as anyone in sixteenth-century England. Together, they embodied the two streams of Tudor life: the untrammelled broking of power through violence, threat and political flexibility; and the cleansing of the mind through education and integrity. William Herbert and his wife Anne might be seen as the rootstock of the Wilton Arcadia: its necessary power; its longing for goodness.

William Herbert was a Welsh hardman. He may not have been able to read and could scarcely write his own name – those signatures of his which survive, in an age of sometimes exquisite handwriting, waver and wobble from one letter to the next, unable to distinguish lower from upper case, not even pursuing a straight line across the page, but intent on a flourish here and there, the writing of a bear – a bear with pretensions – into whose paw someone has thrust a pen.

According to Aubrey, Herbert was 'strong sett, but bony, reddish favoured, of a sharpe eie, sterne looke' and his portraits confirm that stark, bullish quality, his feet planted four-square beneath him, his eyes cold, his impatient face scarcely connected to the finery in which he had been dressed, one hand holding gloves but ready for the sword, the other clasping the staff of office as if it were a stick he might hit someone with. Everything is fixed, obdurate, immovable, the man as substantial as the material world to which his life and passions had been directed. He was the acquirer of riches and the founder of a dynasty. The Elizabethan historian William Camden called him 'an excellent man, who was in a manner, the Raiser of his own Fortunes', and Aubrey 'of good naturall parts, but very colorique'. He was an English condottiere, with a hatchet mouth and an unforgiving eye. Spirit barely flickered inside him. He was no Arcadian but without him Arcadia could not have flowered.

Neither William Herbert, nor his descendants, wanted to see themselves as arrivistes. They wanted to look as if they had always been at the heart of significance and throughout the sixteenth and seventeenth centuries the Pembrokes did their best to cover up some slightly flaky origins. In the fourteenth and fifteenth centuries they had been entirely Welsh. Not until the late fifteenth century were they even called Herbert (no one knows where the name came from). Instead, out of the mists of Wales and time, emerged Jenkyn ap Adam who begat Gwylym ap Jenkyn, who begat Thomas ap Gwylym, who married Gladwys, the Star of Abergavenny (her dowry was a park full of deer) and together they begat William ap Thomas, who took a large body of Welsh archers to Agincourt. His son, Gwilym Ddu, 'Black Will', marauded and burned his way across England in support of the Yorkist cause in the Wars of the Roses and as his reward was made Earl of Pembroke by Edward IV. This slashingly successful warrior, the first Welshman to become an

English peer, who for years ran the whole of Wales as his fiefdom, had several illegitimate children, one of whom, Richard, had as his lordship the poor, steep Vale of Ewyas in the Black Mountains, a place that is still full of small, edge-of-subsistence farms, houses pushed into the hillside, heart-stopping beauty and unrelenting rain.

No one could ever imagine that Ewyas was the threshold of power but it is the place from which the young William Herbert, Richard's second son, emerged to conquer his world. From a modern perspective, it is not surprising as a background to a tough, violent, imposing and driven life: a grandfather of heroic proportions; a present, near-fatal lack of social standing; the stain of illegitimacy; and the fate of the second son: disinheritance even from his own father's small patrimony.

That essentially meritocratic view was not how it was seen at the time. When William Herbert was made Earl of Pembroke in 1551, he did not boast of his climb to power, nor call himself the first Earl. There was no honour in that. As far as he was concerned, he was the twentieth Earl of Pembroke, heir in line direct to the previous nineteen, of nine different creations, who had battled their way across the Middle Ages. It was the grandest of inheritances. The pretentious George Owen, Elizabethan antiquarian and remote relation of the Herberts, whom he adulated, was still relishing the ancient power of the Earls of Pembroke in the late sixteenth century. The Earldom of Pembroke, Owen wrote, 'was in auncient tyme a County Palatine', not subject to any king's power. The earl 'had the commanding and leading of all the people of his country to make warres at his pleasure. He had within his Country nine castles of his owne and twelve seigniories or manors which were parcell of his Countye . . .'

In an era of increasing bureaucratisation of government, and an emasculation of the old magnates of medieval England, there was a frisson to this manly independence, which a mere created earl or baron could scarcely rival. It is not surprising than any memory of the illegitimacy of William Herbert's father was quietly soothed away. Here was a man conducting his life as a power-broking baron in the mould of his ancestors.

What Owen does not mention in his catalogue of honour is that the first time this William Herbert made his mark on the world, it was as a murderer. His father had died in 1510 when William was three, and the boy went to live in the household of his relation by marriage, the Earl of Worcester. Worcester was a warrior, administrator, diplomat and the great producer and showman of Henry VIII's court. He was responsible for the tournament ground and pasteboard palaces set up for the meeting of Henry VIII and François I at the Field of the Cloth of Gold in the summer of 1520. It was Worcester who arranged for five thousand people to be shipped across the Channel to France to arrange this event. Vast quantities of timber and glass were brought to the site. Three hundred knights took part in the tournament, over which Worcester himself presided as one of the judges. William Herbert, aged thirteen, was at his side, as his page, learning the intimacy of power and glory.

Worcester died on 25 April 1526 and that year William Herbert appears as a 'gentleman pensioner' at the court of Henry VIII. It was the lowest rung of court life. One could be a gentleman pensioner and still be thrown into jail for debt, or be arrested on suspicion of treason, but it was the necessary first step on the road to significance. But then Herbert's career came adrift. On Midsummer Eve 1527, a time for drinking and feasting, bonfires, high spirits, sex and violence, there was an incident in Bristol, the great seaport already spreading its networks to the New World, which might have destroyed him.

The Mayor of Bristol – a man known as Thomas or 'Davy' Broke, later described by the hostile Protestant preacher George Wishart as 'a knave and gorbely [fat] knave' – together with his 'brethren' – perhaps 'that droncken Gervys, that lubber Antony Payne, & slovyn William Yong, and that dobyll knave William Chester', all leading Bristol merchants and all identified by Wishart as Broke's associates – were coming back into the city after some duck shooting. Unexplained, William Herbert, already with the reputation of 'a mad fighting young fellow', was there with a gang of Welshmen to meet them on the bridge. They began to talk and 'for want of some respect in compliment' fell into an argument and then a rage. A fight broke out and Herbert killed one of the merchants, a man called Richard Vaughan from an old and distinguished Bristol family.

The incident fits. Herbert's origins in South Wales were just across the Severn. The Bristol men would have known he was an illegitimate son. Herbert had by now spent most of his life in the heady atmosphere of court, wearing the badge first of his kinsman the Earl of Worcester, then of the king himself, acquiring the sheen and courteousness of that world. His own honour would have been both high and tender in his mind, and now he found himself insulted by a party of midsummer, drunk, duck-hunting, Bristol merchants. Of course he turned to his knife.

Herbert and the Welshmen who were with him 'fled through a gate into the Marsh and escaped in a boat with the tide.' After that, wanted for murder, named in a Bristol coroner's report as the man who did it, Herbert disappeared. Nothing is known of him for the next seven or eight years. John Aubrey thought he had gone to France, to the Valois court, but as Herbert in later life was unable to speak French, that is unlikely. Maybe he went to ground in Wales, surrounded by the protective world of his Herbert connections, sheltered by the common understanding that Welsh fighters had long since been killing fat Bristol merchants. Either he, or someone else called William Herbert, killed 'one honest man' in Newport in South Wales in 1533 and his servant was convicted of killing yet another Welshman the following year. Brutalism lay at the centre of his life.

In 1534, Herbert was still being described as a 'late gentleman of the household' but soon after that he returned to court, was re-admitted to the glowing circle near the king and in 1535 promoted to become 'an esquire of the body', an honorific title but one that implied a further penetration of the layers surrounding the sovereign. The story of this family over more than a hundred years is hinged, at least in part, to that bodily geometry: closeness to the king, to his actual body, his breathing presence, is the one variable which governs their fortunes. Thuggery and exile among the ancestral comforts of South Wales was one thing; sharing the same physical space as the fount of all honour and the source of all lands was quite another.

On returning to court, he met Anne Parr, the woman he would marry. She and Herbert may have fallen in love. Neither had any fortune to bring to the marriage. Both were orphans. Both were making their own way in the world of the court. And Henry VIII's court in the 1530s was one where love and courtly love were both admired and practised, as necessary and civilising elements of the Italianate courtier's life. The most beautiful lines written in Tudor England are by Thomas Wyatt, in his poem bemoaning the unArcadian, treacherous courtly world of calculation and disloyalty ('They fle from me that sometyme did me seke'), describing just such a moment of unadorned and immediate love,

> When her lose gowne from her shoulders did fall
> And she me caught in her armes long and small
> Therewithal sweetly did me kysse
> And softly said 'dere hert, howe like you this?'

Love itself might also be seen as a form of Arcadia, a private place in which the fever and anguish of being is soothed away.

Will Herbert was about eight years older than Anne Parr and a drawing by Holbein, probably made when she was about twenty in 1535, shows her as she was when he fell in love with her. As an image, it is a universe apart from Herbert's tense and wary assertion: calm, pure and controlled, with a clarity and directness about her eyes, and a firmness but no meanness in her mouth, she seems all spirit. It was a marriage of opposites. It is a strikingly Protestant image, nearly shadowless, a form of portraiture which is motivated by truth and clarity, a product of the Reformation, the removal of the dark and its substitution with the clear-eyed, clear-skinned vision of Englishwomen such as Anne Parr.

In 1531, as an orphaned sixteen-year-old after her mother died, she had come to court to serve as a maid-in-waiting to Henry VIII's sequence of queens. She was the daughter of a gentry family, of no great wealth or standing, but one which since 1483, over four generations, had served England's queens. Her mother, Dame Maud Parr, had been both confidante and lady-in-waiting to Henry's first queen, Catherine of Aragon, and now both Anne and her elder sister Katherine were serving in the household of Catherine's daughter, Princess Mary. Sir Thomas Parr had died in 1517 and both girls had been brought up with their brother William by the formidable Dame Maud. She was fluent in French and maybe also in Latin, a manager of lands and contracts, an educational theorist and friend of the humanist scholars Thomas More and Roger Ascham. She had provided her daughters with the richest possible humanist education, setting up a small school in their house in Leicestershire. Its methods had been modelled on the programme Thomas More had ordained for his own family, teaching the children philosophy, mathematics, Latin, French and Italian, chess, the study of coins and art theory, medicine and a rigorous training in the scriptures. Anne had emerged a scholar. In later life she would become patron of fellows at St John's College, Cambridge. She sent two of her sons to Peterhouse. Roger Ascham, who became Elizabeth I's tutor, borrowed her copy of Cicero and quoted Ovid in the letters he wrote her. The fineness and purity that glow from the face drawn by Holbein was no illusion.

Both Anne and her sister would become champions of the reformed religion which swept through England in the 1530s. It is difficult to escape the conclusion that their education in the highest and most sophisticated form of Renaissance humanism prepared the ground for a sceptical attitude to the inherited ways of the

Church. Anne Parr, in other words, looks like a Protestant in the making. She also looks like William Herbert's better half. They were probably married late in 1537, when she was twenty-two and he thirty-one.

No one could have predicted that they would be the foundation of one of the great families of England. She had remained no more than a maid-in-waiting, a body servant, to the evolving sequence of queens; he was still an Esquire of the King's Body. They were without any prospect of inheritance, landless, disconnected from that great engine of power, but playing their hands in the life of the court, the only place where that condition could be altered. 'Upon the bare stock of their wits, they began to traffic for themselves.' Over the next twenty years, the two of them played that game more success-fully than anyone else in England.

William's attitude to religion would remain equivocal for the rest of his life. He changed as circumstances required him to change. He believed in the religion which the king or queen of the day required him to believe in, no more and no less. Such changes of religious allegiance were no rarity in sixteenth-century England – many justified it openly on state grounds – but his volte-faces were among the slickest and the sweetest. In the 1590s, the old, slippery smooth courtier, the Marquess of Winchester, was

> questioned how he stood up for thirty years together amidst the changes and raignes of so many chancellors and great personages. Why, quoth the Marquess, *Ortus sum ex salice, non ex quercu*, I was made of the plyable willow, not of the stubborn oak. And truly the old man hath taught them all, especially William, earl of Pembroke, for they two were ever of the King's religion, and ever zealous professors.

Meanwhile, the two young Herberts, as if in a game of grand-mother's footsteps, were making their slow and careful approach to the centre of power. Anne became a Gentlewoman of the Queen's Household and William one of fifty new Gentlemen Spears, as they were called, an extravagantly equipped honour guard, with gold

chains and gilt pole axes, an elite band of strong young capable
courtiers among whom Henry felt at ease. Will Herbert soon rose
again to become a Gentleman of the Privy Chamber, at a stipend
of £50 a year, one of a set of efficient, tough, educated officials of
royal government, entirely dependent on the favour and will of the
king. They were no palace popinjays or playthings of the king
but for him essential information-gathering, will-enforcing tools of
government, diplomacy and war.

In the spring of 1539, the abbey at Wilton was among the 800
dissolved in England and Wales. Much of the rest of the year must
have been taken up at court with speculation on who the recipient
of this wonderful place and its lands might be. In May 1540 the
door opened: William Herbert received a twenty-one-year lease of
the site of Wilton Abbey; in July he was appointed chief steward of
all the abbey's lands. He was knighted, Anne became Keeper of the
Queen's Jewels and that autumn their son Henry was born.

For three years, Wilton remained the property of the crown but
in April 1542 it was given, by Henry VIII's 'mere motion', as it is
described in the enormous Exchequer document prepared for the
King's Remembrancer, the official whose task it was to remember
everything that had been done by the king or in his name, to 'our
beloved Servant William Herbert Knight and Anne his wife'. The
document is vast because it lists the vastness of the gift. The house
and site of the abbey 'now dissolved' and all our 'messuages houses
edifices dove houses stables mills barns orchards gardens waters
ponds parks lands soil and hereditaments whatsoever' were to go
to the chosen couple. The list rolls on and on: manors, lordships,
tithes, corn sheaves, grain, hay, 'fisheries and the fishings of our
waters', the 'twenty and five quarters of salt annually extracted from
the salt pits' in Dorset, the 'granges mills tofts cottages meadows
feedings pastures waste furze heath and marshes,' as well as all sorts
of 'fees farms annuities and pensions' which the 'last abbess and
convent' had been entitled to. The list of places, and of everything
in them, was a hymn to accumulation, the beauty of materiality,

satisfying the deepest possible lust for land and property. The King's Remembrancer was transferring the ownership of an entire world and its driving force was the 'mere motion' of regal power, a fiat, a breaking of bonds that had persisted for centuries. Herbert was now in possession of what John Aubrey would call 'a countrey of lands and Mannours', a fiefdom, a power-base and a landscape.

This was good but it was not everything: no more than a grant for their lifetimes. After their deaths, as things stood, the great estate would revert to the crown. But in July 1543, the world of the Herberts changed. Anne's elder sister, Katherine, to whom she was exceptionally close and who shared with her a passionate attachment to the reformed religion, married the king. She was a beautiful widow and the king fell in love with her. Both William and Anne Herbert attended the wedding, at which Henry shouted 'Yea!' when asked if he wanted to marry her. Anne helped her sister prepare the black silk nightdresses the king liked his brides to wear and William Herbert suddenly found himself the royal brother-in-law. Lands, offices and cash began to flow towards him. As their London house, the new queen gave them the great old palace of Baynard's Castle on the Thames. With it came the right to bind any traitor 'at low tide to a pillar in the Thames near the Castle Wall, leaving him there for two floods and two ebbs.' The totality of royal power was lapping at their shores.

Wilton and its train of beauties became Herbert's and his family's for ever in January 1544. Royal stewardships in Wales followed and in 1546, Herbert became Joint Chief Gentleman of the Bedchamber, the place with the steadiest and most regular contact with the king in his most private moments, the soft, potent heart of monarchy.

In the summer of 1543 Herbert started to erect his new house at Wilton, 'a large & high built square of hewen stone'. It was in some ways a Tudor muddle, with pediments and onion domelets, classical busts in circular frames, scallop shells, out-of-scale columns and pilasters, a collection of ideas borrowed from the Renaissance, with Corinthian capitals and exquisite entablatures all finely executed but with little understanding of the system of which they should have been a part. Herbert liked to wear a large ring on each of his index fingers and his new house at Wilton was rather like that: expensive, flashy and big. Its lead rainheads and downpipes were decorated with a rich and barbaric mixture of green men and beautiful acanthus leaves twisted into elegant knots. All over the building, as you can still see if you creep in under the attic spaces of the later additions, brilliant colours and gilding, armorial beasts and legendary figures encrusting the walls. It was an adaptation of the abbey, probably based around the abbey cloister, but still it cost more than £10,000. Sixteen acres of five- and six-year-old coppice trees were felled to provide the fuel to burn the lime to make the mortar with which the stones were bound together. Those stones came either from the partly demolished abbey itself or from the ancient site of Old Sarum, carted in to the palace by the River Nadder all summer long.

Parts of the Tudor house remain embedded in the seventeenth- and nineteenth-century additions, and one porch was preserved by Inigo Jones as a fine example of early Renaissance style, but the effect of Herbert's showiness can be measured by an account of it set down in 1635 by a Lieutenant Hammond, who was touring the west of England. He found Wilton as it was after the great seventeenth-century garden had been created but just before the transforming Jonesian work on the house had begun. It was a building larded with richness: a gallery, 'richly hung and adorn'd with stately and faire pictures'; cloth of gold hangings, 'over the Chimney peece the statue of King Henry 8th richly cut and gilded ouer', 'the great Dyning Chamber, very richly hang'd'; in it 'a most curious Chimney Peece, of Alablaster Touch-Stone and marble, cut with seuerall statues, the Kings and his lordships owne armes richly sett out.' Accounts have survived of marble and jasper doorcases as well as 'eight great tables' imported from France.

Buried inside this gilded case was the hidden fist, still there, remarkably, in 1635, something which, Lieutenant Hammond felt, 'may well compare with any in the Kingdome:'

That is a most gallant Armory, which is 60 yards in length, the number of Armes therein will compleatly furnish, and fit out 1000 Foote, and Horse: besides 30 Glaues [lances], 30 Welsh Hookes, 60 Black Bills, 20 Holy water Springers [?], and 60 Staues, which were weapons to guard the old Lord's Person, with many other Offensiue, and Defensive Armes as Coats of Maile &c.

In a special room at the end of this huge private arsenal were the great suits of armour Herbert and his son collected: one made in Greenwich for Henry VIII and another for Edward VI, complete suits of Milan armour, 'the Lord William his Turkish Scymiter, or sable, and his whole armour for his Horse richly grauen and gilded.'

Could the foundations of power in an English country house have ever been quite so graphically displayed? By the time an inventory was made of the house in 1683, there was both a 'new' and an 'old armory'. The new had some pistols, blunderbusses, bullet moulds and 'bullet guns' stored in it, but the old spoke of an earlier world. Piles of muskets, too many for the surveyor to count, were in there among the 'hollster pistols' and 'bandiloes' – a broad belt from which something heavy could be slung. Alongside them, twenty-six bills – hooks to be used for slashing at hedges or men – twenty 'holboards' – halberds, a combination of axe and spear on the end of a seven-foot pole – 260 pikes, ninety-two other pikes and, most chillingly of all, 'dog chains'.

Outside the door this hardman established his own Arcadia. A garden was made with walks, fishponds and fruit trees and a stable built for eighty horses. The abbey's dovecote, forge, mill and giant grange for the grain rents from the estate were all left standing. The entire village of Washern, across the Nadder from the site of the abbey, as well as the vicarage of Bulbridge, was enclosed in a new park and demolished. What had been both common land – the open fields – and 'several' land – closes belonging to individuals – was shut up in the park and denied to the people who had farmed it 'time out of mind'. Herbert planted a copse and an avenue of trees where the people of Washern had previously grown their food. The avenue would later be called 'Sir Philip Sidney's Walk', as it was there he would stroll, composing the *Arcadia*. Within the park, among the 'diverse et pulchre perambulaciones,' as a surveyor in 1566, described it, half English, half Latin, Herbert built 'unum Standinge' – a platform – 'in quo dominus stare potest ad super vivendum diversa loca pro placito suo' – in which the lord can stand so that he can overlook the various places for his pleasure.

Those few actions, and the few sentences used to describe them, represent the conflict of the two Arcadias. The ancient abbey is destroyed; a palace is built in its place; the poor have their ancient rights kicked away and their houses demolished; and a beautiful stretch of parkland, adorned with trees and pleasure buildings, is installed where their ancestors had lived. The purpose is 'pro placito suo', to calm the great man's troubled mind and to provide the lord with an easing vision of pre-lapsarian bliss.

The pleasure park erased the custom of the manor. It wasn't done entirely illegally. Where lands were taken from common grazing, or even from the open field, and enclosed in a park (Herbert would have seven parks in all by the 1560s, and employed a full-time 'Regarder', whose job was to travel round the parks looking at them to see all was well) the peasants received compensation, usually in the form of lowering of rents or a relaxation of the services due to the lord. At Wilton, a seven-acre field called Lampeland was enclosed in Herbert's park. In compensation for its loss, Herbert no longer required the villagers of Washern to pay 7 shillings 8d every year for a marsh or meadow called Woodmersh.

That is all very well, but in a system where pressure on food and resources was tight, and where the balance of arable land with hay-growing meadow was finely tuned, removing seven acres of growing ground, not to speak of demolishing houses in a world so deeply dependent for its sense of meaning on the form and pattern of use of the landscape hallowed by custom, was a form of dispossession which went far beyond the removal of an economic asset and resource. Why was it done? Not only to feed the vanity of a Tudor magnate but to provide a place of peace and calm in a life of extreme anxiety and stress. The sufferings of the villagers of Washern are a direct product of the tensions and struggles at the Tudor court.

The silent presence in this life is that of Anne Parr. Her portrait bust appears opposite William Herbert's on one face of the 1540s porch, said to be designed by Holbein, which still exists today in the Wilton garden. But her voice does not survive in the documents. At least at court, one can be sure that she played her part in protecting her sister, the queen, in the great crisis that threatened the Parrs and the future of the English Reformation in the summer of 1546. The sickening and increasingly short-tempered Henry VIII had turned against the revolutionary forces he had unleashed through his break with Rome. In this subtly murderous atmosphere, conservatives at court, led by Bishop Gardiner, had tried to frame Katherine as a radical and a subversive. Agents and spies had rifled through the queen's apartments, looking for proscribed books and pamphlets in cabinets, chests and drawers. She kept them, in fact, in the garderobe and when the threat became too hot, had them smuggled out to her uncle's house, only retrieving them after Henry had died. Anne Parr, who was Keeper of the Queen's Jewels, a passionate believer in the reformed religion, and well practised at secrecy and courtiership, was central to preserving a network of Protestants right at the heart of Whitehall. For a time, in 1546–7, Katherine Parr's chambers were the centre of the English Reformation.

John Foxe, the great chronicler of that revolution, described the atmosphere in which Anne Parr lived. The queen was

> very much given to the reading and study of the Holy Scriptures, and that she, for the purpose, had retained divers well learned and godly person to instruct her ... [and] every day in the afternoon for the space of an hour one of her said chaplains in her privy chamber made some collation to her and her ladies and gentlewomen of her privy chamber, or

others that were disposed to hear; in which sermons they ofttimes touched such abuses as in the church then were rife.

In February 1546, Katherine ordered some new coffers for her chamber, with new locks, metal hinges, corner bands and handles with nails: the tools of survival. People around her were being picked off by Bishop Gardiner. In May, a young aristocratic Protestant, Lord Thomas Howard, was summoned before the Privy Council and charged with 'disputing indiscreetly of Scripture with other young gentlemen of the Court'. Later that week, it was demanded that he 'confess what he said in disproof of sermons preached in Court last Lent and his other talk in the Queen's chamber and elsewhere in Court concerning Scripture.' Others of her servants, the courtiers, yeomen and physicians who attended her, were arrested and imprisoned for holding erroneous opinions and engaging in 'unseemly reasoning'.

In the last two weeks of July, Bishop Gardiner attempted to close the trap on the Parrs. According to John Foxe, the Protestant martyrologist, Gardiner came to the king and whispered in his ear that Katherine and her ladies were holding, discussing and propagating views which even by the king's own laws were heretical. More than that, 'he, with others of his faithful councillors, could within short time, disclose such reasons cloaked with this cloak of heresy, that his majesty could easily perceive how perilous a matter it is, to cherish a serpent within his own bosom . . .'

'They rejoice and be glad of my fall,' the queen had written two years earlier in a set of private prayers.

> They be assembled together against me. They strike to kill me in the way before I may beware of them. They gather themselves together in corners. They curse and ban my words everyday, and all their thoughts be set to do me harm. They watch my steps, how they may take my soul in a trap. They do beset my way, that I should not escape. They look and stare upon me. I am so vexed that I am utterly weary.

The Protestant condition had martyrdom at its heart. Its self-conceived purity was isolated in a world of sinners. A court was a nest of enemies, and only in the sacredness of the soul's relationship to God was there any refuge. At some level, there was a connection here – one that will run throughout the story of this family – between a Protestant desire for safety away from the failings of the world and the ideal of Arcadian bliss, a place devoted to the demands of love and purity of motive. Protestantism and Arcadianism in that way sat hand in hand, bridging the secular and religious cultures of early modern England. Both were driven by the demand for retreat and for a stilling of the clamour. Each represented an equal and opposite reaction to the disturbance and trauma of modernity: the speeding up of the flywheel; the sense that the world was getting old and corrupt; and beggars on every street and every corner. If inflation and debasement of the currency were rife, simplification was good. It seemed that the ancient was a refuge, that rents did not produce what they had in the past, that order was under threat, that bread was too expensive, that old systems of authority looked creaky and irrelevant, that there was no calm in the world.

One seventeenth-century puritan preacher, Ralph Josselin, an Essex clergyman, saw the grave itself as a gazebo, or a place like the Standinge in the park at Wilton, as somewhere drenched in peace. 'Your Wives, your Husbandes, your Sonnes and Daughters, whose departing you so much lament,' he told a funeral congregation, 'are but stept aside into their retiring rooms, their cool Summer-parlours, the shady cool Grove of the Grave to take a little rest by sleep . . .' Rest; the end of the drama; and silence: Renaissance England wanted nothing more. It is the subject that Hamlet dwelt on again and again: searching for somewhere in which the agony was over, where the flesh which he described either as too solid, too sullied or too sallied – all three readings are relevant – would at last melt and resolve itself into a dew. He was a Protestant prince but he was also an Arcadian, at home not in the world of strife to which his ancestors had all belonged, but in the place of reflection and quiet. The soliloquy was itself an Arcadian form.

The natural end of Gardiner's plot against Katherine Parr and her circle was the arrest, interrogation and execution of the queen and those about her. It reached its climax in the first week of August 1546. Gardiner's men had been into the queen's apartments. Anne Parr's closet, as well as those of the other gentlewomen of the chamber, had been searched but nothing found. The books were well away. Nevertheless, Gardiner felt he had enough evidence against her to persuade the king to issue a warrant for her arrest and committal to trial. Katherine guessed nothing, but by chance the warrant, at least according to John Foxe, fell out of the pocket of her enemy the Lord Chancellor, Sir Thomas Wriothesley. It was found on the paving stones by one of the queen's pages, or perhaps her doctor, and immediately brought to her.

Her courage left her and she fell into a fit of hysterics, took to her bed and when the king came to see her, spoke to him without guile, asking what it might be that she had done wrong. The next day she had recovered, went to him in his chamber, told him she was 'a silly poor woman' – meaning not that she was stupid but that she was innocent – and the king was her 'only anchor, supreme head and governor here in earth, next unto God, to lean unto.'

But there was no certainty in this court and Gardiner continued with his plot to destroy Katherine Parr. She and the king then moved to Hampton Court, and it was there that the final act was played. Henry, Katherine Parr, Anne Parr and the other gentlewomen of her court were in the Privy Gardens, when suddenly, without warning, Wriothesley himself appeared among the gravel walks and box-lined beds. He had forty armed guards with him and together they approached the royal party. Katherine watched for the king's reaction. By this stage in Henry's life, no one could be certain which way he would turn or which set of loyalties he would respond to. The needle, quite arbitrarily, could flick either way. Would this, as it had been for other queens, be the moment of denial? Or had her confession of weakness and dependence been enough? Her life and future hung in the balance as Wriothesley approached down the gravel paths. But for Henry, there was no hesitation. The king, in an apoplectic rage, took Wriothesley roughly aside and shouted at him. 'Knave! Arrant knave! Beast and fool!' Wriothesley was ordered from the palace with his men and Gardiner's plot collapsed. The radical Protestant party, of which the Parrs were a central element, would be safe for the rest of the reign and what the Herberts had, they would keep.

At court, Sir William Herbert continued to make headway, thriving under the wing of his sister-in-law the queen. More land in South Wales, in Worcestershire and Cheshire, the control of Cardiff and Aberystwyth Castles, and the keepership of Baynard's Castle in London all came sluicing his way. He bought those lands which weren't given to him, acquiring manors and estates which had previously belonged to the dissolved abbey at Shaftesbury. As Henry VIII slid towards his death, Herbert was among those who colluded in the changing of his will to their own advantage. There had been a whispering conspiracy as the old king died and the councillors best placed to profit from his death concealed it from the world while they made the necessary arrangements. 'Remember what you promised me in the gallery at Westminster,' one of Herbert's allies, Sir William Paget, later wrote to the young king's uncle, the Lord Protector Somerset, 'before the breath was out of the body of the king that dead is. Remember what you promised immediately after, devising with me concerning the place which you now occupy . . . And that was to follow mine advise in all your proceedings more than any other man's.'

The boy king Edward VI succeeded his father and Herbert was of the central governing interest clustered around Protector Somerset. In 1548 he was made a Knight of the Garter and Master of the Horse, acknowledged as a born commander, with the natural ability to impose order through violence.

In April 1549, reports began to come in to the Privy Council in Westminster of peasants creating havoc in many parts of the country. There was nothing new in that: a long tradition of English violence had bubbled away for generations. But there was no doubt that the 1540s were a desperate time in southern England. Not only were there many estates in which the lax government of the abbeys had been replaced by hard-headed modern men, harder than most. The underlying economic situation was desperate too. The population of England, now at about 2.75 million, had increased by some 35% over the previous century. The cost of living had risen by 50% in the previous fifty years. In 1545, the harvest had been catastrophic and the economy was still reeling from the after-effects. The rich, gathering up the pickings from the dissolution of the monasteries, were getting richer, and the poor, their numbers burgeoning against a static food supply, were getting poorer.

On top of that, the Duke of Somerset, Regent and Lord Protector while Edward VI was still a minor, had issued proclamations to the effect that landowners should return to the old ways of doing things, that they should consider themselves, as the orthodoxy would continue for decades to come, as stewards and fathers of their little commonwealths. Enclosures of what had either been open field or common land, either for private gain, or for the pleasure a park could afford, ran against this communitarian ethic. In Somerset's hands, the custom of the manor was making a renewed claim against the lordly Renaissance desire for spreading parkland.

In addition, the long history of English radicalism, founded on that element in the Bible which saw men as equal in the sight of God, fed the sense of outrage. If Isaiah could warn, 'Woe unto them that join house to house, that lay field to field, till there be no place [left], that they [i.e. the landowners] may be placed alone in the midst of the earth', it was inevitable that the rioters would demand 'Why should one man have all and another nothing?' What was there to stop the people of Washern, who had been evicted from their houses and had the seven acres of Lampeland taken from them, reclaiming what was theirs in the sight of God and apparently of the Lord Protector?

On 25 May 1549, a Norfolk gentleman, John Paston, wrote to his cousin the Earl of Rutland: 'there is a great number of the commons up about Salisbury in Wiltshire, and they have plucked down Sir William Herbert's park that is about his new house and divers other parks and commons that be inclosed in that country.'

It was the people of Washern taking their revenge. They threw down the new oak palings which Herbert had set up to enclose the deer and exclude the people, and slaughtered what deer they could catch. For three weeks, they occupied the ground on the other side of the Nadder from Herbert's new house. They may not have known quite what they were taking on, since in those weeks, as they attempted to rebuild their houses on the old sites – there was a mistaken belief widespread in England than any man who could build a house and light a fire in the course of a day had the right to remain in it – Herbert was away in Wales. There, from his Glamorgan estates, drawing on the 'affinity' – the band of his tenants who could be relied on to fight for him when summoned – he marched back into Wiltshire. Approaching Wilton, he attacked his invading Washern tenants as if they were an enemy and 'slew to death divers of the rebels'. News of Herbert's fearsome response reached the young king, who recorded in his journal how the men of Washern had created trouble and chaos and how 'Sir William Herbert did put them down, overrun, and slay them'.

The park where Sir Philip Sidney would within thirty-five years wander with the dreams of Arcadia in his head was now restored to wholeness and if you stand on the lawns outside Wilton House today staring across the elegance of the park and its gentlemanly accoutrements, you are looking at one of the heartlands of Arcadia: a stretch of landscape in which the people who claimed some rights over it were murdered so that an aesthetic vision of otherworldly calm could be imposed in their place. It is an early, English, minia-ture version of the clearances on the great Highland estates in

Scotland or even of the National Parks in the wilder parts of America: calm, beautiful and empty landscapes, not because God made them like that but because the people who belonged there were driven off, killed or otherwise dispensed with.

It is worth pausing for a moment to consider exactly what was done here in the service of Arcadia. Remember the dog chains in the old armoury, the bills and pikes, the halberds with which you could spike a man and then cut him. Almost certainly Herbert would have used a sword on his tenants. The favourite and usual strokes in the sixteenth century were not fencing-like thrusts – a slightly later, European development – but rather more wood-manlike slashing and severing: the cutting of the head from the shoulders; the cutting off of an arm or a leg; and the slicing stroke down through the head. This could be dramatic. There are records throughout the Middle Ages of sword cuts leaving the severed halves of the head hanging down to left and right on either shoulder. Sometimes the sword was smashed into the head with such violence that it cut down through a man's torso to his hips, his body folding apart like a carcass in an abattoir. Skeletons from medieval battles, unearthed and examined, often have multiple wounds: both legs cut off, sometimes apparently from a single sweeping blow with the sword; parts of the skull cut away in several pieces; occasionally many wounds of which any one would have been fatal; bodies left halved.

There is a disturbing echo in this story of the use of a park as a place for a hunt. The king's phrase – 'put them down, overrun, and slay them' – is curiously reminiscent of the account of a successful pursuit of a quarry. This was the manly excitement of the hunt taken to its ultimate, a point of view summarised by one Richard Blome, the author of the late seventeenth-century *Gentleman's Recreation*. Hunting, as Blome described the tradition,

> is a commendable *Recreation* . . . a great preserver of *Health*, a Manly *Exercise*, and an increaser of *Activity*; . . . it recreates the *Mind*, strengthens the *Limbs*, and whets the *Stomach*; . . . no

Musick is more charming to the *Ears* of *Man*, than a *Pack* of *Hounds* in full *Cry* is to him that delights in *Hunting . . .*

Hunting was universally seen as a training for war, or rather more than that as a form of nostalgic and pre-technological war which reminded its noble participants of what war must have been like before an awkward, ugly modernity contaminated it. Sir Thomas Elyot, the Tudor theorist of government, had recommended that sixteenth-century Englishmen should only use the javelin in the hunt, because that is what Xenophon had recommended in ancient Greece and it alone would preserve the nobility of the exercise. James I, a passionate huntsman, would have no gun come anywhere near the parks where he pursued the deer because the use of guns, as he told his son Prince Henry, was a 'theevish forme of hunting'. Grandeur was antique.

When in the following decade William Herbert paraded through London (the old dowager Queen of Scots, Mary of Guise, was visiting), he had with him 'a hundred great horses, mounted by a hundred horsemen', their coats lined with velvet, gold chains around their necks, white feathers in their hats, wearing the Pembroke badge of the wyvern, the winged dragon, 'and every [man] havyng a new gayffelyns in ther hands.' That is a word to raise the hackles on one's neck. Was it javelins the men and women of Washern were hunted with, as Elyot recommended, that summer afternoon in 1549? Was it a kind of pig-sticking? The elision was commonplace in the sixteenth century of any difference between a working man and a brutish beast. Shakepeare's Venus uses a 'javelin's point a churlish swine to gore' – and one is left in no doubt that her churlish swine, with his brawny sides, his hairy bristles and short, thick neck, living in his 'loathsome cabin', is a kind of animal Caliban, a dirty commoner, to be gored by the lovely, javelin-wielding elegant men, with feathers in their hats, chains around their necks and beauty in their faces.

William Herbert's pursuit and slaying of the tenants who had

presumed to enter his park represents the most disturbing com-
paction of the binary worlds of Arcadia and violence: a dreamlike
killing of people in a consciously aestheticised place, the reality of
human death for once taking over from the play-acting of deer-
death, the heart-pumping chase, the satisfactory conclusion, the
restoration of calm and of people accepting their suppression.

Having used his Welsh tenants to kill his Wiltshire tenants,
Herbert then took them to war. He was certainly – and from the
point of view of his own interests rightly – excited by it. The summer
of 1549 would turn Herbert from a successful adventurer into one
of the central power-brokers of the Tudor state. He brutally sup-
pressed a Catholic rebellion in the west country and emerged from
it at the head of an army which effectively deposed Somerset and
established Herbert at the heart of government. When Somerset was
executed, his lands, in the most primitive accumulation of spoils,
were distributed among the victors, Herbert among them. The
Council allowed Herbert to mint 2000 lbs of silver into coin, keeping
the difference between the value of the metal and the value of the
currency, making him a profit of £6,709 19s. And rewards continued
to flood towards him. During Edward's reign, Herbert received lands
worth £32,165 in capital value, including fifty-three manors in Wales,
nine in Wiltshire, five in Gloucestershire, two in Sussex, and one
each in Middlesex, Devon and Hertfordshire. And on 10 October
1551, the second son of the illegitimate gentleman from the Vale of
Ewyas was created Baron Herbert of Cardiff. The following day he
became the Earl of Pembroke.

At the end of February 1552, his wife Anne Parr, Countess of
Pembroke died at Baynard's Castle in London. She was thirty-six,
the mother of two sons and a daughter, and was buried with huge
pomp in Old St Paul's, next to the tomb of John of Gaunt, where
her memorial described her as 'a most faithful wife, a woman of
the greatest piety and discretion' and 'her banners were set up over
her arms set on divers pillars'. The earl undoubtedly loved her.
When he came to write his own will, despite having married again,

he said he wanted to be buried 'nere the place where Anne my late wife doth lie buried' in St Paul's. In a perfectly literal sense she had brought legitimacy to the Herberts. If he had vigour and ruthlessness, she gave the family grace and courage. When Edward VI re-granted the manors to the Pembrokes, it was explicitly 'to the aforenamed earl, by the name of Sir William Herbert, knight, and the Lady Anne his wife and the heirs male of their bodies between them lawfully begotten.' She was the joint creator of this extraordinary enterprise. A stained window in a Wilton church shows her kneeling before an open prayer book or Bible – no signs of religious imagery in evidence – in a long armorial mantle on which are embroidered the many-quartered arms of her distinguished ancestry. It was that Parr-derived inheritance which gave the family any claim to ancient nobility. She knew it. On her tomb in St Paul's the epitaph said that she had been 'very jealous of the fame of a long line of ancestors'.

William Herbert, Earl of Pembroke, had now become one of the rulers of England, a man without whom no power settlement could be made. He was precisely the sort of figure – independent, dangerous and unforgiving – whose standing the governments of Elizabeth and the Stuarts would need to erode. His power had been derived from royal patronage, but he had so managed the gift that it had now outgrown its source. Astute buying of lands, the exercise of violence or the threat of violence and the subtle, flickering understanding not only of the best alliance to make but the moment to desert an ally: all of this had placed him at least partly in control. The Earl of Worcester, the Parrs, his Wiltshire neighbour the Duke of Somerset had all provided another step up, and at each turn the earl had learned to combine toughness with flexibility, to be the willow not the oak. He knew, in other words, how to run with the fox and hunt with the hounds. The Machiavellian truth of Tudor England was that unless men of Pembroke's substance plotted to remain in power, others would plot to remove them. It was a business principle: either growth in the enterprise, or collapse.

The young Edward VI spent time down at Wilton, hunting, getting lost and being entertained by Pembroke as though he were visiting the palace of an eastern potentate. 'The King was served in vessels of pure gold,' the imperial ambassador Jehan Scheyfvre wrote to the Queen Dowager of Spain, 'his Council and Privy Chamber in silver gilt, and all the members of his household, down to the very least, in silver. All this plate belongs to the earl, who presented the King on his departure, with a very rich camp-bed, decorated with pearls and precious stones.'

Pembroke habitually carried the sword of state before the sovereign. The untrammelled roughness of his Welsh ancestry (he spoke fluent Welsh himself and was educating his son Henry in the language and its poetry) proved an asset at that brutal court. The Imperial ambassadors spread the gossip through Europe: Pembroke could speak no other language than English (untrue), could neither read nor write (probably untrue) and stood at meetings of the Privy Council 'shouting at the top of his voice', in which mood no one dared contradict him (almost certainly true). The memory of 1549 and his assertion of military power was never far from the surface.

As Edward VI sickened, Pembroke and his ally the Duke of Northumberland plotted for a Protestant succession to the throne which would deprive the Catholic Princess Mary of the crown. Their candidate, Lady Jane Grey, was Henry VIII's great-niece and according to the old king's will was to be the next heir after his own children. She had been a girl in the Parr household and had become a passionate Protestant and a Greek scholar there, reading Plato's dialogues in the original for pleasure, denouncing the Roman Church as the home of Satan. According to her parents' wishes but against her own will, she was quickly married to Northumberland's son, submitting only 'by the urgency of her mother and the violence of her father, who compelled her to accede to his commands by blows.' Her sister, Lady Katherine Grey, was married at the same time to Pembroke's eldest son, Henry.

Once again, Pembroke held the fate of England in his hand.

Edward died on 6 July 1553. Three days later, Lady Jane was told she was queen; Pembroke knelt to kiss her hand, at which the sixteen-year-old fell weeping to the floor, speaking of her inadequacy. On 13 July, Northumberland left London to capture Mary who was in Norfolk, with an army and support gathering around her. Once again, Pembroke bent like the willow, sniffed the wind, heard that the people were gathering to Mary's banner in Norfolk and at this critical juncture abandoned Lady Jane Grey. He got his son Henry to repudiate Katherine Grey and turned against Northumberland, his friend and ally. Pembroke gathered a group of like-minded lords in the great rooms overlooking the Thames at Baynard's Castle on 19 July. He asked them to join him in supporting the Catholic princess even then making her way with her army to London. It was another occasion for shouting. Pembroke bellowed to the assembled lords, holding his battle sword in front of him, 'This blade shall make Mary queen, or I will lose my life.' There was no denying him and the party went out into the streets of London where they had Mary proclaimed queen, Pembroke throwing up his jewelled cap and tossing his gold-filled purse into the crowds.

Mary was crowned queen in October, and Pembroke was there, carrying the sword of state before her. Lady Jane Grey, Northumberland and his son Guildford Dudley were all executed. Henry Herbert, Pembroke's son and heir, rejected Katherine, Lady Jane Grey's sister, and wrote to her vicious letters in which he called her a whore.

Pembroke became the leathered brawn for the new regime too, facing down a Protestant rebellion in London in 1554, fighting a series of largely ineffectual wars on Mary's behalf against the French, bringing the spoils back to Wilton and entrenching ever more his power-base in Wiltshire and Wales. Wilton served as a a perfect tool in his display of significance. He spent more time there than in London, entertained foreign ambassadors in his exquisite landscape, took them out hunting and hare-coursing on the downs, and displayed the vast assemblages of men and money which were the undeniable evidence of his standing.

'The handsomeness and commodities of Wilton, with the good appointment and the good furniture thereof, in all things whereof the better has not been seen,' were as impressive as anything England could offer. The most sophisticated Europeans were not entirely taken in. The Venetian ambassador wrote a witty and sceptical account of the strange manners of the English to his masters in the Venetian Senate in August 1554. 'The nobility, save as such are employed at court, do not habitually reside in the cities' – the Venetian began, his eyebrows raised,

> but in their own country mansions where they keep up very grand establishments, both with regard to great abundance of eatables consumed by them [the ambassador had witnessed the groaningly vast supper and breakfast offered at Wilton to a Spanish marquis and his men] as also by reason of their numerous attendants, in which they exceed all other nations, so that the earl of Pembroke has upwards of 1000 clad in his own livery. In these their country residences they occupy themselves with hunting of every description and with what-ever else can amuse or divert them; so that they seem wholly intent on leading a joyous existence, the women being no less sociable than the men, it being customary for them and allowable to go without any regard either alone or accompanied by their husbands to the taverns, and to dine and sup where they please.

This, in part, reads more like the description by an Englishman of the pleasures of Renaissance Italy: its slight air of loucheness, the sunshine in their lives, the apparent ease and equality of men and women in the aristocratic milieu. The English by the 1550s had absorbed much of that campagna culture. But here it is clamped to what is also late medieval behaviour, the great gang of the affinity, the display of power, the pre-modern guarantee of luxury through overt threat and strength. When the King of Spain himself arrived at Southampton to marry Queen Mary, the earl went down to meet him with two hundred mounted gentlemen in black velvet wearing heavy gold chains, accompanied by a body of English archers, their yellow tunics striped with bands of red velvet, the livery of the House of Aragon. This is the social and multiple equivalent of the way the earl himself appeared. Here is the fighting body dripping in pearls, velvet and gold. It is the essence of Tudor England: luxury as the medium of power; power as the underpinnings of beauty; beauty as the companion of threat.

To a great extent Pembroke came to believe his own propaganda. Where the descent of the crown itself was full of uncertainties and illegitimacies, where the claim on power was not a matter of genetic formality but an exercise in politics and force, then the legitimacy of the Pembrokes as magnates who could raise formidable armies of their own was not in question. They had as much right to be sources of power in their own countries as the sovereign did in the nation as a whole. Magna Carta did not mean nothing. Noble power, in an atmosphere where there was so much harking back to the myths of the Middle Ages, to the Arthurian romance, must have felt like a reality. In a 1566 survey of his estates, Pembroke's surveyor, after discussing the 'free' tenants – those who owed the manor no duties – and the 'customary' tenants – those whose lives were ruled by the custom of the manor – asked 'which of them could be tallaged [taxed] as serfs *ratione sanguinis nativi*' – by reason of their native blood. It was still legitimate in 1560s England to ask whether the ownership of a manor and a piece of land involved the ownership of human beings who came attached to that land as soil-bound slaves.

Pembroke's name in England and Wales came surrounded by a halo of threat and power. In 1556, one Thomas White, arrested and interrogated by the Council, reported a conversation he'd had secretly, one evening in an inn with a man called Ashton. Ashton had said

> he had a noble gentleman able to bring a great part of Wales at his tail. I asked him if it was lord Pembroke. He said, 'Tush for him, for he is more feared than loved.' I said, Two of the best in England are not able to drive him out of there, being the Queen's friend as you say he is, and she having the trust

in him you say she has. He said, all his trust was in his great horses, but with 5,000 or 6,000 footmen, he would wait with stakes sharpened at both ends.

This muttered, half-obscure, secretive talk feels like the last whimper of the Middle Ages, of great armed power-barons stalking the land and holding the central authorities to ransom. That January Pembroke received a special commission to levy troops for Mary's defence of Calais, a thousand from Wiltshire, a thousand from North Wales and a thousand from South Wales, by far the largest commission given to any nobleman in the country.

Still, for all this potency, the old Wiltshire nobility knew exactly who he was. They treated him as a parvenu. His servants and those of the old Lord Stourton, part of the ancient nobility of Wiltshire, brawled in the villages and in the streets of both Salisbury and London over the meaning of nobility. The stories were still current in the seventeenth century when John Aubrey heard them. Whenever Lord Stourton was returning home from the assizes in Salisbury, his way ran straight past the gates of Wilton. The old man would never lose the opportunity to 'sound his Trumpetts and give reproachfull challenging words: 'twas a relique of Knighthood Errantry.'

Mary Tudor died in November 1558 and another of Aubrey's stories, hinged to that moment and certainly untrue, nevertheless reveals what Wiltshire thought of this Pembroke: coarse, vulgar, a shifter, an object of ridicule as much as terror, a man in some ways humiliated by his greed for wealth and power.

> In Queen Mary's time, upon the returne of the Catholique Religion, the Nunnes came again to Wilton abbey, and this William earle of Pembroke came to the gate with his Cappe in hand and fell upon his knee to the Lady Abbesse and the Nunnes crying peccavi [I have sinned]. Upon Queen Mary's death, the Earle came to Wilton (like a Tygre) and turnd them out, crying, 'Out ye Whores, to Worke, to Worke ye Whores, goe Spinne.'

Elizabeth succeeded her half-sister and Pembroke apparently seamlessly transferred his allegiance from the Catholic to the Protestant queen. He had been among those who had first acclaimed her, but the relationship between sovereign and magnate very quickly shifted. A strained correspondence between them survives from the very first weeks of her reign, thick with a sense of fearlessness, a prickly manoeuvring but no form of self-abasement. Both Edward and Mary had appointed him Lord President of the Council for Wales and the Marches, a powerful official in a part of the kingdom which anyway formed some of the Pembroke heartlands. But this queen was to be different. 'I have received your letters,' he wrote to her from Wilton,

> perceiving your grace has been informed that the counties and marches of Wales (for want of a president and others of ability and reputation resident there) are grown to much disorder and like to fall into greater inconveniences if speedy remedy is not provided. As you are minded to take the presidency from me (which I never sought) I am ready to yield. Where it liked you to have my advice of one or two for that office, pardon me, for the world is such nowadays as if I should meddle I might be thought of some (that have not yet learned to speak well) very partial, having presently both friends and kin there in trouble.

It was a fairly graceless withdrawal, and on 5 August, his bastard nephew, also called William Herbert, was to feel the sting of royal power. A letter came from the queen at Richmond to the Sheriff of Glamorgan: 'We are informed that William Herbert of Cogan Pill, Glamorgan, has disobeyed several letters from our privy council. Immediately apprehend him and send him hither to the council under safe custody at his own charge.'

This William Herbert was thrown in the Fleet prison next to the Thames in London, but all this was a sign of the world changing, of the warmongering Tudor magnate no longer casting any kind of shadow over the central authority of queen, Council or her sheriff

Open grassland on the Downs above Broad Chalke (*top*); burred oaks in the ancient hunting forest of Grovely Wood (*above*); and (*left*) the clear-running waters of the Ebble: the ingredients of the Pembrokes' Arcadia.

The deer around the Ranger's
Lodge in Grovely Wood (*above*),
as drawn by the first Earl's
surveyors in the 1560s; the hay
harvest (*right*), one of the pinch-
points of the community's year;
and the community flock (*above
right*), folded at night in
temporary, hurdle-fenced
enclosures, so that the dung
could enrich the soil.

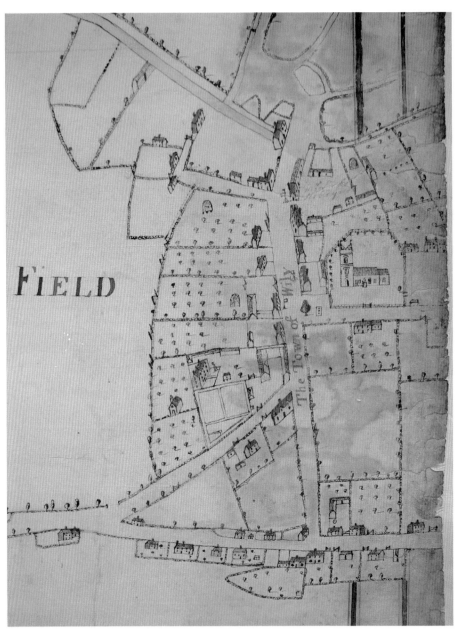

The Pembrokes' village of Wylye: each house has its yard or 'backside', an orchard and one or two closes. There are haystacks and stacks of unthreshed grain. Stocks stand in the village square. It is a place of control, as neat as a sampler.

William Herbert, first earl of Pembroke (*left*), perhaps painted to celebrate his elevation to the Garter in 1548, when he was about 42: the hybrid of Renaissance prince, medieval magnate and a man on the make.

A drawing by Hans Holbein (*below left*), of a woman of about 20, perhaps Anne Parr, wife of the first earl: clear-eyed, protestant, cultivated, bringing grace and refinement to her husband's unbridled aggression.

The first earl of Pembroke (*below*) as one of the great Tudor power brokers, an English condottiere, on a medal cast for him in 1562 when he was 56.

Tudor Wilton (*above*) encased the remains of the abbey in a pedimented courtyard house, as drawn on the vellum rolls of the first earl's 1560s survey.

OPPOSITE Henry, second earl of Pembroke, failed to achieve his father's dominance and was overshadowed by his wife, Mary Sidney, 'the sweetest daughter of the sweetest Muses, the brightest Diamant of the richest Eloquence, the resplendentest mirrour of Feminine valour.' Her brother, Philip Sidney, (*opposite below*) at his most powerful: carried to his burial in St Paul's in February 1587. As the revered author of the *Arcadia*, Sidney was far more powerful than when alive.

William, third earl of Pembroke, (*left*) carrying the staff of Lord Chamberlain, painted by Daniel Mytens in about 1615 when he was 35. A man of balance, dignified, the cultural heir to his uncle Philip Sidney. His racier younger brother Philip, (*below left*) made earl of Montgomery by James I, painted by William Larkin soon after becoming a Knight of the Garter in 1608, aged about 24.

Philip's second wife, Lady Anne Clifford, (*below*) wears in her ear a single pearl suspended from a black thread, in memory of one of her dead children: 'Having many times a sorrowfull & heavy heart, I may truly say I am like an owl in the desert.'

in the wild lands of Wales. Sir Henry Sidney, a royal servant of no great wealth, too poor to be elevated to the peerage, was appointed in his place.

Never in Elizabeth's reign would the queen call on the powerful but dangerous capacity in her great noblemen to provide her with armies. Her avoidance of war was not only a means of saving money. It was a way of preventing the dispersal of power into the hands of those mighty subjects. The story of Elizabethan England is in part one of the emasculation of the nobility, the turning of real warriors into toy warriors, fighters into frustrated lovers, the condottieri of Tudor England into the wan and beautiful princes drifting through the fields of Arcadia, an aestheticisation of nobility which buttressed rather than menaced the power of the state.

Elizabeth's was a new form of monarchy, appealing to a wider constituency than the nobles she might have gathered around her, using them but not relying on them. A sign of how this new world was to work had already appeared clearly enough in April 1559. She went one afternoon

> to Baynard's Castle, the Earl of Pembroke's Place, and supped with him, and after supper she took a boat and was rowed up and down the river Thames, hundreds of boats and barges rowing about her, and thousands of people thronging at the waterside to look upon her Majesty, rejoicing to see her and partaking of the music and sights in the Thames, for the trumpets blew, drums beat, flutes played, guns were discharged, squibs hurled up into the air, as the Queen moved from place to place. And this continued till ten o'clock of the night, when the Queen departed home.

This was the most elegant form of emasculation, diminishing the nobility by means of a supper-party and some fireworks, the defeat of Tudor brutalism by glamour and politics. From now on, the great old magnates of medieval England, the Cliffords, Nevilles, Percys and Talbots, were left to fester in their huge estates, remote from the levers and rewards of power.

Pembroke, too, suffered from the marginalisation. One last attempt was made by the old earl in the late 1560s to influence the state in the way he had at the height of his career. He was keen for the Duke of Norfolk to marry the Queen of Scots, by then a captive in the north of England. Elizabeth heard rumours of this suggestion, Norfolk was sent to the Tower and Pembroke was arrested. But then two of the old northern magnates, the earls of Westmorland and Northumberland, had raised armies from their affinities in order to release the Queen of Scots from captivity. Pembroke seemed to Elizabeth to have been involved in this re-assertion of noble power. For their own purposes, that is what the two earls were claiming. A little pathetically he wrote to the queen in December 1569

> From my poore Howse at Wilton
>
> My name is moast falselye and wickedly abused by the wicked Protestation of those two traitorous Erles.
>
> I do reverently before God, and humbly before your Majestie, protest that in all my Lief I was never privey to so muche as a Mocion of any Attempte either of these bankcrupte Erles, or of any Mans ells, against either Religion (in defence whereof onelye I am redie to spill my blood) or yet your Majesties Estate or person; and that I am redie against them, and all Traitors to make good with my Bodie when and howsoever it shall please your Majestie to commande: For God forbid that I should lieve the Houre, now in mine olde Age, to staine my former Lief with a spot of Disloyaltie.

There is the willow bent full double. Of course he had never changed sides; of course his only interest was in the validity of true religion; of course he had never plotted with any other grandee about how they might steer the riches of England into the strong chests in the strongrooms and armouries at Wilton. God forbid than anything so impure had ever passed though his mind!

John Aubrey, listening to the Wiltshire gossip about the first earl seventy-five years later or more – this was a story from his great-uncles, one of the Brownes of Broad Chalke – heard that 'in Queen

Elizabeth's time some Bishop (I have forgot who)' – it was in fact the Bishop of Winchester – 'was sent to him from the Queen and Council' – actually of his own accord – 'to take Interrogatories of him', to ask him some legal and technical details about his land holdings. The bishop, although Aubrey didn't hear this detail, wanted to get back the manor of Bishopstone in the valley of the Ebble, just to the east of Broad Chalke.

> So [the bishop] takes out his pen and inke, examines and writes.
> When he had writt a good deale sayd the Earle, 'Now lett me see it.'
> 'Why,' quoth the Bishop, 'your Lordship cannot read it?'
> 'That's all one, I'le see it,' quoth he, and takes it and teares it to pieces. 'Zounds, you rascall,' quoth the Earle, 'd'ee thinke I will have my throate cutt with a pen-knife?'
> It seems they had a mind to have pick't a hole in his Coate, and to have gott his Estate.

This wonderful story, as if folk tales were being constructed even in sixteenth- and seventeenth-century Wiltshire, has a deep moral and historical truth to it. This is nothing but the modern, literate, bureaucratic state trying to take back from the unlettered warrior, the ancient earl who depended for his standing on his physical presence, his leadership of men and his native cunning, the lands on which his existence relied. Here, in a few lines, modernity, legal and lettered, nibbles at the ancient conditions. The historical truth of the story is that the bishop attempted to have a private Act of Parliament passed but a covey of Pembroke-sponsored MPs in the House of Commons saw him and his Bill off. But the emotional and metaphorical truth is not in that account. It is here in the Brownes' memory and Aubrey's delighted retelling of it: the sense that the modern world was a clever cheat, the ancient earl a blind and muscled colossus, capable still of a growl and the tearing up of paper.

The same anxiety fuels Aubrey's final remembered story of the earl, which shares the same dreamlike emblematic quality. As he lay dying in early 1570, one desperate phrase, the end of all his dreams and nightmares, was on his lips, repeated again and again: 'They would have Wilton, they would have Wilton.' Underneath that armoured carapace, and never given voice in the official record, only remembered here in the gossip of the chalkstream valleys, was a desperate anxiety over the status and the lands for which he had lusted and fought for so long. It is a recognition that his noble power, his gathering of armies, his assembling of crowds of liveried and chain-bedecked followers, his country of lands and manors was, in truth, as fragile as a vase.

On 23 December 1567 'remembering the uncertainty of man's life and to how many perils and casualties the same is subject' – something of which Pembroke would have been all too aware – he had made his will. He left £400 each to the poor of the ward around Baynard's Castle, in Salisbury and in Hendon near London where he had yet another house. Apart from a few legacies to his other children, he left everything to his son Henry.

But late on the evening of 16 March 1570, in his apartments in Hampton Court, feeling death coming near, he had his younger son Edward and the Earl of Leicester, son of his old friend Northumberland whom he had betrayed, come to his bedside. Death had given him a conscience. His second wife was to keep her own clothes and her jewels, which would otherwise have gone to Henry. He left his 'newest fairest and richest bed' and his greatest jewel to the queen, to Leicester his best gold sword and to his brother-in-law William Parr, Marquess of Northampton, his second-best gold sword.

Leicester then left the bedside, and the dying earl was alone with his son Edward and the physicians. His final thoughts are recorded. His second wife, Mary Talbot, who had been married for her money and her connections – she was the daughter of the Earl of Shrewsbury – was to be looked after, to be allowed to stay in Baynard's Castle, his daughter Anne was to be given £500, but more than that, anxiously and insistently, the ordinary men who had been with him and looked after him during his life were to be cared for by Henry, Lord Herbert, his heir.

> That my lorde Herbert do consider Thomas Gregorie and Tidie with money for their travaile and paines beside that he hath bequeathed to them in annuity that he speciallie do appointe to Francis Zouche and Charles Arundell fit and good annuities for them. That he have special care of Henrie Morgan George Morgan Phillipp Williams Robert Vaughan and Thomas Scudamore and either entertaigne them into his service payinge them their wages beforehand or else appoint them sufficient annuities That he do entertaigne his household and keep them together.

It was his last stated wish that his son should keep his affinity together. Philip Williams was his secretary, Robert Vaughan his treasurer, Thomas Scudamore one of the gentlemen who carried his coffin. He died the following morning, aged sixty-three, the climacteric, thought to be the most dangerous year of one's life, being the product of the two magic numbers, nine and seven.

His funeral on 18 April 1570 was the greatest possible statement of the man he had become and of the dynasty he had created. The reverse of a beautiful portrait medal of the earl cast in 1562 showed a Welsh dragon or wyvern by a classical tempietto and carried the motto: 'Draco Hic Virtus Virtutem Custos' – *This dragon the true guardian of the virtues.* That is how he saw himself; the man of violence protecting the good: the humanist inheritance which Anne Parr had brought to this family; the radical Protestantism in which, for all the necessary trimming, they almost certainly shared a belief; and the people of his lands whom he had in part abused and for whom he felt a deep affection.

Two yeoman conductors with black staves led the procession, followed by a hundred poor men, walking 'ij and ij'. Mr William Morgan, one of the many Welshmen in London for the funeral, carried the earl's banner, ahead of 'the Defunctes gentlemen ij and ij', that is the greatest of his gentry tenants from all those lands spread across England and Wales. Two secretaries followed, as befitted a man of business, then all the knights and squires who were beholden to him, and then the chief officers of his household, his steward, his treasurer and his comptroller. In all of this, it was a funeral indistinguishable from a king's. Another banner carried by his neighbouring Wiltshire knight, Sir George Penruddock, from Compton Chamberlayne in the valley of the Nadder, who had been with Pembroke fighting the French for Queen Mary, then the York Herald with Pembroke's coat armour, carrying his helm and crest, the Chester Herald carrying the shield on which Pembroke's arms were emblazoned, the Richmond Herald carrying his sword and finally the Garter King of Arms carrying his coat of arms, accompanied by two 'Gentleman Ushers' with white rods. One of these gentleman ushers, dressed up for the occasion, was in fact Roger Earth of Dinton just across the valley of the Nadder from Compton Chamberlayne, who had been arrested in August 1553, described as 'Servaunt to The'erle of Penbroke' and thrown into the Fleet prison for fighting with one of the servants of Lord Stourton in the streets of London. Gentleman usher or brawling member of the affinity: in this life they were the same thing.

The coffin itself was carried by eight gentlemen, some from his Welsh lands, some from Wiltshire, and eight yeoman assistants, including a ranger of his forests and men from Wylye and Broad Chalke. Further knights and gentlemen, all hooded, processed into St Paul's, followed by the young Henry, the new Earl of Pembroke, followed by the great of Elizabethan England: the Lord Chancellor, Sir Nicholas Bacon, the Earl of Leicester, Sir William Cecil, Lord Howard of Effingham, Thomas Sackville, Lord Buckhurst. Finally came the long, long line of the dead earl's yeomen, the copyholders of his estates across the breadth of the realm, and the servants of other noble men and gentlemen mourners, all of them in black, 'ij and ij', for minute after minute through the great west door of St Paul's.

As a formality, this accumulation of people was the definition of nobility. It was the household in full performance, the medieval community in commemoration of death. Everything about this funeral procession enacted the realities of sixteenth-century power: the spread of lands and of people on them; the conspicuous expense of such elaborate obsequies; the intimacy with the great of the court and the royal administration; the sense that if this was not, in actuality, a fighting band, it was not long since it had been. There were men here who had been with the earl on the bridge in Bristol in 1528; who had helped him destroy the papist images in the 1530s; who had stood with him against the rebels in 1549; again in the streets of London at the accession of Queen Mary; again when Thomas Wyatt had threatened the Catholic queen in 1554; again on the battlefields of France when the great suits of armour were brought home to Wilton; and who had, of course, chased with him, day in and day out across the Arcadian hunting grounds of Wiltshire.

At the end of it, after 'a certain collect' had been read and the chief mourners had departed, the officers of his household were left alone to see the body buried. 'Which officers did put the defunctes staff into the graue and brake each of their own staves and cast them into the graue with him.' The founder of the dynasty was dead and his authority over.

5

Customarie Services and Composition Piggs

The workings of downland society

WHAT WAS the reality of life on those great estates, of the people who assembled for their moment of theatre at the funeral of the first earl? It so happens that a great deal can be known about that world in the late sixteenth and early seventeenth centuries because in the early 1630s, the earl had his domain carefully surveyed. Unfortunately no map survives, even if it were made, but many enormous written documents were preserved from those surveys, recounting the names, family relationships and tenancies of hundreds of people in the chalkland valleys. An extraordinarily detailed picture emerges from them: the shopkeepers, millers, clothiers, smiths, 'husbandmen', cheats and laggards who were the earl's tenants and dependants; the houses, yards and barns these people occupied; his 'Lands, Woods, Meddowes and pastures', the marshes, orchards, warrens, 'lawns', bottoms, bowers, breaches, hedges, coppices, crofts, furzes, lanes, moors and ditches that made up the estate; the farm animals that were such intimate co-occupants of these places; and the extent to which the great estate, with its own manorial courts, its own police system, its own punishments and its own deeply embedded hierarchies, was its own, self-reflective world.

In Broad Chalke, for example, the village arranged on either side of the Ebble, where John Aubrey would later delight in its tunable bells, there were thirty-six copyhold tenants in September 1631. The first to be named were Thomas Randoll, fifty-seven, and Avice, who was two years younger and was probably his sister. They lived together, in a single-storey house of four rooms, with storage lofts over the rooms, but it was not an isolated dwelling. The house was surrounded by a 'four-room' barn, a stable, a cowhouse and 'other houses fit for husbandry'. It was, in other words, a small farmyard, just off North Street on the north side of the village, above the line of clay where the springs bubble up and run down through the meadows to the river. The Randolls had kept everything in good repair, as they were required to, and next to the buildings they had a backyard, called 'a backside', a small orchard and a vegetable garden. Below them, on the wet ground by the river, they had a half-acre 'close of meadow or pasture' called the East Close – a small hedged field which they would either keep closed for hay, to be cut and made in July, or, if they had calves or a thin 'rother', a cow due to go out to grass, they would graze them here in the spring. 'It is the pasture lards the rother's sides,' Shakespeare's Timon says, 'the want that makes him lean.' Above the house and yard stretched the open fields in which the Randolls had their arable strips: fourteen acres in the East Field, ten acres in the Middle Field and eleven acres in the West Field. On these fields, after the barley and wheat harvest had been taken, and on the fallow fields, the Randolls had the right to pasture three horses, four cows and a calf. Above that, on the chalk, they could keep eighty sheep with the village's communal flock.

Everything was fixed. There was no idea that the enterprise should grow or change. This was how it was, an ingeniously inter-locked system, which had been like this for a long time and no one could see why it should not continue like this for ever, just as it seemed to have come out of a distant past 'time before mind'. Their father John Randoll had entered into this agreement with the Pembrokes in 1596 and John had named Thomas and Avice as the two other 'lives' in the copy. They were entirely secure here for as long as they lived. In 1596, John Randoll had given the earl £20 as entry money to the property, quite a high 'fine' as it was called, the equivalent of the annual stipend for a vicar, and had agreed a rent of eighteen shillings a year, about the annual wage of a girl servant, or the price of about ten turkeys. In effect, the copyholder bought a lease on which the rent was both low and fixed as long as the three named people remained alive. It is a measure of life expectancy in early modern England that three lives were thought to be the equivalent of twenty-one years. The Randolls had done well: in 1631 they were thirty-six years into their copyhold and still going strong.

The rest of the village repeated much of this pattern: the copyholders occupying neat small farmsteads, lined out between the arable fields and the wet land by the river. The house of the old lady Goody Dewe was here, from whom Aubrey would later hear about Edward VI getting lost while hunting. She and the other Dewes lived on the south side of the river, with her husband Bartholomew (sixty-six years old in 1631) and their two sons Thomas and John, their house one room smaller than the Randolls', but otherwise similar in all its arrangements and appurtenances.

There were signs of optimism. A fifteen-year-old boy, William Lawes, and a ten-year-old, John Penn, were both named as lives on copyholds. There can have been no expectation there of an early death. And there was no sense that women were excluded from the system. Widows continued to have unassailable rights in their properties after their husbands died; and there was a pair of sisters, Anna and Mary Fish, occupying one ten-acre farm on the north side, off High Lane. Anna was married, but her husband had no part of the tenancy, and it was Anna herself who would become a member of the 'homage' or jury of the manor court.

It isn't difficult to imagine how beautiful a place Broad Chalke must have been on a summer day in the 1630s. Its interlocking of private property and common interest, the sheer neatness of the relationship of downland fields, meadow, river and village, laid like a tapestry sampler across the dip of the valley, the presence of the animals as an extra layer of life in the village – 'A farme without stocke,' John Norden had said, 'is like a piece without Powder, or a

Steeple without bells': all of that exudes a sense of health and coherence. 'About Wilton and Chalke,' Aubrey mused in his memory, 'the downes are intermixt with boscages that nothing can be more pleasant, and in the summer time do excell Arcadia in verdant and rich turfe and moderate aire ... The innocent lives here of the shepherds doe give us a resemblance of the golden age.' There was a real financial basis for this sunny view of life in the downland villages. Between 1540 and 1640 inflation affected all goods – the price of timber tripled, building materials went up by 2½ times, metals doubled in price and textiles went up by 150%. But at the same period, prices for farm produce in southern England rose by a factor of four or five. It was a good time to be in farming.

The Pembroke estate made sure that through an increase in entry fines it relieved the tenants of some of that profit, but the three-lives copyhold meant that the fixed annual rents were very soon out of date. In 1631 one old widow, Anne Witt, was living in a four-roomed house in Broad Chalke, with the usual barn, cowhouse, orchard, garden and 13½ acres of arable strips, according to an agreement made by her now-dead husband seventy-one years before in 1560. She was paying a very low, uninflated 11s 6d rent a year. The village as a whole in the 1630s was undoubtedly experiencing a wave of wellbeing on which tenants and landlords both rose.

In the list of possessions made on householders' deaths, one can begin to visualise the way in which these copyholders lived. In the Pembrokes' village of Wylye, on the north side of the Grovely ridge, one of the copyholders, William Locke, died in February 1661. At the time of his death he was eighty-two. Like the other copyholders, his house, with three rooms and lofts above them, was on the street side of his backyard, which was surrounded on the other sides by a barn, a cowhouse and stable and a separate kitchen. Much later buildings are still there on the same site opposite the Bell Inn but they are arranged exactly as they were in the seventeenth century.

The bay size of the Lockes' timber buildings, probably using small oak trees, roughly adzed to shape, would have been about fourteen feet square. Both house and barn would have been single-storey, thatched buildings about forty-two feet long and fourteen wide. Less room was devoted to human habitation than to buildings designed to keep the farm enterprise going. But the Lockes were clearly living in comfortable conditions, even with some pretension to them. The house had a room called the 'hall', with a dining table and a side table, three chairs, three joiner-made stools and a pair of cushions. William had six tablecloths and two dozen napkins with which to make the room elegant, as well as six pewter dishes, two candlesticks also in pewter, which can take a high polish, two salts and sixteen silver spoons. In the smallest possible way, there is a dignity of self-possession here, of a man and his family conceiving of themselves as living an honourable life. Upstairs there were two bedrooms, plenty of sheets and pillowcases, blankets, pillows, bolsters and hangings for the beds, as well as a rug, a good set of towels and two chamberpots.

Alongside these best rooms were the harder-working parts of the farmstead. It was a crowded and busy place. In the cowshed, there was a cow and a bullock. Three pigs lived in the stable and five shillings worth of poultry pecked their way about the yard. There was a haystack here – the winter food of the stalled cow and bullock – with some peas also stored with it, two woodpiles, one very large, worth £10, and one small, and a stack of timber, maturing, which had been cut into planks and posts. There was also a 'wheat-rick' in the yard, the corn still in the ear, waiting to be threshed on the threshing floor in the barn and then stored in the 'old garner' – the granary which was also somehow within the barn. Threshing equipment, ladders, sacks for flour and winnowings 'and some other baggs' were all kept here too, along with the barley, part of it threshed when Locke died, part still waiting to be threshed.

This sense of the busy, small-scale farm enterprise invaded large parts of the house too. The hall was flanked by the buttery on one side (barrels, five pounds of lard, a meat safe, a cheese press, three flitches of bacon, a flagon and 'other small things') and the brew-house (a furnace, vats, pails, bowls, iron bars, hooks and halters), a place in which more washing was done than any beer brewed. Unmentioned, but certainly here, were the willow baskets in which the washing was taken to the line to dry, perhaps out in the vegetable garden or in the orchard beyond it

The kitchen had all the equipment needed for cooking over the wood fire: chains, hooks, pots, kettles, skillets, spits, forks, frying pans, dripping pans 'and other lumber'. In the loft above it, which must have been warm and dry, the Lockes kept their wool equip-ment: a pair of scales, some 'liden waits' and 'one pair of way beames', 90 lbs of wool worth £4 10s, as well as still more 'other lumber'. The state of attics in the seventeenth century was not very different to any other period.

Beyond this dense concentration of carefully gathered, materially significant and valuable objects – no mention of a book, a painting or a musical instrument – was the land: a vegetable garden, an orchard, a set of little closes and the 27½ acres in the common fields. Only ten acres of wheat was sown in them when William Locke died in February. A third of the land had been left fallow as usual, and the barley for the other third, once it had been threshed in the barn, would be sown by his heirs in the spring as usual. He had £3 of hay 'in the fields', his contribution to the communal hay stack on which the communal flock was feeding during the winter, and 'two dozen of hurdells' with which to fold the sheep on the arable that would soon begin to sprout. It is a depiction of an exactly ordained life, a rootedness.

Of course this is not the whole story. The village was both a sustaining and a fierce, demanding, exclusive and excluding organ-ism, but what is here undoubtedly feels good. The poorer families are scarcely mentioned. Some families right in the middle of the village were sharing these small houses and barns, which can't have been easy. Ralph Street and his son John, farming a mere three acres, lived in 'a dwelling house, sometimes called the stable'. There was a tiny cottage, of two rooms, with a little garden and orchard, right out on the eastern edge of the village, called the Hermitage, for which the annual rent was four shillings, the price of a dozen candles. Strikingly, and unexplainedly, this is the earliest-known figurative use of that word in English (the next was in 1648). Was it a joke? There are certainly other half-jokes in seventeenth-century Wiltshire place-names. Out on the open ground on the other side of Broad Chalke was a cluster of houses called 'Little London'. The seventeenth-century hovels belonging to the landless labourers who lived here have gone now, but judging from equivalent places in Wiltshire, called sardonically Little Salisbury, Ireland, Scotland or Cuckolds Green, this would have been the living-place of the poorest of the poor, Broad Chalke's own slum, single-roomed hovels only ten or twelve feet square, some even ten feet by eight, in which families would attempt to maintain their lives. The floors were often no more than straw on mud. Transient labourers and their families, often, as those place-names imply, from the poorer margins of the British Isles, clustered at the edge of these elaborately instituted villages like dogs at a camp.

Although necessary and tolerated as the source of casual labour for those copyholders who were too old or infirm to do the farm-work themselves, villages such as Broad Chalke loathed and despised the slum-dwellers existing on the margins of their pretty villages. Hundreds of petitions were presented by parishioners to have these sheds and their contents removed, often 'by reason of the soyle' – the dung – 'for the said Cottage so built doth stand unto a water-course, which watercourse runneth into a well which is used by the most parte of all the Inhabitants to fetch there water. And further the Children [living in the hovel] have a Loathsome decease called the White Scurfe which is infeccious.' Villagers often wanted such human sties pulled down, but this example, from a 1628 petition of the parishioners of Melksham in the north of Wiltshire, is significant not only for the village policing its physical and moral health, but for the proper procedure they went through in doing so. They didn't simply demolish the house but applied to the justices to agree to let this sick, poor family have another house in a better place:

> We th'inhabitants of the said parish whose names are under-written, Knowing that he hath lived as an honest and poore man . . . and pittying his Distressed estate in regard of himselfe, his wife and Five small children who are likely to perish through want of harbour, do hereby Signifie both our contents unto his disyres, and that we conceave that it wilbe a worke of greate mercy to satisfie his humble request.

That is the manor working as it was meant to, as a social organism which nurtured the weak while carefully protecting the communal resources and wellbeing of the village itself. It was a quality of rural life which George Herbert would also celebrate in the 1630s.

At Broad Chalke, in addition to those copyholders, there was a single tenant of the demesne farm – that is the land which the lord in the Middle Ages used to keep for himself. In 1631, he was Anthony Browne, a gentleman, John Aubrey's great-uncle, the source of endless stories which his great-nephew would greedily write down. His deal with the Pembroke estate was not by copyhold at all, but by indenture, a modern rental agreement, which was an almost purely financial transaction between him and the earl. In 1601, he and his wife had bought the lease, which was to run for the rest of his life, for £40. On top of that he had to provide the lord every year as rent thirty quarters, or very nearly a ton each, of wheat and barley, slightly less of oats, twenty-four geese, twenty-four capons, which were castrated cocks, and a hundred pigeons. By a separate contract, for which he had to pay rent of £20 a year, he had some extra bits of grazing and the 'warren of conies', whose meat Aubrey would come to love so much – the highly profitable fat rabbit farm – on the downland to the south of the village.

Here, already, is a sign of the transitional nature of these arrangements. The key-money to be paid on getting into the lease was a straightforward amount of cash; the annual rent was meant to be in kind. But instead of the pigeons, cheeses, capons and rabbits,

Browne in fact gave the earl £13 14s 8d a year. Only the grain he owed continued to be paid in kind. The wheat, barley and oats would have gone to the earl's barns and granaries at Wilton: ten quarters filled a cart and so every August, seven or eight cartloads would have made their way out of Anthony Browne's yard at what is now Manor Farm in Broad Chalke, across the Ebble at a wide ford, into the northern part of the village, past the farmyards of the Laweses and Randolls and then up the long dusty white chalk track, climbing 300 feet to the top of the downland ridge, before dropping to the valley of the Nadder at Burcombe, and turning east through South Ugford and Bulbridge, joining the tens and maybe hundreds of others creakingly bringing the rent to the lord's store at Wilton.

It was part of the agreement between the earl and his tenants that in delivering rent in kind 'to the Capital mansion house of His lord at Wilton', they should take 'meat, bread, & drink, at the Lord's cost whensoever they come.' The summer carts gathered outside the barns, the carriers and labourers from the downland villages sitting on them in the midday sun, the refreshments provided by the earl's men, overseen by the steward or more likely his deputy: all of this was a perfectly real financial relationship in action in the early seventeenth century, but it was also a Virgilian scene, working to the rhythms of Arcadia.

Something else is also in play here. The same document, pre-served in the Pembroke papers, which describes the meat, bread and drink that will be given to those bringing the rent to Wilton, also says that the tenants of the land 'out of their Benevolence, or good will, shall every year carry Houseboote [timber for repairs] & Fireboote [firewood]' to Wilton's capacious stores. 'Benevolence' and 'good will' are, of course, code for no payment. This is another imposition, for which a free lunch would have been scarce rec-ompense. Arcadia continued to have steel in its core.

Browne had a very pleasant set-up in Broad Chalke: a house with fifteen rooms, a big barn next to it, a cowhouse, stable and pigeon house, a carthouse, a garden and a one-acre orchard. He had thirty-four acres down in the valley, much of it sweet, rich grass-growing meadow, about 270 acres in the arable fields, of which a third was left fallow each year, eighty acres sown with wheat and a hundred with barley; and the right to keep 1200 sheep in the communal flock up on the downs. This was a serious enterprise on a different scale from that of the copyholders.

But this was more than just business: this was also the working of a community and Browne would have found himself intimately entwined in the life of the copyholders around him. Manor Farm in the seventeenth century was surrounded by a positive nest of obligations and duties inherited from the Middle Ages, the obligations owed by custom, time out of mind, to the lord's farm, of which Browne was now the tenant.

First, in June or early July, the copyholders had to wash and shear 1000 sheep and then mow and make the hay in the meadow down by the Ebble called Long Meade, which was 4½ acres in extent. At harvest time, in high summer, late July or August, the 'customary tenants' had to find thirty reapers for a day, to cut and bind Mr Browne's corn. Most of them would have 'found' themselves to do the work. They then had to find thirty carts and wagons plus the teams of horses or oxen to pull them, to carry the corn from the fields into the barns.

In return, there were the obligations which Browne had towards the community. First, there was the vicar. He was to get '6 akers of the best wheate which he can make choice of out of 80 akers.' One can imagine that scene well enough, the parson touring the fields, Mr Browne, perhaps, guiding him towards the slightly less than best, the parson knowing already exactly where the best was to be found. Once he had made his choice, Mr Browne had to 'reape and carrie the same home into his Barne for him'. After the harvest and up until Martinmas on 11 November, Browne then had to provide the vicar with grazing for sixty lambs, then weaned from their mothers, for free. He had to give eight bushels of wheat to the Chief

Forester of Cranborne Chase (from whom he received two acres of wood each year, for firewood and with which to make sheep hurdles, cut from the earl's coppices in the Chase) and Browne's note says that he is meant to pay more wheat and barley to the underforester, 'Which Corne hath been demanded but hath never been paid by me hitherunto.'

While the customary work was being done by the tenants, Mr Browne, standing in for the lord of the manor, effectively acting for him in this tiny community, gave meat and drink to the reapers while they were doing their hot days' work on the fields. More meat and drink was provided for the men carting the sheaves back to the barns. While they were cutting the grass and making the hay down in Long Meade, he gave the reapers a ram and eleven gallons of beer to be divided between them. The ram, in many of the chalkland villages, had a strange custom attached to it. The animal would be placed in the middle of the field, the tenants around the edge. If it remained quietly there, they could keep it. If it escaped or wandered off, it remained the lord's. What was this? An entertainment? A piece of theatre? A dramatisation of the potency of lordship and the impotence of tenancy? In the *Surveior's Dialogue*, John Norden had his freeholder, discussing the virtues of freehold, tell the surveyor, 'It is a quietnesse to a man's minde to dwell upon his owne: and to know his Heire certaine. And in deed, I see that men are best reputed that are seized of matter of inheritance: Leases are but of base account.' But dwelling upon one's own was not available to the vast majority of the population. Maybe the lord's escaping ram, a taunting form of largesse, was a means of telling the copyholders exactly where they stood.

Browne also had to provide the customary tenants with good food at Christmas. A quarter of beef (which meant what it said, a quarter of an animal) was to be shared out among the tenants on St Thomas's Day, 21 December. On the same day he had 84 lbs of wheat baked into bread and distributed to his neighbours, plus sixteen gallons of barley baked into 'horse bread' for their animals, and a large expensive cheese (£4 16s 0d) cut up and divided around the village. Two one-year-old pigs, called 'Composition Piggs' by Browne, meaning that they were payment instead of tithes owed to the church, were given to the parson every year.

In his own accounts Browne calculated his yearly income from the meadow grass, the wheat and barley and the sheep at about £272, and his annual costs £127, but he gave no money value either to the work he received freely from the copyholders, or to the food and supplies he gave them each year. All of that was beyond money, merely the mutual obligations of an ancient community, each part reckoned intuitively to balance the other. And he wrote a note to that effect in his papers: 'I doe accompt these Customarie services are but equally valuable with what Custom they reseve [receive] from me in Lue [lieu] thereof.'

This was the nature of the Wilton universe. It was, for the beneficiaries, a model of conservative wholeness, a set of economic, agricultural and social arrangements which reflected the ideals of Arcadia itself: full at least of the possibilities of an integrated society; with no expectation that anyone would do any better than any other; with a level of mutuality which urban, commercial and courtly life could scarcely tolerate (but nevertheless longed for); and which instituted the lord of the manor as a king in his own domain.

It was a system which provided the political classes with a metaphor for the country: England itself was a manor, with the principle of inherited and customary law at its heart; where its sovereign lord, according to the ancient constitution, was powerful only in response to the law as it had been handed down and only in consultation with the representatives gathered not in the manor court but in parliament; where a tyrant would ignore that mutuality but a king would recognise it as the identifying quality of this society.

This was the ideal and these the principles to which figures as diverse as Philip Sidney, Shakespeare, John Norden, George Herbert, the two brothers who became the third and fourth Earls of

Pembroke and the gathering of poets whose lives and writings they supported at Wilton would all appeal in the coming decades. It was, as Aubrey called it, 'a countrey of lands and Mannours', one of the limbs of the body of England.

6

I'll be a park and thou shalt be my deer

The making of the Pembroke Arcadia
1570–1586

THIS WAS THE WORLD that Henry, the new Earl of Pembroke, inherited on his father's death in 1570. On that day he became the richest man in England, but with the change in generations, the atmosphere of the story changes too. Henry had been used by his father as a tool in the advancement of the family. First, as part of the great plot to disinherit Mary Tudor and to install Lady Jane Grey on the throne, he had been married to Lady Jane's sister Katherine in 1553, and then just as rapidly unmarried from her, on the grounds that the marriage had never been consummated. Henry, as an unattractively loyal son, had written cruelly to the poor girl, telling her without any kindness that she had no claim on him. Next, he had been married to the Earl of Shrewsbury's daughter, Katherine Talbot, for her money. Quite smoothly, the pliable willow principle at work, the old man had steered his son around the labyrinth of aristocratic lands and royal influence.

As his third wife, after Katherine Talbot had died, Henry married the most brilliant woman of her generation. Mary Sidney was so sparkling a catch that according to Aubrey's salacious and voyeuristic gossip, Henry's father, the old trimmer himself, thought she was bound to cheat on him. 'The subtile old Earle did see that his faire and witty daughter-in-lawe would horne his sonne, and told him so, and advised him to keepe her in the Countrey and not to let her frequent the Court.' As often with Aubrey's tales, this one is impossible. The old earl had been dead seven years by the time Henry married Mary Sidney, but there is a poetic and emotional truth to it which goes beyond the simple facts. Henry's personality disappears under the intense glamour and interest of those who came to surround him at Wilton.

Certainly, from this distance, Wilton under the new regime turns from being the creation of the canny and potent dynasty-maker to the setting and frame for the sparklingly jewel-like presence of Elizabethan England's greatest woman patron and greatest woman poet. She drew around her a dazzlingly literate court. She was the dedicatee, sponsor, completer and publisher of the greatest prose romance of the age, was a distinguished translator of the Psalms, the author of political tragedies, the champion of Spenser, the friend of Shakespeare and the sustainer of the Arcadian vision.

Her father, Sir Henry Sidney, an impoverished but distinguished servant of the state, had been brought up as a classmate of Edward VI and had held the boy-king in his arms as he died. Sidney had been unable to accept a peerage because he did not have the income to support the condition, but he was a member of that rising upper-middle band of intelligent, vividly Protestant Englishmen who became the vertebrae of the Tudor state. On her mother's side, Mary Sidney was connected, dangerously, to greatness. Her mother's father was John Dudley, the Duke of Northumberland who had attempted with Pembroke to make Lady Jane Grey Queen of England, whom the first Earl of Pembroke had deserted at the crucial moment, and who together with his son Guildford Dudley and Lady Jane Grey had been executed by Mary Tudor. Mary Sidney's uncles, Robert Dudley, Earl of Leicester, Ambrose Dudley, Earl of Warwick and their sister Katherine, Countess of Huntingdon, had been disgraced, imprisoned and impoverished, but had survived to flower again in the sunshine of Elizabeth's reign. This Dudley milieu – attuned to power, close to the throne, increasingly attached to the fervent cause of active and aggressive Protestantism both in England and in Europe, thinking of themselves as the core of that interest in England – this was Mary Sidney's inheritance. Using the enormous wealth of the Pembrokes, she would make Wilton the heart of that other England, a place dedicated to preserving the country against the erosions of an increasingly powerful court and crown. It was under Mary Sidney's influence that Wilton became the heartland of the English Arcadia.

Her co-champion and co-promoter of the cause was the man who gave this enterprise its name, her brother, Philip Sidney, the author of *Arcadia*, which was largely written at Wilton and dedicated to his sister, the woman who was in effect its queen, or as the poet Gabriel Harvey would call her,

> the dearest sister of the dearest brother, the sweetest daughter of the sweetest Muses, the brightest Diamant of the richest Eloquence, the resplendentest mirrour of Feminine valour; the Gentlewooman of Curtesie, the Lady of Vertue, the Countesse of Excellency, and the Madame of immortall Honour.

Over two generations in this family, the women whom the bluff, difficult and choleric men married were the ones who brought the civilisation of Renaissance England into the rooms and garden walks at Wilton. Anne Parr had brought humanist grace to Herbert drive. Mary Sidney brought Renaissance glitter to Henry's conformity. She had been educated to the highest level: fluent in French, Italian and Latin, with a smattering of Greek and Hebrew. The medieval discipline of rhetoric – figures of speech, the understanding of decorum, the different forms of language suitable to different purposes and different occasions – complemented theology and a reading of the classics. She could sing and play the lute and was famous for the lace she wove.

She was more than twenty years younger than her husband and it was no love match. Mary had been at court since 1575, a hand-maiden to the queen, and her uncle Leicester had arranged her marriage to the thirty-nine-year-old Henry in 1577. The dowry which the Pembrokes required was an enormous £3000 – her father had to borrow a large chunk of it from Leicester himself. As for

Henry Pembroke, he seems, if anything, a little overawed by the massive, remembered presence of his father. He had behaved as required as a young man, welcoming as a thirteen-year-old the Spanish envoys to Wilton with an elegance which was noticed at court, acting with the propriety his bullying father would have insisted on, but doing little more in the end than maintaining the role he inherited. No very distinguished image of him survives, nothing compared with his father's, mother's, wife's, sons' or grandsons' portraits. In the one picture that survives at Wilton, the man himself seems shrivelled inside his clothes. He wears the ribbon of the Garter, he has a little sword, his sleeves are fashionably puffed. Nothing is larger in the landscape than that huge inherited coat of arms. Neither handsome nor authoritative, he looks like a man acting a role with which he does not quite identify. It is inconceivable that this figure could ever have held the future of England in his hands.

Instead, Henry found a role as the agent of royal power in the western provinces where the Pembroke lands lay and where his father had raised armies and decided fates. He became Lord Lieutenant of Wiltshire, Shropshire, Somerset, Worcestershire, Herefordshire and twelve Welsh counties. He was Lord President of the Council for Wales, responsible, with the sheriffs, for the performance of justice, the preparation of the muster rolls by which the militias were called out, summoning those trained bands and supervising the military stores. He was, in other words, the local agent of a centralising state, accepting the diminution of the nobility against which his father had railed. The difference between the first and second Earls of Pembroke is the difference between a very late medieval warlord and a very early modern official. 'My dogs wear my collars,' Elizabeth had said. Henry Pembroke was one of them.

The state papers are peppered with complaints about Henry's inefficacy and his own slightly querulous notes in reply. Local Wiltshire gentlemen badger him to become his deputy. 'All men cannot be deputy lieutenants,' Henry writes back. 'Some must govern, some must obey.' The Privy Council in Westminster intervenes. Henry needs more than one deputy lieutenant because he is 'for the most part resident in Wales'. The Privy Council took to appointing captains of the trained bands in Wiltshire without consulting him. Henry complained, removed the Westminster appointees and put his own in their place. Without hesitation, the Council told him to reinstate the originals. He was ticked off for the inadequacy of the Wiltshire militia, hopeless both in men and equipment. Henry said that the Wiltshire gentlemen didn't want to contribute money or men. He was told to 'be more earnest with them'. He was carrying a great name and title, but was he up to the task? England was now at war with Spain; some vigour was required.

Henry, as his father had done, organised the representation of Wiltshire in parliament, trying to ensure that he always had a body of MPs who would act as his own pressure group at Westminster. But even this he allowed to slip out of control. Sir John Thynne, an ambitious north Wiltshire gentleman, cheated and bribed his way into one seat against Henry's wishes and against the candidature of Henry's steward, George Penruddock of Compton Chamberlayne, the son of the first earl's great standard bearer. Henry wrote Thynne a sad and spineless letter:

> I would have all gentlemen to have their due reserved unto them, which from tyme to tyme as Parliaments fall out to be chosen: now some and then some, as they are fit, to the end they may be experimented in the affairs and state of their country, not thinking that you meant to be one, for that you were last and latelie . . . if you have a liking to be of the house I shall willingly further you to any place I have or can gett for you.

This is good behaviour, concerned with the balance and regularity of the political community, even treating the gentlemen of Wiltshire as if they were his sons to be educated in the ways of the world; but it is scarcely the correct response to having been outmanoeuvred by a man on the make.

Instead, Henry, when back from his summer expeditions to Wales, plunged into heraldry and bloodsports, the longstanding consolations, over many centuries, for grandees not quite up to making their way in the political world. 'Henry Earle of Pembroke was a great lover of heraldrie,' Aubrey remembered, 'and collected curious manuscripts of it, that I have seen and perused; e.g. the coates of armes and short histories of the English nobility, and bookes of genealogies; all well painted and writt. 'Twas Henry that did sett up all the glasse scutchions about the house.' A slightly pedantic nostalgia marked an ebbing of the fire.

He had one of the richest hunting establishments in England, an enormous enterprise: Arab stallions and mares, racehorses, horses for 'stagge-hunting, fox-hunting, brooke-hawking, and land-hawking.' For hounds the earls had the biggest, the 'harbourers', whose morning task it was to find 'a runnable stag' in its 'harbour' in the wood. There were bulldogs which were put in 'to break the bayes of the stagge' at the end of the chase when the animal had run itself into its final corner; there were also bloodhounds to find the wounded deer, foxhounds and the smaller harriers, 'that kind of dog whom nature hath endued with the virtue of smelling, and draweth into his nostrils the air of the scent of the beast pursued and followed,' who would put up the hares, and 'tumblers', small greyhound-like lurchers, which could be sent off to hunt alone and would fall or tumble in catching the rabbits or hares. 'His Lordship had the choicest tumblers that were in England, and the same tumblers that rode behind him he made use of to retrieve the partridges.' There were 'setting-doggs' – 'a certain lusty land spaniel', setters – which would put up the partridges 'for supper-flights for his hawkes'. Greyhounds were kept to run in the Hare Warren, 'as good as any were in England'.

Henry set up a famous horse race on the downs above Wilton, four miles long from the start at the Aubrey farm in Broad Chalke to the finish by his father's Hare Warren outside the park at Wilton. He presented a golden bell worth £50 to the winner. The first to win it in 1585 was one of the great glamour men of Elizabethan England, George Clifford, Earl of Cumberland, adventurer, tournament champion, passionate Protestant, enemy of Spain and practised robber captain on the high seas, one of Queen Elizabeth's state-sponsored pirates. Once, after a trip to the Azores he arrived back at Falmouth, where he 'unladed and discharged about five millions of silver all in pieces of eight or ten pound great, so that the whole quay lay covered with plates and chests of silver, besides pearls, gold, and other stones which were not registered, elephants' teeth, porcelain, vessels of china, coconuts, hides, ebon wood as black as jet, cloth of the rinds of trees very strange for the matter and artificial in workmanship.'

That is the kind of figure with which to fill the rooms of Elizabethan Wilton, a place in which Henry Earl of Pembroke is present but not quite dominant. He was too much his father's son and had not absorbed the central place that beauty and glamour had taken in the exercise of power.

It happens again and again in the history of cultures. A generation of severe, rigorous, demanding and ambitious parents, who establish a form of order and riches, gives way, in the next generation, to a more evolved world, one more intent on fineness than propriety, happy to spend what the parents had earned, indifferent to debt, more interested in display than restraint, more attuned to brilliance and intricacy than mere obstinacy and assertion. The difference between mid- and late-nineteenth-century Britain and between mid- and late-seventeenth-century Holland appeared in the change that occurred between mid- and late-sixteenth-century England. The Wilton which in the 1580s became the dream landscape of Elizabethan England, the heart of a full-blown Arcadia, came out of the armoured toughness of an earlier age. Everything William Herbert had done to his tenants and his rivals, his enemies and friends, laid the foundation for a place of the highest and most lightly conceived civilisation and literary art. Under Mary Sidney's tutelage, the Arcadian butterfly emerged at Wilton.

Roger Ascham, the humanist and educationalist, correspondent of Anne Parr, had described the men of the first earl's generation, admiringly, as 'grave, steadfast, silent of tongue, secret of heart'. Perhaps, in his shouting tempers, those words do not quite fit the first earl, but the seriousness and secrecy of purpose, the care with which the willow had to bend with the wind, the self-limitation, the imposition of will: all of that describes the making of the Pembroke fortunes; and all of it was transformed in the following generation into something that was very nearly its opposite.

You can see what happens in the portraiture. The shape of people's mouths, from the tight drawn line in the world depicted by Holbein, the unforgiving straightforwardness of eye and jaw, the sense that each face is a mask over a mind of fixed intent, gives way, particularly in the second half of Elizabeth's reign, to something far less certain. The faces portrayed by the Elizabethan miniaturists turned from that unaccommodating and manly blankness, the defended façade of a calculating mind, to something subtler, more nuanced and more penetrable, coloured by doubt and delicacy, a feminisation of the ideal. Men's clothes became gay and brilliant; shoulders were no longer held four-square to the viewer; a doubting finger rose to the lips; the sobriety and resistance of the difficult years had been left behind. Fineness replaced assertion as the definition of nobility. The wars, threats of war, revolts and religious struggles engaged in by the makers of dynasties in the years of Henry, Edward and Mary now became play-wars in the ever more elaborate shows of tiltyard and tournament, even longed-for wars, wars not as the necessary assertion of social and political dominance but as the fulfilment of personal destiny. Life for the Elizabethan elite was strung between these ideals: the elegance of an existence without war, increasingly nostalgic for the days of chivalry, combined with a sense that sweetness was not enough, that the world had turned away from manliness and truth towards the honeyed, jewelled toys, the pearl-embroidered doublets, the glamour houses from which the lights at night glimmered through the branches of the surrounding woods 'not unlike the beams of the Sun through the crannels [crevices] of a wall'.

The height of this Elizabethan dream-glory was the moment in 1575 when the queen went to visit Kenilworth Castle, decorated by her favourite and sometime lover the Earl of Leicester, and lit up like a liner sailing through the Warwickshire woods:

> every room so spacious, so well belighted, and so high roofed within, so seemly to sight by due proportion without: by day time, on every side so glittering by glass; by nights by continual brightness of candle, fire, and torch-light, transparent through the lightsome windows, as it were the Egyptian Pharos reluent unto all the Alexandrian coast ... or else radiant as though Phoebus for his ease would rest him in the Castle, and not every night so travel down into the Antipodes.

At its most self-loving moments, it seemed as if the sun had come to rest in Elizabethan England, to spend the night there, its beams stealing out from the bedroom windows into the surrounding night, illuminating it like the candles and torches at a feast.

At the end of September 1574, Elizabeth came to Wilton and Wilton put on its most entrancing show. A full five miles away from the house, Henry Pembroke met her in her carriage out on the beautiful downland grass 'accompanyed with many of his honourable and worshipfull friends, on a fayre, large, and playne hill, having a good band of men in all their livery coates.' As a boy, Henry had been there when his father had done the same for Philip of Spain en route to his wedding with Mary Tudor. Henry knew what to do:

> Men, well horsed, who being placed in a ranke in order, from one another about seaven foot, and about fifteen foote from the highway, occupied a great way; and another rank of the earle's gentlemen servants, about a stone's cast behinde their masters stood on horsebacke in like order. And when the Queen's majesty had ridden beyond the furthermost of the earle's men, those that began the ranke, by three and three,

rode another way homeward on the side of a hill, and in like
order the rest followed and lastly the gentlemens servants.

This was landscape as theatre, the cast cleverly disappearing behind
the scenes, only to appear, magically, at the next glorious display.
As the queen arrived at the house, riding in through the gateway to
the first outer courtyard, 'Without the inner gate the countess with
divers ladyes and gentlewomen, meekly received her highnesse. This
utter court was beset on both sides the way with the earles men as
thicke as could be standing one by another, through which lane her
grace passed with her chariot and lighted at the inner gate.'

It might have looked like the assembling of the affinity, the great
gathering of the magnate's forces, the re-enactment of noble power,
gracefully welcoming a sovereign, but everyone would have known
the reality. Henry was a functionary. His offers to raise his troops
for the defence of the kingdom would not be taken up by the Privy
Council. He received letters from them telling him to attend more
closely to his duties in Wales, instructed by the Privy Council 'to
reside half the year at Ludlow' – the headquarters of royal government in the Welsh marches – an instruction Henry resented 'as
though I wanted discretion to discharge the like trust which had
been committed to all others [who had held the post previously];
or were unworthie to have any regard had of my health. I will not
despaier of her Majesties goodness: I haue waited onlie on her:
I haue not by factions sought to strengthen or by future hoopes
endeuered to foster my selfe: and therefore from her Maiesty as
I onely dezerwe; so by her Maiestie I only expecte to be conforted.'

All he really wanted was 'some princelie bountie', which he
didn't really need and which never came. In these letters one can
see very precisely something which might otherwise be quite intan-
gible: the growth of the state, the concentration of power in the
hands of the crown and the converting of the aristocracy into agents
of regal power.

Meanwhile, the Wilton show rolled on, the sugared crust over the rather different underlying realities. 'Her Highnesse lay at Wilton house that Friday night, the Saturday and Sunday nightes following; and on Monday after dinner her grace removed to Salisbury; during all which time her majesty was both merry and pleasant.'

That final phrase carries within it the expectation that she might have been neither. Elizabeth had been schooled in the world where the first earl had also learned the lessons of survival. Her enormous and defended authority, reserving all options from foreigners and rivals for power, whether in England or abroad, was the great iceberg around which the world of Arcadia was framed. Arcadia looked for openness, mutuality and a sense of power residing not in the crown but in the balanced organism of the commonwealth of which the crown was merely the head. Any sense of that mutuality or balance in the government of the kingdom was no part of Elizabeth's statecraft.

The first earl had been appointed in 1553 to the office of Warden and Keeper of the Park of Clarendon, to the east side of Salisbury, 'that delicious parke (which was accounted the best in England)' according to Aubrey, as well as Launder or keeper of the grazing there and Lieutenant of the Conies. Henry had inherited the post and the entire party went over there at the weekend. It had been the queen's decision.

> On the Saturday her highnesse had apoynted to hunt in Claryngdon Park. Where the said earle had prepared a very faire and pleasant banquett[ing house made of] leaves for her to dyne in; but that day happened so great raine, that although it was fenced with arras, yet it could not defend the wett, by meanes whereof the Quene dined within the lodge; and the lords dined in the banquet house; and after dinner the rayne ceased for a while, during which tyme many dear coursed with grey hounds were overturned, soe as the tyme served, great pleasure was shewed.

The atmosphere of this hunting was not the red-cheeked, pink-coated high spirits we might associate it with now. There was something much more consciously elevated about this Elizabethan hunt, a heightening of the world rather than a coarsening of it, as if on the hunting field, or at least in the huge hunting world of the Wiltshire downs and their long horizons, one could taste some element of an Arcadian reality.

Inside a park, the pursuit and killing of the delicate fallow deer, an animal from the east, which had been kept in parks in Persia when England was little but mud and wildwood, and had travelled to Europe via Minoan Crete and Norman Sicily, was an engagement with nature on the most refined and feminine of levels. Here, with bow and arrow, is where the women of the household, or the unathletic and scholarly men, would pursue the hunt, often shooting deer that had been driven by men and hounds into convenient corners for them. They might not even engage in the hunt itself, but simply watch as the animals were killed before them.

The hunting park was in that way conceived as a place of delicious femininity, full of an erotic charge, heightened by its sense of enclosure, of a nature shut in but still quite wild. It was never more seductively or entrancingly expressed than by Shakespeare's slightly fat, slightly old, slightly overheating Venus, trying again and again to persuade her lovely young beardless Adonis to enter the sweetness of the enclosure she had to offer. She is lying next to him on a primrose bank.

> Sometimes her arms infold him like a band:
> She would, he will not in her arms be bound;
> And when from thence he struggles to be gone,
> She locks her lily fingers one in one.

> 'Fondling,' she saith, 'since I have hemm'd thee here
> Within the circuit of this ivory pale,
> I'll be a park, and thou shalt be my deer;
> Feed where thou wilt, on mountain or in dale:

> Graze on my lips; and if those hills be dry,
> Stray lower, where the pleasant fountains lie.

To that extent, deliciousness was what the park was for. It was a place full of the ambiguities of Arcadia: power and delight, freedom and control, simplicity and sophistication, all overlapping and intersecting in the richest possible cultural landscape. Every aspect of that Arcadian complex would have been in play when the queen came to be merry at Wilton, and in the rainy enclosures of Clarendon Park. The earl was merely her ranger here, her servant. But he derived huge income from the post, one anyway which he had inherited from his father. He was in control but he was there to serve her. He provided the deer for her to shoot at, with her bow, but the deer were hers anyway, his hounds her hounds, his standing her standing. His need of her was more than hers of him. He might have been surrounded by hundreds of men in his livery but he wore her collar; she certainly didn't wear his (although she did like to wear, on occasion, a miniature of Robert Cecil, her secretary in her last years, on her shoe).

And yet, overlying this picture of dominance, which would be less nuanced if she had been a man, was a small charged theatre of the erotic, of Diana the huntress queen, her taunting and powerful virginity somehow set in play by her role as huntress, a merging and muddling of genders and potencies. James I expressly forbade his Queen Anne from hunting deer, but a Queen Regnant was different. She was, in her womanliness, even more removed from those around her than a king would be. Perhaps because of the necessary distance to be kept between male power-brokers and her own body, any sense of intimacy with her authority was stilled at birth. No man could get close enough to be anything more than emasculated in her presence. And that denial of access to power was one of the conditions in which an appetite for Arcadia – which was the absence of tyranny – would thrive.

The Countess of Pembroke's elder brother, Philip Sidney, was a proud, clever, often slightly touchy, ambitious, well-travelled, fiercely Protestant, ingenious, funny, story-telling, highly educated, charming and occasionally violent man. He once told his father's secretary that he would 'thruste my Dagger into yow' because the secretary had been opening the young man's letters. But he was a complex figure and Dr Moffet, his friend and the Pembrokes' physician at Wilton, thought Sidney 'possessed a gentle, tender disposition'. One thing he hated was hunting, thinking it an unnecessary and tyrannical brutality. According to his friend Edmund Spenser, he was capable of melancholy but he was also 'made for merriment/Merily masking both in bowre and hall'.

Sidney had been born in 1554 and was his father's treasured son. As a young man he had swum into the mainstream of English cultural life: Raleigh, Raleigh's half-brother the adventurer and explorer Humphrey Gilbert, Dr Dee, the great mathematician and cartographer of Elizabethan England, the historian William Camden, Richard Hakluyt the chronicler of English expansionism across the world's oceans, Francis Walsingham, the Protestant zealot and spymaster, the poets Fulke Greville, Edmund Spenser and Edward Dyer: all were part of Sidney's circle, which was literate, literary, politically and materially ambitious, highly Protestant, courtly and chivalric. Sidney had travelled through Europe, where he had fallen in love with the works of Titian, Tintoretto and Veronese and had himself painted in the modern Italian style, and across northern Europe had conversed at length with Protestant princes and scholars, as if he were their equal. It was the training for a life of significance.

But Sidney wasn't much liked at court and was distrusted by the sage heads around the queen for an immoderate turn of mind, a readiness to argument and an inflated idea of his own importance, derived from his connections to his uncle the Earl of Leicester and the respectful treatment he received from Protestant leaders abroad. They saw in him possibilities of an Englishman who might lead England into the religious wars against the Roman Catholic powers of the continent. Nothing could have been more unwelcome to the queen.

Sidney's life was strung between literature and politics. He was born with a gift for fluency, a rhythmic ease which flooded English sensibility with a new and extraordinarily influential feeling for the beauties of the flowing phrase. Largely through him the current of English poetry and romance turned from the blocky, rough-cut directness of mid-sixteenth-century poetry to something sweeter and more liquid. He thought of himself as someone on whom the service of his country and his faith lay as a duty. He was an elegant man, but pock-marked, his face scarred by smallpox when he was a boy, as his mother's had been. Among the mottoes which he would later carry as a knight in the tiltyard was one which said of himself, 'Spotted to be known'. Ben Jonson thought his appearance revolting; 'Sir P. was no pleasant man in countenance, his face being spoiled with pimples and of high blood and long.'

By his mid-twenties he was already chafing at his failure to be more engaged with a serious career. He took to arguing, angrily, with other courtiers over matters of status and honour. He even spoke forthrightly to the queen herself over her neglect of the dignity of gentlemen such as himself at court. By the late 1570s, his frustrations finally led him away from court, where he was unwelcome, to Wilton, its delights and consolations. In 1579, an argument over precedence with the Earl of Oxford, who had rudely ejected him from a tennis court at Greenwich mid-game, and his authorship of a manuscript letter arguing that the queen should not marry a Catholic Frenchman, led to his banishment to the country. He was already attuned to the power and potential of pastoral and in that same year he had given the queen, as a New Year's present, a cambric smock, the dress for a shepherdess, an invitation to the simplicities of Arcadia.

At Wilton his sister, Mary Pembroke, who loved him immoderately, took him in. Aubrey's strange, half-transmuted, gossipy memories had it that the two of them slept with each other and that the Philip who would become the fourth earl was their misbegotten son, named after his father-uncle-godfather. That cannot be true, but the gossip, as ever, addresses a deeper truth. There is something warmer, closer and more loving in the relationship of

Mary Pembroke and Philip Sidney than there ever was between Mary and Henry, the hunting and heraldry-obsessed earl who married her.

There are several versions of *The Countesse of Pembroke's Arcadia*, probably begun in 1578 but revised over many years. The first was a gentle romance, in which an undertone of politics played throughout the pastoral, the second a more violent and less clear-cut epic and the third, completed by Mary after Sidney's death, something of mishmash between the two, perhaps with additions of her own. All of them were dedicated to her. It had begun in a challenge from her to him, daring him to write a romance in English, something to match the *Arcadia* written by the Neapolitan, Jacopo Sannazaro, almost a century before, and which Sidney had bought on his Italian travels. 'You desired me to doe it, and your desire to my heart is an absolute commandment,' Philip wrote. 'Now it is done onely for you, onely to you.'

She had been involved from the start. It was 'but a trifle, and that triflingly handled,' Sidney wrote with conventional self-deprecation, a 'modesty tropos'. 'Your deare selfe can best witnes the manner, being done in loose sheetes of paper, most of it in your presence, the rest, by sheetes, sent vnto you, as fast as they were done.' Written, then, partly at Wilton, partly in London, perhaps partly at the Sidney house at Penshurst in Kent.

Sidney's Arcadia is, at least to begin with, a vision of escape. It is a land of fertile valleys and rich pastures, where the houses are 'lodges of stone built in the form of a star'. The inhabitants – and it does not take much to translate this into the circumstances at Wilton – are either great princes or poor shepherds. There is nothing much to do but fall in love and have adventures. Olive trees grow here; there are sandy beaches by turquoise seas. From time to time they might come on a 'sleeping lyon' or 'a she Beare not far from him, of litle lesse fiercenes', but that is not the dominant tone, which is one of sweetness, conversation, ease in the shade, time for love, some 'burning kisses', 'sweete kisses', 'cold kisses', 'many kisses',

'kisses oft' and all under 'the Palmetrees, (which being louing in their own nature, seemed to giue their shadow the willinglier, because they held discourse of loue)'.

This unthreatened, easy perfection was the realm of Arcadia. It was a place where the grief and tension of existence had been eased away and stilled. Sweetness was the face it showed to the world. So often do honey and sweetness appear in Sidney's *Arcadia* that they seem at times like a joke. The grass on which the sheep nibble is sweet, the words which the princess murmurs through 'the cherry of her lips' are invariably sweet and increasingly honeyed. She is, according to the stricken knight, 'the sweetest fairnesse and fairest sweetnesse: with that word his voice brake so with sobbing, that he could say no further.' Her 'breath is more sweete then a gentle South-west wind, which comes creeping over flowery fields and shadowed waters in the extreme heat of summer, and yet is nothing, compared to the honey flowing speech that breath doth carry ... She had no sooner ended with the joining her sweet lips together, but that the shepherd who lay before her recorded to her music this rural poesie: O words which fall like summer dew on me / O breath more sweete, than is the growing bean / O tongue in which, all honeyed liquores be ...'

It is an Edenic, wish-fulfilment world. A young prince finds himself naked but 'this nakedness was to him an apparel'. Scene after scene unfolds in the liquid language which became one of the Elizabethan idioms. Handfuls of words pour forth as smoothly continuous as the broad backs of the downs over which he had been wandering. It is all slightly absurd, the mind on holiday. One can only guess what the old earl might have made of it. But, that said, there is also a dance-like sensation, or ballet-like sensation, that this is a realm in which beauty for once might be allowed its freedom. It is the language and the images of youthfulness and release, emerging from under the carapace of a tough-headed, Polonius-like generation of elders, who had been all too insistent for all too long on the proprieties and duties and self-improvements and self-controls to which older generations are chronically prey. This, for all its weakness and over-sweetness, is the freedom of writing as if the writing itself were making a new world, discovering a light-hearted engagement with some freely invented thing (the models for which Sidney had, of course, read in Virgil and Theocritus, and seen on the walls of the Italian villas and places he had visited a couple of years before).

'Reade it then,' he told his sister,

> at your idle times, and the follies your good iudgement will finde in it, blame not, but laugh at. And so, looking for no better stuffe, then, as in a Haberdashers shoppe, glasses, or feathers, you will continue to loue the writer, who doth exceedingly loue you, and moste heartilie praies you may long liue, to be a principall ornament to the family of the *Sidneis*.
> *Your louing brother,*
> *Philip Sidney.*

Not, intriguingly, of the Pembrokes or the Herberts, whose violent, vulgar, grasping Welshness perhaps did not compare with the noble refinement of the Dudley-Sidneys. For something which Sidney revised and struggled over for years, this is the pose of *sprezzatura*, an assumption of ease laid over a life of hidden purpose.

As Virginia Woolf wrote in her affectionate essay on the *Arcadia*, 'the life that we invent, the stories we tell, as we sink back with half-shut eyes and pour forth our irresponsible dreams, have perhaps some wild beauty; some eager energy; we often reveal in them the distorted and decorated image of what we soberly and secretly desire.'

Founded on the autonomy of desire, Sidney's *Arcadia* is fiercer than a mere soft-edged dreaming of a sunlit holiday. He was a disappointed man. To his friend Edward Denny he wrote from Wilton that 'the vnnobl constitution of our tyme doth keepe vs from fitte imployments'. The queen would not let him have a position at court; nor with the Protestant armies in Europe, where he had been offered the governorship of the Protestant provinces of Holland and Zeeland by William of Orange; nor even in the New World, to all of which he was drawn. The experience of authority in sixteenth-century England was one either of uncertain success or certain humiliation. Arcadia, of its essence, was a place in which to escape authority and enter the world in which desire was king.

Desire, which colours page after page of the romance, is a world beyond power. Both beneath power and indifferent to it, desire was where the self could find an unadulterated and uncompromised being, a form of life beyond the humiliations of hierarchy. Queen Elizabeth's dogs may have worn her collars but not in Arcadia. Arcadia was beyond the submission to a pre-defined destiny. It was a form of transcendence into a world of beauty whose essence was freedom. In the romance, there is a deep and pained longing, expressed far more intently than the warblings of shepherds and their oaten pipes, for an age before consciousness, before moral codes, before grief and sorrow, before a man could be disappointed by his own life:

> Many times haue I, leaning to yonder Palme, admired the blessednes of it, that it could beare Loue without sence of paine. Many times, when my masters cattle came hether to chewe their cudde, in this fresh place, I might see the young Bull testifie his loue. But how? with proud lookes, and ioy-fulnes. These beasts, like children to nature, inherit her bless-ings quietly; we, like bastards, are layd abroad, euen as foundlings to be trayned vp by griefe and sorrow.

But that longing to escape into the world of desire, Sidney knew to be not enough. In his great sonnet sequence, *Astrophel and Stella*, probably also written at Wilton, Sidney dwelt, as any number of melancholic Elizabethan young men would also dwell, on his dis-grace with fortune and men's eyes, on the triviality of his life and occupations. His great friend and mentor the French Protestant divine Hubert Languet had written to ask him if it was 'honourable for you to be lurking down where you are, while your country is begging for the help and support of her sons'. Sidney answered in a sonnet:

With what sharpe checkes I in my selfe am shent [shamed]
   When into Reason's audite I do go:
   And by just counts my selfe a banckrout know
Of all those goods, which heav'n to me hath lent:
Unable quite to pay even nature's rent,
Which unto it by birthright I do ow, . . .
My youth doth waste, my knowledge brings forth toyes . . .

This is the seriousness of Arcadia, buried inside its sugar. A sense of honour and conscience drove him towards a political life which he felt it was his duty to take up. The knowledge that he came from a governing family was a powerful force for Sidney. In families like his lay the guarantee of freedom for the country. Only a powerful, crown-denying nobility could preserve the country free from tyranny. His brother-in-law Henry Pembroke may have been meekly submitting to the crown's control of noble power, but for Sidney and the many readers of his manuscripts among the elite, that submission was not enough.

No question in the sixteenth century was more alive than the relationship of the crown to the governing class. All over Europe, it seemed clear historical limitations on the sovereign, largely guaranteed by an ancient nobility, were under threat. The great struggle for the Low Countries, out of which the glories of the Dutch Republic would come in the seventeenth century, was precisely this conflict between an assertive Spanish state and the old liberties of the Dutch dukedoms which Charles V the Habsburg King of Spain had inherited. In Italy, one small principality after another had been transformed from a consultative, self-limiting form of government to one in which the prince, having read his Machiavelli, imposed his absolute will. In France, that same influence had had its play. 'Is it better to be loved than feared, or the reverse?' Machiavelli had asked in *The Prince*. 'The answer is that it is desirable to be both, but because it is difficult to join them together, it is much safer for a Prince to be feared than loved.' Fear, and an abandonment of the assumption of good intent, which was behind the layered structures of the inherited medieval custom, were the foundations of tyranny. 'It is necessary for him who lays out a state and arranges laws for it,' Machiavelli had written in the *Discourses*, 'to presuppose that all men are evil and that they are always going to act according to the wickedness of their spirits whenever they have free scope.' That was not the custom of the manor. Fulke Greville, Sidney's friend, disciple and follower, had heard Sidney himself bewail the influence of modernity on France, 'how that once well-formed monarchy had by little and little let fall her ancient and reverend pillars – I mean parliaments, laws and customs – into the narrowness of proclamations or imperial mandates.' That is precisely what Sidney, his uncle Leicester, his father-in-law the spymaster Sir Francis Walsingham and others of the Protestant party in England feared. A modern, absolutist monarchy would lift England away from 'her ancient legal circles' and 'our ancient customs and statutes'. The custom of the manor, the very mutuality of the time-honoured workings of the country, was a model of the workings of Arcadia. And the environment at Wilton, for all its self-delusions, was a model of the ideal state. Hubert Languet, the only real person named in *Arcadia*, had in his great book *Against Tyranny*, published in 1579, addressed the central political Arcadian question to a tyrant: 'Just because someone has made you a shepherd for the sake of the flock, did he hand over that flock to be skinned at your pleasure?'

No: the shepherd needed to love his sheep; just as the lord needed to love his tenants, and they him in return.

For Languet, who might have been speaking of Henry Pembroke and his diminished condition, the modern tyrannical state had eaten away at the nobility who were the guarantee of a real freedom and had clothed them in the fancy dress of the tiltyard and the tournament:

> You speak of peers, notables and officials of the crown, while I see nothing but fading names and archaic costumes like the ones they wear in tragedies. I scarcely see any remnant of ancient authority and liberty . . . let electors, palatines, peers,

and the other notables not assume that they were created and ordained merely to appear at coronations and dress up in splendid uniforms of olden times, as though they were actors in an ancient masque, or as though they were staging a scene from King Arthur and the Knights of the Round table.

Here, already quite clearly articulated but sixty years early, are the phrases that would be used in the English Civil War. The state had put collars on its dogs and an emasculated nobility felt tyranny creeping across the land. This was not about democracy but the fears of the old ruling class sensing the growing power of the state. An uncontrolled crown would destroy the customs of England. Only with balance, and the organic integrity of a country which had head, body and limbs in harmony, would England be what it always had been.

This Arcadian heartland is a mysterious place for us: consciously elitist but fiercely Protestant in religion; prepared – just – to countenance the overthrow of kings but courtly to a degree in manner and self-conception; political in its removal from the political world; aristocratic, community-conscious, potentially rebellious, literary, martial, playful, earnest, antiquarian, English, Italianate and nostalgic. But this is the essence: Arcadia sees an aristocracy not as an element of a controlling establishment but as an essential organ in a healthy state, a check and balance on the centralising power of the crown and the true source of authority and care in the lands it owned. The vision of Arcadia is not far from the desire for wholeness which the communities of the chalkland valleys wished in their elaborate and ancient constitutions to embody.

Alongside his written versions of *Arcadia* – they were never printed during his lifetime but circulated in manuscript – Sidney also enacted his vision of courteous rebellion and independent purity at court. Before the French ambassador, on Whit Monday and Tuesday, in the early summer of 1581, Sidney, his friend Fulke Greville and two other young men, who were prepared to spend their fortunes on the performance, put on a show in the tiltyard in

Whitehall. They called themselves 'The Four Foster Children of Desire', that word glowing in the context of Elizabethan show as an acceptable and oblique stand-in for what in the language of Arcadia it really meant: rebellion, or at least self-removal from the structures of power.

They had the gallery at the end of the tiltyard, in which the queen would stand, redecorated and called 'the Castle or Fortresse of Perfect Beautie'. It was a game of mock rebellion by young men who believed that the queen and court, then considering a French and Catholic marriage for the queen, were neglecting the habits and structures of an older England, even moving towards a kind of tyranny which the land of desire could never tolerate. Sidney had written a speech dense with scarcely concealed meaning which was to be addressed to the Fortress of Perfect Beauty:

> Forasmuch as her highnesse should be there included, whereto the said foster children layde tytle and claime as their due by discent unto them. And upon denial, or any repulse from that their desired patrimonie, they vowed to vanquishe and conquer by force who so should seeme to withstand it.

This extraordinary pantomine of mock rebellion stands midway between the realities of 1549 and 1642. The same elements were at stake: patrimony, nobility, a crown which seemed to betray the best of a noble inheritance, courteous men, in some ways desperately dependent on the crown for their standing, in others proudly independent of it, holding the crown to account, showing no respect, threatening violence. Here it was a game, whose frisson depended on its approach to reality. The four knights sent a boy to issue their challenge to the queen as she came from Chapel. 'Without making any precise reverence at all, he uttered these speeches of defiance, from his masters to her Majestie "These foure ... do will you by me, even in the name of Justice, that you will no longer exclude virtuous Desire from perfect Beautie."'

It was, they said, in a breathtaking double bluff, 'a plaine proclamation of warre':

If beautie be accompanied with disdainful pride, and pride
weighted on by refusing crueltie, then must I denounce unto
you that ... they will besiege that fatal Fortresse, vowing not
to spare (if this obstinacie continue) the sword of faithfulnesse,
and the fire of affection.

The speech tells it straight. The queen and her government were
proud and disdainful. Their cruelty consisted in refusing a place or
a role to Philip Sidney and others like him who not only owed the
country their duty, but had the strength, the independent strength
within them, to attack that fatal fortress and its hideous obstinacy
with the sword of faithfulness – that is the Protestant religion – and,
in an astonishing yoking together of disparates, 'the fire of affection',
which is to say Arcadia's burning desire. Here, quite clear, even if
buried under ceremony and courteousness, like a dramatised version
of a jewelled New Year's Day emblem, was the rebellion of the
Arcadian lords. Needless to say, this show was so weak and so
marginal that it had no effect at all. Any impact would have to wait
for different circumstances in the following century.

Sidney's *Arcadia* had argued for action and for giving powerful
and glamorous roles to the nobility and their supporters. Elizabeth's
reluctance was motivated not only by a desire to avoid war and its
expense but also not to give her great subjects ideas above their
station. Finally, in 1586, after years of pleading and under the command of Leicester, an English expeditionary force, paid for with
Dutch money, went over to the Netherlands to fight for the Protestant Dutch against the Spanish. Sidney was appointed Governor
of Flushing, one of the three ports the English received from the
Dutch as guarantees against their paying the costs of the expedition.

It was in a small engagement in that war, at Zutphen on
23 September 1586, that Sidney was wounded. He had left off his
thigh armour, either, as his friend and biographer Fulke Greville
said much later, as an act of theatrical courage, so that he would be
no better protected than the other gentlemen around him, or maybe
because a lighter armour would have given him some added

mobility on the battlefield: 'So he receiued a hurt by a musket shot a little aboue the left knee, which so brake and rifted the bone, and so entered the thigh vpward toward the bodie, as the bullet could not be found before his bodie was opened.'

As the wound turned gangrenous, Sidney turned towards God. The wound was 'a loving and fatherly correction' from the source of loving justice. In the light of this lesson, Sidney promised to 'addict myself wholly to God's service, and not to live as I have done. For I have walked in a vain course.'

Those words cast a chill over the delights at Wilton. But they were the words of a dying and wounded man. The truth is that as an inheritance, as a dead man, Sidney, and his association with the free-flowing landscape of Arcadia, with its combined vision of Protestant freedom and noble authenticity, in a world away from the corruptions and failures of the court, were more potent than they had been when he was alive. In death, for England as much as for his family, he became 'an Angell Spirit:' – the phrase was his sister's – 'so rare a iewell of vertue and courtesie.'

Theatricality did not desert Sidney in death. His body was taken back from the Low Countries, covered with a pall of black velvet. The pinnace that brought him home, right into the Pool of London, where his body was disembarked at the Tower, had 'all her sayles, tackling and other furniture coloured black and black cloth hanged round about her with Escouchions of his Armes.' It was the ship of sorrow and the death of hope. But this image was the guarantee that everything Sidney had ever believed would survive him. He had made the Arcadian amalgam central to the English nobility's view of themselves as the inhabitants, at least in potential, of a sweet and beautiful world, free of tyranny, whose freedoms were guaranteed by their own independent virtue within it.

In the reign of his sister Mary, Wilton would become the focus and reliquary of that ideal.

7

Little Earths kind of Paradise

Mary Pembroke's court at Wilton
1586–1601

THE COURT which Mary Sidney gathered around her at Wilton was filled with wits, poets, thinkers and scientists. She and they made it the centre of Renaissance England. Almost the entire family was writing poems. Her other brother, Robert Sidney, who became Governor of Flushing on Philip's death, wrote a sequence of poems addressed to Mary. Her son William and her niece, also called Mary Sidney, both became poets. The only silent members of the household were the increasingly ailing and curmudgeonly Henry, and her younger son Philip, both of them devoted to their hawks and hounds.

She had not been admitted to her brother's funeral and afterwards she withdrew to Wilton in her grief for two years. Sidney had made her his literary heir. She was in possession of the manuscripts of *Arcadia*, *Defence of Poesy* and the sonnet sequence *Astrophel and Stella*. Over the coming years, from her base at Wilton, she would oversee the publication of all of them. But her role was far more than a keeper of the flame. Before his death, Sidney had been translating the Psalms into sophisticated English lyrics. He had reached Psalm 43 and Mary set herself the task of completing the remaining 107. In doing so, she helped shape the religious lyric of the seventeenth century, steering the atmosphere at Wilton away from the rather flat-footed hunting-and-hawking to which Henry her husband was devoted, and towards a higher, more spiritualised world.

'Religion,' John Donne, the friend and admirer of both Sidneys,

LITTLE EARTHS KIND OF PARADISE

would say in a sermon, 'is a serious thing but not a sullen' and the translations of the Psalms which Mary Pembroke would make over the next few years were acknowledged by him and others as the most ingenious and mostly richly poetic of any made in English. Donne certainly drew from them, as would George Herbert for the great religious poems he would write here in the early 1630s when vicar of Bemerton.

In the part courtly, part Protestant world of Wilton, with its twin presiding deities of Calvin and Castiglione, the translation of the Psalms was a fusing of those universes. The task of the poet, as Ben Jonson said of translation, was 'to draw forth out of the best and choicest flowers, and turn all to honey', and that is what, at least in part, Mary Sidney did with the Psalms, applying the sweetness of Arcadia, its courtly concern for graceful precision and sophisticated invention, to the great poetry of the Hebrew Bronze Age. Religious verse, in her hands, as it would be in George Herbert's, did not exist in a compartment separate from urbanity and courtesy; it was an extension of those qualities, not a denial of them.

The Psalms were thought to be the work of King David, royal poems, and that high religious and kingly standing played its part in the Wilton Psalms. 'Hee,' Mary wrote later, meaning her brother Philip, 'did warpe, I weav'd this webb to end / the stuffe not ours, our worke no curious thing . . .'

She was binding her life in with her dead brother's, both of them in service at a court at which no Tudor monarch held sway, the highest court of which man could conceive. Here, in the Arcadian-Protestant amalgam, is another subtle form of subversion, a demotion, at least by implication, of all the pretensions to greatness which a worldly court might make.

Mary Sidney would have had before her the Psalms as translated by Miles Coverdale in 1535 and distributed throughout the country in the Great Bibles which Henry VIII and Archbishop Cranmer required each parish to hold. Here is the language of Coverdale's Psalm 139, addressing the power of God:

Yf I saye: peraduenture the darcknesse shal couer me, then shal my
night be turned to daye.
Yee the darcknesse is no darcknesse with the, but the night is as
cleare as the daye, the darcknesse & light are both alike.

Mary Sidney took that plain and workmanlike statement and gave
it a kind of dancing elegance, at the same time elevating and refining
its tone, making it courtly, maintaining its seriousness but banishing
its sullenness, eliding Calvin with Castiglione:

> Do thou best, O secret night,
> In sable veil to cover me:
> Thy sable veil
> Shall vainly fail:
> With day unmasked my night shall be,
> For night is day and darkness light,
> O father of all lights, to thee.

'In dancing,' Castiglione had written in *The Courtier*,

> a single step, a single movement of the body that is graceful
> and not forced, reveals at once the skill of the dancer. A singer
> who utters a single word ending in a group of four notes with
> a sweet cadence, and with such facility that he appears to do
> it quite by chance, shows with that touch alone that he can do
> much more than he is doing.

This is the heartland of *sprezzatura*, the nonchalance that stems
from discipline and rigour. The apparently effortless movement of
the dancer is just the effect Mary Sidney was aiming for here, not
as a form of worldly refinement but as an aspect of prayer and
worship.

The Sidneyan Psalms are far more than a mere sweetening of
the sacred note. They put on a bravura display of different voices
and different tonalities, different verse forms and rhyme schemes, a
deliberate compendium of inventiveness which veers from coyness
to savagery, from the most stylish of dance-tunes to the most unforgiving of homilies. Psalm 52 as translated by the Geneva Bible of
1587 was a traditional Puritan exercise in straight talking to the great

of the worldly world: 'Why boastest thou thy selfe in thy wicked-
nesse, O man of power? the louing kindenesse of God indureth
dayly. Thy tongue imagineth mischiefe, and is like a sharpe rasor,
that cutteth deceitfully. Thou doest loue euill more then good, and
lies more then to speake the trueth.'

Mary Pembroke had no difficulty in outstripping the Presby-
terian divines in the uncompromising attack of her translation:

> Tyrant whie swel'st thou thus,
> Of mischief vanting?
> Since helpe from god to us,
> Is never wanting?
>
> Lewd lies thy tongue contrives,
> Lowd lies it soundeth:
> Sharper then sharpest knives
> With lies it woundeth.
>
> Falshood thy witt approves,
> All truth rejected:
> Thy will all vices loves,
> Vertue neglected.

This is the counterpoint of that earlier, dancing lightness: the ham-
mering, Puritan contempt for the corruption and vanity of power,
spoken with the authority of a countess, her own court around her,
and the moral strength of her dead martyred brother allowing her
no compromise in language or grammar. Truth-telling of this kind
can largely dispense with verbs and adjectives. The Psalm in Mary's
hands has become a naked, noun-based charge-sheet of worldly
failing.

The poets Samuel Daniel, Abraham Fraunce, Fulke Greville,
Edmund Spenser, Michael Drayton and Thomas Nashe all became
part of the Wilton orbit. They lauded Sidney's sister as the 'Arabian
Phenix, wonder of sexe', 'the inheritor of his wit and genius', the
miraculous re-appearance of his genius in another guise, 'the happie

and iudiciall Patronesse of the Muses', of which patronage needless
to say these poets were the grateful recipients. The slightly desperate
and wayward minor poet and anthologist Nicholas Breton, whose
career wavered from one patron to the next, left an account of life
at Wilton under Mary Pembroke which at least hints at its combination of courtliness, literariness and piety. It was the nearest England had ever come to the gatherings of genius around Elizabetta
Gonzaga, the Duchess of Urbino celebrated in Castiglione's *The
Courtier*. 'Who hath redde of the Duchesse of Vrbina,' Breton wrote
to his patroness,

> may saie, the Italians wrote wel: but who knows the Countesse
> of Penbrooke, I think hath cause to write better: and if she had
> many followers? Haue not you mo seruants? And if they were
> so mindfull of their fauors? Shall we be forgetfull of our duet-
> ies? No, I am assured, that some are not ignorant of your
> worth, which will not be idle in your seruice.

Breton, for whom life did not always run smooth, had been 'a poore
Gentleman in the ruine of his fortune' but when Mary Pembroke
turned towards him, he found Wilton to be a 'little Earths kind of
Paradise'. It was everything of which an Elizabethan literary man
might dream: 'Her house being in a maner a kind of little Court,
her Lord in place of no meane commaund, her person no less then
worthily and honourablie attended, as well with Gentlewomen of
excellent spirits, as diuers Gentlemen of fine carriage.'

Everything was as it should be, 'God daily serued, religion trulie
preached, a table fully furnished, a house richly garnished, honor
kindly entertained, vertue highly esteemed, seruice well rewarded,
and the poor blessed relieued.' Despite this lavish larding of praise,
Breton, for some reason or other which remains obscure, fell out of
favour. Such gatherings of dependants in large and highly emotion-
alised households, as Wilton clearly was, will tend to argument and
rivalry. There are suggestions that Breton may have been something
of a drinker. His own account blamed 'the faction of the malicious,

the deceitful working of the enuious, and the desart of his owne unworthinesse.' The fateful moment came on a winter's day when, as he described in the third person, he had decided to leave the pressurised Wilton household and go wandering on the downs:

> Taking leaue for a time, to trauaile about a little idle business, in a cold snowy day passing ouer an vnknowne plaine, not looking well to his way, or beeing ordained to the misery of such misfortune [the Calvinist note], fell so deepe down into a Saw-pitte, that he shall repent the fall while he liues.

That's all he says. Had he been drunk? Or sunk into a kind of ridiculous melancholy, not looking where he was going, bringing dishonour on the household? It was certainly the most Sidneyan of mistakes, a wandering man, out on the wide snowy plains of Wiltshire, dreaming of a better world than this. Whatever his misdemeanour, only after a few years of apology and crawling was Breton re-admitted to the charmed circle.

Others, more confident in this challenging world, survived more easily. Sir Walter Raleigh's half-brother, the slightly sinister inventor and 'chymist' Adrian Gilbert, joined the household, as did Dr Thomas Muffet (or Moffet or Mouffet), physician and entomologist, a school friend of Edmund Spenser's, graduate of Basle, a follower of the Earl of Essex, the first man to write authoritatively about the migratory habits of English wild birds and the editor and compiler of the first English study of insects. His heavily worked Latin manuscript is now in the British Library – one real moth which was flying around the park at Wilton in the 1590s survives squashed between its pages – decorated in the margins with Muffet's beautifully observed drawings of bees, worms, flies, beetles, butterflies, gnats, mosquitoes, the long-legged flies called 'shepherds' in Wiltshire and many, many spiders. These were later reproduced as woodcuts in the 1634 edition of his book, the *Theatre of Insects*.

Sidney had often dabbled in chemical experiments, as would

Mary's son, William Herbert, the third earl, and in this slightly dilettantish and amateur way Wilton was part of the first stirrings of modern science in England. There is also another intriguing possibility, perhaps the most familiar of all survivals from Elizabethan Wilton. Dr Muffet, the most famous spider expert in England, had a daughter called Patience. It may be that Patience was Little Miss Muffet and her father's spiders are the originals of the spider which one afternoon on the banks of the Nadder in the 1590s sat down beside her.

> Little Miss Muffet, sat on a tuffet,
> Eating her curds and whey;
> Along came a spider, who sat down beside her
> And frightened Miss Muffet away.

The rhyme is not recorded before 1805, two centuries after Dr Muffet's death, well after the death of Patience Muffet's great-grandchildren, but it is not, I think, stretching too much of a point to see in it a tiny, concentrated piece of Arcadian drama. Here is Miss Muffet, sitting in all her innocence, on a tiny piece of downland, calmly spooning the milk and honey of Arcadia into her mouth. She is in the dreamy, dairy-based heaven for which all Arcadianists long. But into this vision erupts a dark, frightening, complex, hairy, unpredictable and ugly thing, all too real and all too unsettling. He is so big, this spider, not teetering fearfully from one anxious corner to the next, but settling himself down like a man with a pipe, a pint of beer and an opening line about the weather. The pastoral dream is banished, fineness has gone, Patience is driven from her tuffet and the scene ends with an absent heroine, a brute in possession of an otherwise empty stage, and a sense of the spell having been broken. The arrival of the spider is an act of violence. It undoubtedly carries sexual overtones – the black hairy leggy thing invades the milkiness of innocence – but also preaches the repeated lesson: Arcadia is not enough; it cannot survive the impact of reality. Perhaps reality itself is the end of childhood. The essence of the dream is its fragility and fragility, like childhood, does not last.

Muffet wrote a charming verse tale for his beloved countess about his passion for bugs ('I sing of little Wormes and tender Flies') but he also turned his hand to some elaborate Latin verses in memory of Philip Sidney. They were written in 1593, on Mary Pembroke's instructions, as a homily to young Will Herbert, the thirteen-year-old heir to this huge cultural inheritance, who that year went up to Oxford. The weight of expectation imposed on the boy's shoulders was immense and it is clear that he was not entirely happy with the burden being placed on him. Again and again, Muffet tells Will that his uncle when he was a boy preferred his books to his games. At school 'his bedroom was plastered with elegant epistles of choice Latin which he had stuck up on the walls.' Twice he became ill through studying too much – a habit of Mary's too – and when he was at university and then at court, Sidney kept his passions under control. Sloth, greed, self-seeking and sensuality: all of them this paragon avoided. He was not without lust, but he controlled it.

Muffet did admit that the young Sidney spent far too much on 'Christmas festivities and joustings, at which he was magnificently appointed, and then, with ceaseless liberality, on learned visitors.' But he was both modest and regal, and rose by his seriousness as well as by 'wit, grace, elegance, learning and influence'. Other courtiers – more sidelong glances at Will – 'chose to live in clover at home, to hunt wild animals, to follow a hawk, to wallow in every sensual pleasure.' Only our hero, it seemed, gave up 'love, poetry, sport, trappings, lackeys, pages and carriages inlaid with ivory' for the sake of helping a neighbour country 'where without fear he ran into fire as soon as he reached the foreign shore'. It doesn't take much to imagine the thirteen-year-old groaning under the propriety of the model being held out to him. Will was the 'growing shoot'. He was 'the flower of the Sidneys'. He was given, as his own *impresa*, the motto *Stat messis in herba* – the harvest is in the green stalk. He was the second Sidney, their perfect man in embryo. 'Therefore,' Muffet, with his eye of course more on the mother than the child, told the boy, 'do you embrace and cherish him, your second self.'

The sense of urgency in Mary, needing to steer her son and heir towards the otherworldly perfection of her dead brother, was driven, it seems clear, by Will's inclination to the very opposite. He was wandering towards the usual appetites of young men. Even eighty years later, Clarendon, writing his history of the civil war, thought Will had been 'immoderately given up to women'. What becomes particularly intriguing, though, is that precisely this set of circumstances, and the very same set of images that Muffet relied on, would repeat themselves within three or four years at another and more significant level.

There have been many candidates for the beautiful, aristocratic, reluctant-to-marry, sexy young man addressed with such overwhelming passion in the first 126 of Shakespeare's *Sonnets*, but none fits the circumstances as closely as Will Herbert: from a family of immense standing, which was of famous beauty in both men and women; with the initials W.H., those given by the publisher's dedication of the *Sonnets* in 1609 to 'The Onlie Begetter of These Insuing Sonnets'; of exactly the right age (born in April 1580) for an early middle-aged Shakespeare (born in April 1564) to fall in love with in the late 1590s; with a history behind him of his parents commissioning poets, whom they had known professionally, to urge him on to virtuous paths; seen as the 'green shoot' of the family, with the next generation's harvest latent in him, imagery on which Shakespeare memorably drew; and, as it turns out, with a wild and amorous nature but a deep reluctance to marry, exactly the subject of the first seventeen sonnets.

The Pembrokes had almost certainly come to know Shakespeare in the early 1590s when he was writing for a touring company, of no great success, subsidised by Henry and known as 'Pembroke's Men'. Shakespeare had also written *Venus and Adonis* and *The Rape of Lucrece* for another aristocratic patron, the Earl of Southampton.

It would be entirely appropriate, and even resourceful, for Mary Pembroke to turn to this brilliant, youngish court poet to address her increasingly wayward son. The first seventeen sonnets, more conventional than the rest, 'sugared', as they were described at the time, in a Sidneyan way, clearly form a group. Repeatedly playing on the same themes, they urge the young man to marry, to extend his line through children, not to let age destroy his beauty but to further it in children, an extension of the gifts his famous family has given him. The imagery plays around Will's *impresa, Stat messis in herba*. Just as the harvest lies latent in the bud, the passage of the year erodes the beauty of the spring.

> When I doe count the clock that tels the time,
> And see the braue day sunck in hidious night,
> When I behold the violet past prime,
> And sable curls all siluer'd ore with white:
> When lofty trees I see barren of leaues,
> Which erst from heat did canopie the herd
> And Sommers greene all girded up in sheaues
> Borne on the beare with white and bristly beard:
> Then of thy beauty do I question make
> That thou among the wastes of time must goe,
> Since sweets and beauties do them-selues forsake,
> And die as fast as they see others grow,
> And nothing gainst Times sieth can make defence
> Saue breed to braue him, when he takes thee hence.

The setting is polite Arcadia: the herds mill around the house; the woods are shady and the fields produce their harvest. The world turns on its Virgilian axis. This is Wilton, if beautifully animated by that vision of the barley sheaves on their funeral bier, white and bristly in the paleness of high summer, and suddenly shocked by the fruitless summoning of the 'wastes of time' amid this fecundity. For all that, it is courtly and contained. It is also a celebration of the defiance of Time's scythe, the victory of marriage and progeniture over the shadow of age and death. Shakespeare's sonnet, for all its local beauties, is driven by a need to defy time because the family corporation required it. This sonnet, which along with the other first sixteen is patronage poetry, involving no disturbance to any social or sexual hierarchy, was perhaps delivered, it can be conjectured, to Will Herbert, perhaps at Wilton, perhaps with the indulgent overseeing of his mother and father, on 8 April 1597 – there is a great deal of spring imagery in these first sonnets – which was the heir's seventeenth birthday. Shakespeare had taken up where Thomas Muffet had left off, playing a decorous role as prompter of virtue. The poems feel like what they were: a commission, a birthday present, a paid-for imploring, dedicated to the understanding that only by the complex of marriage and negotiation, of getting and begetting, can a person defeat his own mortality. That in effect is the voice of worldliness, of a good deal well done.

Still, Will Herbert would not conform. In 1595, marriage had been proposed between the young Will and Elizabeth Carey. On 25 September that year, the Carey parents were to visit Wilton where 'great preparacion was made for them' but they never came. Will had by then met Elizabeth and the match was broken off 'by [William's] not liking'. Henry was in no position to force him into a marriage he did not like and cancelled the engagement. Sir George Carey was enraged 'that lord Pembroke broke off the match between Lord Harbert and his daughter.'

Next, Bridget, the daughter of the Earl of Oxford and the grand-daughter of Lord Burghley, was suggested. The families manoeuvred towards each other. Burghley sent Mary some special medicine from London and she wrote to him in her increasingly out-of-date and convoluted style:

> Yowr Lordships fine token is to mee of Infinight esteem, and no less in regard of the sender than the vertu in it selfe. It is indeed a cordiall and presious present. Not unlike to prooue a spesiall remedy of a sadd spleen, for of lyke effect do I alredy find what so euer is of likely success proceeding from the cawse whence this proseeded.

That might have been the way to address someone fifteen or twenty years earlier, but the late Elizabethan world had moved on to a quicker and more impatient rhythm. Mary wrote another letter of almost equal inflatedness to Sir Robert Cecil, Lord Burghley's son. 'To bee silent now finding so iust cawse to be thankfull were a wrong to yow and an Injury to my selfe whose disposition hath euer held yow in very worthy regard . . .' In her Wilton outpost, it looked as if Mary Pembroke, still only thirty-six, had lost touch with the ways of the world.

Burghley was worried. His granddaughter Bridget was only thirteen, but there would be no consummation of the marriage until Will had come back from his travels. Would Bridget stay with the Pembrokes then or with her parents? The money was to be discussed by their agents, but the principles were clear. He would give a jointure equal to the dowry, plus a good allowance every year. Oxford himself was keen 'for the ionge gentelman as I vnderstand he hathe been well brought vp, fayre conditioned, and hathe many good partes in hym.' Again, though, the match came to nothing. Henry Pembroke, increasingly ill and short-tempered, had it seems insulted Robert Cecil, perhaps suggesting that the rather recent descendant of impoverished Welsh farmers, as the Cecils were, should not have the pretension to become Viscount Cranborne. The fact of the Herberts' own bastardy was by now well buried.

Mary Pembroke had to try to make good the damage and wrote to Robert Cecil in her high Elizabethan style.

> Sir I vnderstand report hath bin made vnto yow of sum speech that should pass my Lord (not in the best part to be taken) tuching Cramborne. My desire is yow should be trewly satisfied therein, and that in regard of truth and the respect I beare yow, for otherwise I woold be silent. I protest unto yow the report was most vntrue; and upon myne owne knowlidg, word, and honor, do assure yow ther was not any word spoken at any time to which yowr selfe bin present yow could have taken any exception.
>
> Yowr frend as wellwisshing as any M. Pembroke

It was no good. The wickedness of court, its lifejuice of malice and gossip, had broken her designs.

> Lewd lies thy tongue contrives,
> Lowd lies it soundeth:
> Sharper then sharpest knives
> With lies it woundeth.

Henry, now chronically ill, was desperate to see his elder son married before he succeeded to the earldom. If he were unmarried and under twenty-one at Henry's death, the Pembroke estates would fall into the Court of Wards (then in the hands of the Cecils) and his wardship would be sold off to the highest bidder, who would in turn suck from the Pembroke fortunes as much as he could take in the few years that remained before Will turned twenty-one in 1601. Still another marriage, to a niece of Charles Howard, Earl of Nottingham, was suggested, half-arranged, and then failed to materialise, in the summer of 1599.

Meanwhile, in Will Herbert's life, another eruptive passion broke loose. From those first seventeen sonnets, Shakespeare's sequence suddenly comes alive with the reality of his love for this beautiful and feckless young man. Shakespeare, feeling aged himself, is rendered powerless in front of him: 'Some say thy fault is youth, some wantonesse,' he pleaded, pitiably subject to Will's grandeur and carelessness. 'How many gazers mightst thou lead away,/If thou wouldst vse the strength of all thy state!/But doe not so, I loue thee in such sort,/As thou being mine, mine is thy good report.' The poetry leaves behind the formal, dance-like qualities of the Petrarchan world with all its tired reliance on the inaccessible girl of unimpeachable beauty, and replaces her with some of the great truth-telling, homosexual, often brutally misogynistic, wilfully complex and psychologically agonised love poems in the language. It is as if the lid had been lifted on the Elizabethan world, the formality taken away and the reality exposed to air. The fuel for that poetry was not only love, lust, sex and desire but the pains that came in the wake of that desire, a longing for Arcadian peace, a place of resolution beyond the torments of daily existence, beyond all conflict, but also a recognition that time, death and mortality had their place in Arcadia. *Et in Arcadia ego.* Far from urging the boy to a life of heightened virtue, Shakespeare fell in love with him as he was, both the embodiment of delicious and beautiful sexual delight and the occasion for a love which went far beyond the worldly.

Everything in the *Sonnets* drifts into the metaphors of hierarchy, land, inheritance, the law, the court, the embroiled nature of life, as if life itself, in the modernity which swept from one negotiation to the next, was at the same time the great webmaker and the great eroder. We are trapped in its coils and worn down by its relentless challenge. Everything about our negotiated lives is complex and getting more complicated by the minute. And in that complexity, time, without pause, digs furrows in our brows. Life and time remove from us the happiness we thought we had. Even the things that seemed for a moment unapproachably ours are rubbed down and worn away. 'Like as the waves make towards the pebbled shore,/ So do our minutes hasten to their end.'

The great and life-affirming paradox for Shakespeare is that only in the place made by the poem itself, in the actual written poem, can love and beauty remain impervious to time. Only there, in what the poet can do, can things of value be safe. Love itself can hurt but there is a pervasive sense throughout the long sequence of the *Sonnets* that the poem, its making and then its existence, jewel-like, organised like a watch, is itself the Arcadian space, the place in which hurt cannot occur and where perfection is removed from the erosions of weakness and time. The three words that appear more often than any other in Shakespeare's *Sonnets* are 'fair', 'kind' and 'true'. As a fugue on these themes, the sequence is a longing for goodness in a difficult world. It is a realm in which grace has a chance, where truth can be spoken and love remain true. The poem itself is a park.

That itself is a Sidneyan idea. In the most famous paragraph of the *Defence of Poesy*, written by Sidney at Wilton, he makes precisely this Platonic claim: only in art is perfection to be found. Nature can only regard the perfection of art's forms with envy:

> Nature never set forth the earth in so rich Tapestry as diverse Poets have done, neither with so pleasant rivers, fruitful trees, sweet smelling flowers, nor whatsoever else may make the too much loved earth more lovely: her world is brazen, the Poets only deliver a golden.

Only the poets can deliver a golden world. It is perhaps impossible now to read some of these poems as they might have appeared when their first manuscript copies were read by the beautiful boy of distinguished lineage, powerful sexual drives and melancholy turn of mind to whom they were first addressed. But if they do not illuminate the life of William Herbert, which they might, they at least illuminate for sure the world in which he lived, thought and felt, a place in which Paradise might be imagined, or even described, but never quite found.

8

Sweet are the vses of aduersitie

As You Like It at Wilton
December 1603

WHEN THE QUEEN at last died in March 1603, both William Pembroke and his younger brother Philip Herbert, along with hundreds of other peers and gentlemen, hurried to meet the new Scottish king as he made his way south through springtime England. Philip was four years younger than his brother and each of them, throughout their lives, played the complement to the other: William, the older and the richer, the more established, increasingly the more political, the more serious and the more engaged with the Sidneyan inheritance of courtly Protestantism, anti-Spanish and anti-Catholic policies, a poet and the patron of an enormous range of writers, fostering the literary heirs of Sidney and Spenser, allied to a growing interest in the English colonies of the New World as a place in which a vision of Arcadian perfection could perhaps be made real; Philip more glamorous, lighter on his feet, dedicated to the delight and charm of the king and his court, a passionate huntsman and gambler, needing to make his way in the world, hungrier than his brother, no littérateur, but a champion in the tiltyard and at the barriers.

His place as the second son seems to have liberated him from the burden of melancholy which affected his brother. When he had first come to court, he charmed and shone and when James arrived in England, the royal eyes alighted on him. As Edward Hyde, Earl of Clarendon, the Pembrokes' Wiltshire neighbour and later the historian of the civil war, would recall, the beautiful young Philip

Herbert had made an early impact, in a court suddenly liberated from the formalised antiquity of its predecessor:

> Being a young man, scarce of age at the entrance of King James, he had the good fortune by the comeliness of his person, his skill and indefatigable industry in hunting, to be the first who drew the king's eyes towards him with affection; which was quickly so far improved that he had the reputation of a favourite.

> He pretended to no other qualifications, than to understand horses and dogs very well, which his master loved him the better for (being, at his first coming into England, very jealous of those who had the reputation of great parts), and to be believed honest and generous, which made him many friends and left him then no enemy.

Philip may have been the more robust, less troubled and less complex of the two brothers, but there is no sense of William, Earl of Pembroke, living in his shadow. James made William a Knight of the Garter as soon as he had arrived in London. He had been in disgrace during the last years of Elizabeth for making one of her maids of honour pregnant. That was now lifted and there is no doubt of a real warmth and intimacy with the king. At the coronation in August 1604, delayed because of the plague the year before, the Venetian Secretary in England, Giovanni Scaramelli, after watching each of the earls come and kneel before the newly crowned king, had seen 'il Conte di Pemruch, giovane gratioso', a handsome youth 'who is always with the King, and always joking with him, actually kiss his Majesty's face, whereupon the King laughed and gave him a little cuff.'

That moment provides a sudden bridge between William Herbert, Earl of Pembroke – his father had finally died in 1601 – the serious man of court and state business and the Mr WH who would not marry and drove his poet to distraction.

The previous summer, and again in the autumn, from 24 October to 12 December 1603, James and the court had gone down to Wilton. The two brothers were surely there, as was their mother, the widowed countess. Plague had arrived in England and was devastating London. The theatres had been closed. Shakespeare's company, the King's Men, with a new royal patent to their name, were on tour. A payment is recorded for 2 December 1603, when the court was certainly at Wilton, to 'John Henyngs [or Hemminge] one of his Matie players . . . for the paynes and expences of himselfe and the rest of his Companye for coming from Mortlake in the county of Surrey unto the court aforesaid and there presentinge before his Ma[jes]tie one playe. £30.'

Added to that is another tantalising piece of evidence. In August 1865, William Cory, a poet and translator, author of the Eton Boating Song and an assistant master at Eton, wrote in his journal about a letter said to be at Wilton. He was teaching Greek there in the holidays to a young Herbert. The boy's mother, Lady Elizabeth Herbert, told him that 'The house is full of interest: we have a letter, never printed, from Lady Pembroke to her son, telling him to bring James I from Salisbury to see *As You Like It*; "we have the man Shakespeare with us." She wanted to cajole the king in Raleigh's behalf – he came.'

Even though the original of the letter disappeared before the end of the nineteenth century, and has never been seen since, it remains the most suggestive of fragments. If one follows the trail of evidence surrounding the missing letter, it seems at least possible that *As You Like It*, in the form in which it has come down to us, one of the richest statements of the interplay of pastoral and anti-pastoral from Renaissance England, is the version of the play which Shakespeare re-drafted for performance at Wilton on 2 December 1603. The king, the two Herbert brothers and their mother were all in the courtly audience; the play, in some ways, only makes sense if one understands those people to be there, listening and laughing at its jokes. It is a romantic comedy but it is also more than that, a performance designed by the countess, as the letter says, to influence the king's judgement as to the fate of Sir

Walter Raleigh, then in prison some thirty-five miles away in Winchester, recently found guilty of treason, of plotting to remove James from the throne, and awaiting execution. It is one of the moments at which the pastoral, Arcadian idea of peace and forgiveness bites most sharply on the political processes of Jacobean England. The ruse can be shown to have worked. The extraordinary antics to which James subjected Raleigh and his co-conspirators look very much as if they were shaped by his experience of having watched Shakespeare's play.

Raleigh, a long-term enemy of Robert Cecil, who had become the controlling figure of James's government, had been arrested in July 1603, along with Lord Cobham, George Brooke and Lord Grey, for their alleged parts in a conspiracy against the king. Shortly afterwards a Catholic country squire, Sir Griffin Markham, and two unhinged Catholic priests were taken on the same charge in a separate but related plot.

The trials to which they were subjected in November had been a hideous distortion of any kind of justice. The bullish chief prosecutor Sir Edward Coke had been unable to pin anything on Raleigh and had resorted to insult. Raleigh was 'the absolutest Traitor that ever was', the 'notoriest Traitor that ever came to the bar'. 'Thou hast a Spanish heart,' Coke told him, using the offensive second person singular reserved for dogs and servants, 'and thyself art a Spider of Hell.' All that the others did, Coke claimed, 'was by thy instigation, thou Viper; for I *thou* thee, thou Traitor.'

Raleigh replied with the moderation in which courtliness had schooled him. 'It becometh not a man of quality and virtue, to call me so,' he told Coke. 'But I take comfort in it, it is all you can do.'

COKE	Thou art the most vile and execrable Traitor that ever lived.
RALEIGH	You speak indiscreetly, barbarously and uncivilly.
COKE	I want [lack] words sufficient to express thy viperous Treasons.

RALEIGH   I think you want words indeed, for you have
            spoken one thing half a dozen times.
COKE   Thou art an odious fellow, thy name is hateful
            to all the realm of England for thy pride.
RALEIGH   It will go near to prove a measuring cast
            between you and me, Mr Attorney.
COKE   Well, I will now make it appear to the world,
            that there never lived a viler viper upon
            the face of the earth than thou.

At the end of the trials, as was foregone, George Brooke and the two half-mad priests were executed and the others were sentenced to death. According to the gossip of Dudley Carleton, a letter-writer and diplomat at court, Mary Pembroke had once been Raleigh's lover – as a militantly Protestant and romantic adventurer, another of Sidney's heirs, that is not entirely unlikely, although there is no other evidence of it – and she was desperate that his life be saved. 'I do call to mind a pretty secret,' Carleton wrote to his friend John Chamberlain, 'that the lady of Pembroke hath written to her son Philip and charged him of all her blessings to employ his own credit and his friends and all he can do for Raleigh's pardon; and though she does little good, yet she is to be commended for doing her best in showing *veteris vestigia flammae*' – the flickerings of an old fire, a phrase used by Virgil in the *Aeneid*, speaking of Dido, Queen of Carthage, when remembering a long-abandoned but long-cherished love.

Those rekindled flames had produced the Wilton letter, arranged for the King's Men to come to Wilton, Shakespeare with them, to put on a play which might cajole a king into mercy, using every inch of the two brethren's charm to bring the king to Wilton too. He came and it is worth dwelling on the political potency of this moment. The court was gathered in the sequence of rooms in the old Tudor palace. The lords of the Privy Council were there with the king. A violent challenge had been made over the course of the summer to his throne. Those who were plotting to kill him and his family were in custody, sentenced, ready to die. The two priests Clarke and Watson had already been hanged but then cut down still alive, their genitals hacked off, their entrails removed and their bodies quartered. Those quarters had been set up on Winchester's medieval gates and their heads on the first tower of Winchester Castle. Brooke, as a gentleman, had been beheaded in the castle yard.

The atmosphere in the crowded winter rooms at the Wilton court is frantic and agonised. Punishment or mercy? The exercise of absolute power or of forgiveness and hope for the future? 'Whilst these men were so occupied at Winchester,' Carleton wrote,

> there was no small doings about them at court, for life or death, some pushing at the wheel one way, some another. The lords of the council joined in opinion and advice to the king, now in the beginning of his reign, to show as well examples of mercy as severity. Others, led by their private spleen and passions, drew as hard the other way. The king held himself upright betwixt two waters.

By the beginning of December, death warrants had been signed and sent to the Sheriff of Hampshire in Winchester. The condemned men were to take their turns at the executioner's block, at ten o'clock in the morning on Friday 9 December.

A week before that, on 2 December, the countess staged her play, almost certainly in the Great Hall of the Tudor palace, warmed by huge fires against the cold of the winter outside. *As You Like It* was not a new play. Something called *As You Lyke It* had been registered with the Stationers' Company in August 1600, but a quarto of it was never printed. The earliest text is the one printed in the 1623 Folio, dedicated to The Two Incomparable Brethren, William Pembroke and his brother Philip. It is now impossible to tell if the countess chose to stage a play which was peculiarly suited to her purposes or if she had 'the man Shakespeare' adjust his existing play so that it would serve her current ends. She had perhaps commissioned work from him before, those first seventeen sonnets for the birthday in 1597, and there is no reason why the version of *As You Like It* which was collected by the Folio editors was not the Wilton-adjusted text. The two dedicatees of the Folio would have approved. The dedication there says, explicitly, that the two brothers had 'beene pleas'd to thinke these trifles something, heeretofore; and have prosequuted both them, and their Authour living, with so much favour.' Besides, a Wilton audience in December 1603 for *As You Like It* explains the play.

In both play and reality, the court has gone to the country. Those on stage and those in the audience regard each other through a two-way mirror. And this is not any stretch of country: not a single person in the Great Hall would have been unaware that this place was the source and foundation of the English Arcadia, precisely the kind of pastoral nowhere which the Forest of Arden claims to be in the play. But it is a troubled place. In both play and reality, there is an equivocal succession to the throne; in both play and reality there is treachery and usurpation in the air. A usurper rules in the play; in England men have been condemned for plotting against the life of a king, a king who is now sitting there watching in the audience. Unlike almost every pastoral ever written, this is not set in the sweetness of 'the spring time, the onely pretty ring time'. This is set in the depths of winter, because that indeed is where this half-real, half-acted world of the court in Arcadia found itself that December. It is not difficult to imagine how the actors would have played this extraordinary reflective comedy, its meanings bouncing back and forth between pretence, illusion and reflection on the realities of power and purity. And this, of all plays and all situations, is the play in which the world is said to be a stage and men and women its players.

Joke after joke rolls off the back of this double, mirrored situation. 'What's the new newes at the new Court?' someone asks. 'There's no newes at the Court Sir, but the olde newes,' comes the answer. Stale as an interchange on a Southwark stage, the line draws knowing laughter in the new-old court at Wilton. Where had the duke and his court gone? it is asked, and the answer is already thick with cynicism and laughter: 'They say hee is already in the Forrest of *Arden*, and a many merry men with him; and there they liue like the old *Robin Hood* of *England*: they say many yong Gentlemen flocke to him euery day, and fleet the time carelesly as they did in the golden world.'

You only have to imagine these lines spoken in the great gilded and festooned chambers of the Tudor Wilton, to an audience of courtiers, fleeing the plague but bringing with them every dimension of courtliness and its unkindness, scorn, manoeuvring and ambition, to see the smiles with which these words are greeted. Arcadia is an exercise in irony. And the ironies ripple on effortlessly like the leaps and pirouettes of a ballet.

One can take this further. *As You Like It* is stuffed full of brotherliness. There are two pairs of brothers: the real duke is usurped by his brother the wicked duke; and the tough, conformist, court-based Oliver maltreats his sweeter, weaker, Arden-based brother Orlando, a loveable but slightly ridiculous figure, a poet as bad as Sidney on a bad day, dreamy, delusional and something of a joke. His manservant, Adam, was by tradition played by Shakespeare himself. Strikingly, in the context of that treacherous and sexually omnivorous reddish-fairhaired boy of the *Sonnets*, Shakespeare makes this wavering, reddish-fairhaired brother fall in love with Rosalind, a girl (played by a boy) who dresses as a man, but pretends to be the girl that Orlando thinks he loves and goes by the name of Ganymede – straightforward Jacobean code for a rent boy. An extraordinary question raises its head: was Orlando – 'of all sorts enchantingly beloued', as he is ribbingly called – played by and even written, here at Wilton, for William Herbert, Earl of Pembroke, Shakespeare's lover, the young man who would happily kiss the king at the coronation, a bad poet, whose tendency to fall in love was well known even fifty years later?

Every single person in the Great Hall would have known about Will Herbert's 'rustication', as it was called, by the old queen two years before, his groaning self-pity at being consigned to the dreariness of the country after he had made Mary Fitton pregnant. If not by design, it is at least an extraordinary coincidence that the very opening lines of the play, spoken by Orlando, with Adam at his side, refer to his unkind brother who 'keepes me rustically at home, or (to speak more properly) staies me heere at home vnkept: for call you that keeping for a gentleman of my birth, that differs not from the stalling of an Oxe?' This is pretty flat if taken at face-value; if spoken by the richest earl in England, in his own gilded halls, with a real brother who would like to acquire the money and lands he had himself, with a recent history of exactly this kind of complaint, it becomes richly comic. 'Shall I keepe your hogs, and eat huskes with them?' he asks his brother. 'What prodigall portion haue I spent, that I should come to such penury?' For the Earl of Pembroke to be asking the future Earl of Montgomery these questions as he entertains the king would surely have had the audience rocking with a laughter that would roll on throughout the play. 'I prethee Shepheard,' Rosalind begins tentatively at one point, wandering out on to the platform at the end of Wilton's glamorous and enriched Great Hall, 'if that loue or gold/Can in this desert place buy entertainment,/Bring vs where we may rest our selues, and feed.' In these circumstances, *As You Like It* becomes the funniest play Shakespeare ever wrote.

It can be read as a sequence of in-jokes. But it is also a play which is both funny and affecting in the way of romantic comedy, swaying from the poignant to the ridiculous, one as the counterpoint of the other. A belief in the possibilities of Arcadia lies folded together with a distrust of its absurdities. In a pattern familiar from the *Sonnets*, the poetry can without warning take a turn for the serious, acquiring a deeper authority, leaving behind the jokiness and the scepticism, suddenly finding in the old pastoral idea a form of rooted certainty, deriving from nature everything which a more sullied culture could never hope to provide. This is not the Wilton in which the young Will Herbert, rusticated from London, had moped and stultified at its tedium and emptiness; but the Arcadia in which his uncle Philip Sidney had established a pattern of virtue, one which drew on classical sources, but which made for the English a dream of perfection which they never forgot.

The surge and beauty with which the second act begins is the most convincing statement of Arcadia ever made. The old duke, dressed as a forester, makes a speech to the company assembled around him, both on and off the stage: 'Now my Coe-mates, and brothers in exile,' he begins with affection, a sense of society and wholeness, a deeply coded and important allusion to the idea that, in the innocence of the wood, friendship flourishes. In court there might be only flattery and lying; here truth and, in the winter cold, human warmth. 'Hath not old custome made this life more sweete . . .' The Sidneyan honeyed inheritance is bound to the idea that the ancient custom of the manor is what makes it sweet and the old duke expresses the idea not in the form of a proclamation but as a question, in a tone of humility. '. . . Then that of painted pompe?'

The actor could sweep his hand here around the assembled lords in the audience. The play is both at court and not at court. This is the palace in the trees. The two worlds are one. 'Are not these woods/More free from perill then the enuious Court?' They must have laughed at that. These woods *were* the envious court. But perhaps there was some truth in it. The real peril at the moment was not here but in Winchester.

The Duke then speaks of the December cold and its clean, salutary, honest qualities. He continues with a sudden music:

> Sweet are the vses of aduersitie . . .
> And this our life exempt from publike haunt,
> Findes tongues in trees, bookes in the running brookes,
> Sermons in stones, and good in euery thing.

A vision of perfect justice is being laid before the king, one in which there is amity and forgiveness. Orlando himself is also in love with 'the constant seruice of the antique world' which can be found only in Arden. This is not propaganda. It is subtle and nuanced. A little earlier, the play describes to us the melancholy Jaques weeping and commentating 'Vpon the sobbing Deere,' as Sidney himself might have done. The Wilton audience would undoubtedy have laughed at this too, as the gloomy Jaques describes the hunters who kill the deer as 'mere usurpers, tyrants'. But perhaps they might have laughed with a little anxiety? Was the king, so newly come in, to act the hunter in his kingdom? Or was he to pity his quarry, as Jaques pitied the weeping deer, his big round tears coursing each other down his innocent nose? The whole suite of Arcadian ideas – sweetness, rurality, custom, freedom and justice – is set in train here. Perhaps it was part of the countess's intention that the king should be faced with the undoubted potency of these suggestions in her own drawing room. Does the weeping deer stand for the men waiting, condemned, in Winchester Castle?

After the entertainment, the sheer delight of these poignancies and jokes, the play comes to the point Mary Pembroke must have intended. In a final masque, everything is put right. There is clarity, reconciliation, love and forgiveness. It ends with a dance in which unity and harmony bring happiness and increase. All misunderstanding is over and Arcadia has triumphed. That, surely, was the countess's intention, a washing of Arcadian balm over the mind of the king who was drawn to absolutism and tyranny.

Did it work? Is there any evidence that James behaved towards the condemned men in Winchester in ways that were influenced by the play? Maybe. The play itself is full of contrarieties and parallels, of questions held in the balance until final revelations are made, of near-run things and lack of certainties. The shapely aestheticised world of the play does not really take place in the rude obviousness of an Arcadian wood. It is continuous with the world of the court, and once you see the way that James decided to administer his mix of justice and clemency to those who had threatened him with death and those whom he was threatening with death in return, it is possible to detect the world of Arcadian delight in the candlelit halls at Wilton spreading its influence over the world of the executioner's block in the rain at Winchester.

The king, having seen the play, brought about the most elaborately engineered *coup de théâtre* of his reign, a half-comic, half-poignant performance, described by the king to his own courtiers in terms which reflect the half-understandings, the trickeries, doubleness and mirror-making on which this comedy relies. On Monday 5 December, the pathetically deformed and crippled George Brooke was beheaded. When the executioner held up his head and cried 'God save the king', 'he was not seconded by the voice of any one man but the sheriff.' A horrified silence stared back at the headless and distorted body. As far as anyone at Wilton or Winchester knew, most of the other executions, including Raleigh's, were to be carried out the following Friday at ten in the morning.

On Wednesday 7 December, the king wrote a letter at Wilton, privately, at night, describing his intentions for the condemned men. The following day at noon, a messenger, a young Scottish Groom of the Bedchamber called John Gibb, was sent off to Winchester with those secret instructions in his pocket. But there was a near disaster: the king, as he delightedly told his courtiers after events had unfolded on the Friday, gave Gibb the letter but had failed in one particular to make the letter a proper legal document: 'One thing had like to have marred the play, for the letter was closed and delivered him unsigned, which the king remembered himself and called for him back again.'

Theatricality, and a blurred boundary between the invented and the real, was at the heart of James's plan. At Winchester, any royal intervention was kept secret until well on into the morning on 9 December. 'A fouler day could hardly have been picked out,' as Dudley Carleton described it, 'or fitter for such a tragedy.' Sir Griffin Markham, the first to be summoned to the block, was a disenchanted Catholic adventurer and passionate loather of all Protestants, described in the warrant for his arrest as having a 'large broad face, of a bleake complexion, a bigge nose, one of his hands is maimed by an hurt in his arme received by the shot of a Bullet.' He had apparently been promised 'clemency by some secrete messages', but the pardon had not materialised and this morning he was despondency itself. 'One might see in his face the very picture of sorrow; but he seemed not to want resolution, for a napkin being offered by a friend that stood by to cover his face, he threw it away saying he could look upon death without blushing.' He knelt barefaced at the block.

John Gibb was there but in the crush he could hardly get himself noticed. Once again, it looked as if events would take their course without James's message getting through. Gibb had to shout out to the pretty young Sir James Hay, 'one of the king's mignons', as Carleton described him, a favourite, there to observe the executions. Gibb whispered to Hay, Hay whispered to the sheriff and the sheriff led Markham away from the block, locking him into the Great Hall at Winchester Castle.

Then Thomas, Lord Grey of Wilton, a muddle-headed soldier, only twenty-eight years old, with a habit of picking fights, was led out. Today he seemed to Carleton like 'a dapper young bridegroom'. More muddle followed and the sheriff decided that Lord Cobham should come before him. Lord Grey was led back inside. Cobham, now in his late thirties, the elder brother of the George Brooke executed on the fifth, had been a favourite of the old queen and was now generally loathed and despised for his vanity and folly. Cobham prayed for paragraph after paragraph. The spectators were made to stand about in the rain. Then the sheriff interrupted proceedings and all the prisoners were led out into the rain.

> They looked strange one upon the other, like men beheaded and met again in the other world. Now all the actors being together on the stage (as use is at the end of a play) the sheriff made a short speech unto them. He told them of the heinousness of their offences, the justness of their trials, their lawful condemnation, and due execution there to be

performed, to all of which they assented. Then, saith the sheriff, see the mercy of your prince, who of himself hath sent hither a countermand and given you your lives. There was then no need to beg a plaudite of the audience, for it was given with such hues and cries that it went from the castle into the town and there began afresh. In this last no man could cry loud enough 'God save the King.'

Raleigh himself was excused the pantomime of being led out and being withdrawn but he too was spared execution and sent with the others to the Tower. At Wilton an air of apprehension reigned. James had already, in summarily executing a pickpocket that spring, and in making a string of absolutist proclamations about his ownership of all game – entirely against the custom of the country – disturbed the English lords. Was his treatment of the prisoners at Winchester to be another example of harsh, unforgiving, un-English and un-Arcadian government?

James let them stew in their uncertainty – 'The lords knew no other but that execution was to go forward till the very hour it should be performed' – and then decided to expose them to his own unique brand of witty, cavilling intellectuality, a form of addressing a problem which might have been a parody of Touchstone's in the play. 'A certain knight,' Touchstone says, 'that swore by his honour they were good pancakes, and swore by his honour the mustard was naught. Now, I'll stand to it, the pancakes were naught, and the mustard was good.' Which to choose? The king took up where Touchstone left off. Calling the lords before him in his chamber at Wilton,

> he told them how much he had been troubled to resolve in this business, for to execute Grey, who was a noble, young spirited fellow, and save Cobham, who was as base and unworthy, were a matter of injustice. To save Grey, who was of a proud, insolent nature, and execute Cobham, who had shewed great tokens of humility and repentance, were as great a solecism, and so went on in the rest . . . travelling in contrarieties but holding the conclusion in so indifferent balance that

the lords knew not what to look for till the end came out And
therefore I have saved them all.

Everyone was delighted and amazed. The play had ended happily.
The sadness had been banished and the performance could end
with a dance. 'The miracle was as great there [i.e. in Wilton] as with
us at Winchester,' Carleton reported, 'and it took like effect; for the
applause that began about the king went from thence into the
presence and round about the court.'

As You Like It had ended with divine intervention in favour of
love and goodness and a wicked ruler learning clemency from 'an
old religious man' who was living in the skirts of the wild wood:

> *Duke Frederick*, hearing how that euerie day
> Men of great worth resorted to this forrest,
> Addrest a mightie power, which were on foote
> In his owne conduct, purposely to take
> His brother heere, and put him to the sword:
> And to the skirts of this wilde Wood he came;
> Where, meeting with an old Religious man,
> After some question with him, was conuerted
> Both from his enterprize, and from the world:

James had imitated the play. The countess had saved her old lover.
Mercy had been applied to the pathetic if treasonable plotters.
Arcadia had triumphed.

9

So mutable are worldly things

Ancient communities and the threat of modernity

WHAT WAS HAPPENING in the background? What was the life in the world of the chalkstream valleys outside the gilded, witty embrace of *As You Like It* and its sophisticated ironies? Is there any symptom in that other world, that backdrop to the set, of the strains which are apparent in the thoughts and words of the richer, more leisured, more educated and freer, silk-coated figures who claim our first attention in the foreground?

There is a fracture line which runs through the middle of both Sidney's *Arcadia* and *As You Like It*, in fact through the middle of all pastoral, between the idea that the shepherd's universe is a vision of wholeness, which is a reproach to our daily life, and the demonstration that for modern, entrepreneurial, go-getting, Protestant, market-orientated man, Arcadia is not enough. Pastoral and anti-pastoral are each other's mirror image but neither term erases the other. The sweet mellifluousness of the Arcadian world survives the rage and disappointment within it; the entrancing elegance of the woods in *As You Like It* lasts beyond all the joking and teasing to which it is subject. Arcadia can, in that way, be seen as portraying a world in transition, one which both enshrines the old world, the custom of the manor, and dramatises the forces of modernity which are threatening it. Did that fracture line have its counterpart in reality? Was the manor-based system of the chalkstream valleys falling apart just as they were providing a restorative vision of completeness to England's cultural elite?

In many ways, it wasn't falling apart at all. The copyhold, the customary terms on which families held their properties from their landlords, came to be seen as such a valuable commodity, a meal ticket for thousands of yeoman families, that again and again in the inventories you find 'the iron-bound chest', the chest with four locks, 'the stronge chist', 'the greate chiste' which stood in the copyholder's bedroom and was the first thing to be saved in case of fire or flood. The wattle and daub walls of the houses themselves could easily be broken through with sledgehammer or axe, but these defended boxes shielded the papers on which entire families relied for their existence. In the Somerset Levels in January 1607, what is now thought to have been a tsunami burst into the low lands at nine o'clock on a Tuesday morning, 'the sunne being most fayrely and brightly spred', and drowned hundreds of villages. Shepherds saw their flocks sink in front of them. Rabbits clung to the sheep's backs until the wool became heavy with water and the sheep rolled over to drown. A copyholder found his 'deer wife and deerest children, presented to him by the tyrannous stream' all dead, and then, soon after, as a real consolation, the box full of his copyhold papers, floating towards him on the flood, a piece of luck for which ever after he would give thanks to God. Robert Furse, a Devon yeoman, had written a long account of his family and their belongings in the 1590s, telling his descendants that what he had set down 'will be to those that come after you, gret quyttenes perfyt knowledge, and a trewe menes to understond all there evydenses and tyteles.' Quite as much as the elaborate devices of the cultural elite, these copies and the strongboxes in which they were held were the vehicles of the culture, the means by which an organised past was transmitted to the present, a dam against the mutability they all felt and all feared.

Copyhold's place in the law was an underpinning of the continuity they craved. The great jurist, Sir Edward Coke, saw the situation of the copyholder as a form of freedom guaranteed by law:

Copyholders stand upon a sure Ground, now they weigh not
their lord's displeasure, they shake not at every sudden blast of
wind, they eat, drink and sleep securely, (only having a special
care of the main Chance viz) to perform carefully what Duties
and Services soever their Tenure doth exact, and Custom doth
require: then let the Lord frown, the Copyholder cares not,
knowing himself safe and not within any danger.

This approaches a kind of Arcadian centre: a version of freedom
which is dependent not on rights but duties and in which anyone's
good was dependent on everyone's good. People were essentially
not individual but social. Although many manors, including the
Pembrokes', allowed the lord of the manor to set the entry fine
at whatever level he wanted, there is no strong evidence that the
Pembrokes abused this position. In fact, the ideology to which the
world of Sidneyism had attuned them would certainly have set their
minds against exploiting their copyhold tenants, even if the ruinous
costs of life at court would have brought pressures on them to do
so. One sign that they did not is the astonishing level of debt one
seventeenth-century Pembroke after another was prepared to enter
into. With annual incomes approaching £25,000 through most of
the century, none of them died owing less than £40,000.

Needless to say, there was an argument on the other side. Copyhold, with its elaborate burdens, its binding of the copyholder to
an unending series of mutual, community-based duties, was thought
by many to be full of encumbrances. It was innately conservative. Even
John Norden complained of the old yeomen that 'they only shape
their courses as their fathers did', spending their lives in 'a plodding
kind of course.' In this light, the tenurial fetters of copyhold were not
the means of maintaining a community but a way of hampering the
freedoms of free-born individuals. Both landlord and tenant could
see it that way and, in many parts of the country, although not on the
whole on the Pembroke estates, there was a steady drift away from
copyhold to a straightforward leasehold, a purely financial arrangement, one in which each participant was a player in the rental land

market and in which any notion of community came as an optional add-on, not as an integral part of how and where people lived.

In the Pembroke valleys, there are clear signs that community was continuing to work. A statute passed in the reign of Elizabeth had required that any new house should have four acres of ground attached to it, a way of guaranteeing a means of self-sufficiency and of no burdens encroaching on the charity of the village. This was all very well but it meant that the poor, particularly in an era of land hunger, were unprovided-for. There was not enough land to go round and if there was not enough land, there could be no more houses. The poor were driven on to the roads and into the cities where they would beg. A steady stream of petitions was made to the justices for such cases. In Ramsbury, where the Pembrokes had one of their smaller houses, a petition came to the justices at the Quarter Sessions in 1639:

> A poore man but of honest life and borne and bred in Rames-
> burie aforesaid one whom in regard of his povertie it hath
> pleased some of the worthy officers of the Right Honble the
> earl of Pembroke to confirm and bestow upon him a little
> platte of ground to erect and build a howse fitt for habitation
> in and upon the same.

It is a sign of the system working well that the earl and his steward had agreed to provide Lionel Ounter with a piece of ground, but a house could not be built on it without the permission of the Justices of the Peace. The villagers of Ramsbury wrote to them that spring:

> Commiserating this poor man's penurie and desirous to further
> his future good we do in most humble wise desire ye worships
> that you would be gratiously pleased to grante this poore man
> full power and licence to erect and build a Cottage or dwelling
> house in or upon the said Platte of ground and he according
> to his bounden dutie will continually pray for yr prosperous
> estates long to endure.

It remains an intriguingly integrated system: royal justice hears an appeal by a village committee (acting according to the custom of the manor) on behalf of a poor homeless man, for whom the lord of the manor has provided a plot of ground, all framed in the language of obedience and hierarchy, even in certain phrases mimicking the language of the litany ('in most humble wise', 'his bounden dutie'). This is not what a market-based system would have done.

One of the central points about custom as a governing principle of village life was that it should be agreed between the copyholders of the manor, gathered as the 'homage'. Custom did not have to be of any great age. Custom was simply what the village did as a village. As long as those of the homage considered that something might be a custom of the manor, then it could become one. Customary tenure was in that way not pure conservative rigidity, but an adaptive organic system.

In 1632, the people in the Pembrokes' manor at Wylye decided that they wanted to introduce the new-fangled technique of the floated meadow and they did so using the instruments of communal decision-making they had inherited from the Middle Ages. The floating of meadows was a method by which river water was led out over the low-lying grass fields next to the banks, bringing enriching silt down on to the meadows and a seed rain of various grasses to thicken the sward. The comparative warmth of the flowing river water, at something like 55°, would keep the grass growing when the frost would stop it in an unfloated meadow. The costs of setting up the sluices and channels, the gates, banks, distributor dykes and flow systems for these meadows were high: fourteen shillings an acre up front and then a maintenance payment of two shillings an acre thereafter, 'the same to be paid at the feasts of St Thomas the Apostle and the Annunciation of the Blessed Virgin Mary yerely by even and equal proportions.' The flooding of the meadows provided an early bite for the sheep, more hay in summer, making a bigger flock possible, which could manure a larger extent of arable ground. Because of such obvious advantages, large stretches of the valleys of the Ebble, Nadder, Wylye and Avon were converted into watermeadows in the seventeenth century, much of the work encouraged by the Earls of Pembroke and their stewards, recognising, of course, that the value of the estate itself, as well as the incomes of the copyholders, would be increased by the improvements. But the decision to make those improvements could only be made communally because the land of every tenant in the village would be affected by them.

So at Wylye they made an agreement at the manor court on 10 September 1632:

> Which said agreement all the said parties at this courte desired to have entered in the rolles of the courte of this mannor and that thereupon an order should be made for the byndinge all said parties to perform this agreement upon paynes and penalties to be therein expressed, being a business conceived to be very behoofefull and beneficiall to all the inhabitants of this mannor.

As smoothly as the clear waters of the Wylye itself, the ancient community of the manor at Wylye was sliding on to an enriching, technological and modern future.

Happiness finds it difficult to make its way into the records, but for all that, there is an undoubted and even rather subversive note of wellbeing and gaiety which flows through these valleys. There was unlawful drinking and playing at quoits, game-playing on the Sabbath, dancing and music. Particularly in the upstream villages of Broad Chalke and Fovant, there remained a high proportion of Roman Catholics, repeatedly listed as not going to church, and an account even of one man, in 1636, Edward Lucas of Fovant, a gentleman, keeping a schoolmistress in his house (Sarah Overton, a spinster) for at least three months, 'in order to teach his children Popery'. The fact that so much of this starts to appear in the court records in the seventeenth century may be a symptom of an increasing Puritan confidence in taking to court the minor delights and naughtinesses which until then had gone unpunished. When, after the civil war, the Parliamentary Committee for Sequestrations came down to these valleys to discover who had been on the king's side and who, therefore, might have their property confiscated, all kinds of informants came creeping out of the woodwork to snitch on the ways in which their neighbours had been going in for unnecessary delight and even 'injoiinge itt'. The vicar at Bemerton, Dr Thomas Lawrence, did 'permit William Bowlton to play upon his Instrumt (beinge a Treble[?]) at his the sd Doctors Howse and did pmit dauncinge on the Saboth day in his presence and hee did not forbid itt.' Edward Poore, described as a yeoman, had seen him 'dauncinge and bowlinge and kittlinge upon the Sabioth daues at Bemerton.' 'Kittling' means tickling in Scots but probably means playing at skittles here. The priest, they all said, liked to do this with his children.

There is one piece of evidence, apparently almost unique from these valleys, of a song written and sung by a spirited young woman from a house next to the Ebble in March 1631, which describes that other, unspoken life, below the level of official arrangements, of what people bought, owned and sold, earned and spent. It is almost the only equivalent of that world of jokes and laughter, story-telling and amusement which filled the parlours and drawing rooms of the great house at Wilton. In Stoke Farthing, a hamlet just downstream from Broad Chalke, a carpenter called Thomas Holly, one Saturday afternoon, saw Edward Penney, the son of the man who had the demesne farm, a big place with a separate room for the servants to live in and two huge ten-bay barns, coming towards him. Penney gave him 'a certeyne writting in paper wch was made in verce'. Holly could neither read nor write himself and he took it to John White, one of his neighbours, a thirty-two-year-old husbandman, a proper member of the homage, who according to the earl's surveyors kept his house in good repair, to tell him what it said. White read it out to Holly and to two other of their neighbours, the old Walter Whitemarsh and the big farmer himself, John Penney, who clearly hadn't been able to read it himself in the first place. The homage of the village was, informally and ad hoc on a Saturday afternoon, gathering to deal with a small crisis. Only one of them could read, but the ability gave him no particular status. Walter Whitemarsh tooke 'the certeyne writting in paper' away from John White and kept it himself.

Clearly the meeting had decided to do something about it because ten days later, the document was produced before the justices in Salisbury. The author of the verses had been identified. She was thirty-eight-year-old Jane (or Joan) Norrice, the wife of Harry, and the copyholder herself of a very small farm in Stoke Farthing, with an acre of orchard and garden and sixteen acres of arable land in the common fields. It wasn't in good repair. She was clearly hovering on the margins of the respectable community and this 'certeyne writting in paper' did her standing no good at all. The fact that this poor, small, middle-aged woman farmer could write verses and sing them meant nothing. The power of the manor, translated into court Latin in Salisbury, was disturbed that she, Jane Norrice, 'made, fabricated and wrote in the following English words from her own ill will a false, scandalous and obscene libel.' It is in fact a funny account of how the tiniest of chalkstream villages had wickedness going on underneath its proper surfaces:

Rouse braue spiritts boyes and why should wee be sad;
for I haue newes to tell yow the whiche will make yow glad
[If]* yow a wench doe want then vnto Stoake draw nigh sir,
and there for a small [?groat]† a nightes lodgin yow may by sir
Singe boyes drinke boyes why should [we] not bee merry
at Stoake you may haue spoort and play vntell that yow be wery;
Firste to begin at vpper end and soe the street goe downe,
enquire for the Well‡ wench at the end of the towne;
and There yow may be sure to speed§ yf periman¶ be not there,
customers shee hath but few be cause shee is but scrose** Ware

* Illegible in original
† Illegible. A small amount of money?
‡ Or Wells, the town in Somerset
§ Succeed
¶ The pear man?
** Scrow: dog-eared, used

but yf yow will a fine wench haue then vnto Buttwills goe;
but her I thinke without tellinge yow doe already knowe;
for lately shee hath been at court for to make her purgation*;
but firste shee to the taverne went to drinke wine with the passon†;
but yow happen there to miss to shufgroots‡ then resort,
and there tis a greate chaunce that yow may haue somme sport:
or ells with goodman lotes wife§ whom bitehard they doe call sir
wich is a resanable one if not the best of all sir;
but if all these doe happ to miss wich straunge they should doe all,
at next door dwells the old puncke¶ the wich will never faile;
besides the other mans wife which is the old puncke daughter;
for yf that shee should honest be were it not a straunge matter;
now to conclude and make an end, noe more I will now name;
because I will be faultles and be yond of blame;
for though a man be cuckold made he must not now speak of [it]
least that he play at butwills and soe be made [to] pay for it:
Singe boyes [drinke boyes why should we not bee merry
at Stoake you may haue spoort and play vntell that yow be wery;]
Finis.

Henry Norris, husband of the singer and composer Jane, when asked about his participation in the libel said he knew nothing of it. It was all her own work. And what can one say? Tantalisingly, it is not quite possible to make out who in Stoke Farthing Jane Norrice was teasing. Who lurks behind the nicknames? Who was the salty shrivelled up old dame called Lot's Wife 'whom bitehard they doe call'? There are three widows who were copyholders in Stoke Farthing at the time. Ann Penney and Eileen Bryne were both too rich and too big as farmers to qualify, and so maybe Lot's wife was Margaret Savage, her 'bitehard' nickname perhaps having some connection to her real surname? But the others soak back into the soil and we are left with the wit and wickedness of Jane Norrice

* Compurgation: to be cleared of a charge in court on the sworn evidence of others
† Parson
‡ A game, shove-groats, like shove-halfpenny
§ Lot's wife was turned into a pillar of salt in Genesis, Ch. 19
¶ Whore

herself, quite independent of old Harry, possibly married before – she was also known as Jane Clinton – and with a gift for the sly dig and the startling punchline, entertaining all the like-minded others in Stoke Farthing on a cold Friday night in the tippling house in the village, sending up the proprieties, life leaking out from underneath the carapace of control and suppression within which an English village survived. Was she herself, I wonder, the fine wench at Buttwills, who 'without tellinge yow doe already knowe'?

A few years later, just up the road in Broad Chalke, another late winter party fell foul of the law. It too played games with the proprieties, teasing the structures of religion and government. A girl called Jane Lawes was examined on oath by one of the justices, who happened to be John Penruddock of Compton Chamberlayne. She told him that 'on St Iohn his day last att night she was invited to the Myll in Broad Chalke to a daunceinge match where there were divers of the younge men and maidens of ye parishe where as she saith, she saw noe abuse offered or incivility comitted by any dureinge the time of her beinge there.'

That was all, a dancing match, which may not mean a contest here, but simply a gathering, a dancing party in the mill, which apart from the church was almost certainly the largest roofed space in the village. It had been a good party and had gone on all night, until after the candles had burned out, and it was then that others did not have quite such an innocent view of what had happened. Joan Deane was questioned on oath and she said that

> on St Iohnes day last she was invited to the myll as abouesaid where there were many young men and maides att daunce and about two houres before day the candles beinge burnt out she heard some of the maides cry out, but whoe they were that did cry out or did cause them soe to doe she knoweth not beinge in the darke and sittinge by her brother and when a litle time after she and [her brother and] her sister went home about the break of day. and more she saith not.

A third girl was interviewed, Mary Randoll. She too had been

att the myll at broad Chalk on St Iohns day at night where
there were divers of the younge people of the said parish att
daunce and beinge vp in a chamber she saith yt she heard a
cryeinge out sometimes of some of the younger women, but
who they were she knoweth not but saith that one Thomas
Wise who termed himselfe to be the Bishoppe beinge vp in the
chamber, with diuers other young men but what they did she
knoweth not by reason the candles were out and yt they were
lockt in, and could not gett out before it was day, but she her
selfe had noe wronge offered vnto her, but she saith that she
heard divers report that Catherine Sangar of knoyle was sett
vpon her head and was bishopped but by whom it was done
she knoweth not and more she saith not.

One more girl, Aves Gerrett, was to be questioned under oath but
under her name the record is blank. Thomas Wise was a shoemaker,
friend of Edward Targett the miller, who was there with him that
night in the dark upper room of the mill, along with Thomas Deane,
a tailor from the village, and Henry Pen, a husbandman. Were they
raping the girls? Were they playing? What kind of crying out was
it? What exactly does 'bishopped' mean? This was 1640, a moment
at which religious tensions were running spectacularly high. Broad
Chalke had a long and strong tradition of Catholicism, of families
named and fined for decade after decade as recusants, but this is
scarcely about Church politics. It is surely something on the boundary where teasing, drink, bullying, sex and the physical dominance
of men all intersect. These girls would have had to continue to live
in the village and their silence, their retreat into the candleless dark,
is as articulate as any words uttered in court.

Nevertheless, throughout these Wiltshire villages, there are signs
of strain and tension. There is an underlying presence of cruelty and
violence, of an inability to keep the wholeness of the vision intact.
Shepherds appear in the records not as calm philosophers but as
anxious, unsocialised, curt and peremptory outsiders, and the villages
themselves seem like organisms that cannot quite keep their mech-
anisms properly oiled. Early seventeenth-century England begins to

looke like a place of reluctant commitment, where the men are increasingly unwilling to fulfil the unpaid tasks which the government of their manors, the parishes and the county required of them, and a conflict is developing between ambitious landlords and those whose ancient communal rights are threatened by the developments proposed. The great positive statements of Norden about the beauty of a communal world were made against a background in which that communal world was coming under strain. It was a time of technological improvement, of a modernising market system, of a burgeoning population and an uncertain food supply, of an increasing number of vagrants and beggars, a sense that the old structures were not holding up, and of people frantically on the move. A survey of Wiltshire inns in 1686 revealed over 2500 beds available for travellers in the county. Even the small town of Wilton itself had room for over fifty strangers to spend the night there. England had begun to shift.

Increasingly, a national market was eating away at local practices. But even at the highest level, the workings of the market itself were seen, quite explicitly, as the great enemy. The government, in its various creaking efforts at administration, attempted detailed forms of control that would make any modern regulator blanch. The Privy Council, the most powerful political committee in the country, entirely appointed by the sovereign, was intimately involved with, for example, what bakers could and could not do. No one, the great lords of the Privy Council insisted, could be a baker or a miller unless they had been an apprentice for at least seven years. Only farthing, halfpenny and penny loaves could be baked, the size of each set down. A baker could sell 13d worth for 12d – the baker's dozen – but only to victuallers and innkeepers. Outsiders who came to sell loaves where there was already a baker had to make their penny-loaves three ounces heavier in order to protect the business of the local man. The fundamental basis of market behaviour – a better product or a lower price – was ruled illegitimate. Spice cakes, which carried about them an air of the Middle Ages, popery and wrongness, could only be sold on Good Friday – the ancestor of the hot cross bun – and at funerals, consistently the most conservative of all human ceremonies.

One method of ensuring that people did not behave as rational economic beings was the public informer, a mainstay of Tudor and early Stuart economic and social policy. Food supply, farming methods and timings, moneylending, the terms on which an apprentice worked: all of them were subject to government control but the government had no inspectorate. The tax system was radically out of date, inefficient and corrupt. It could never have paid for an army of inspectors and so it encouraged people to set up as free-lance informers for profit. There were even 'informing syndicates', usually with managers in Westminster, where the courts were, and agents in the regions where people were offending against the rules of the regulated market. About two-thirds of those cases brought to court from Wiltshire were the product of professional informers or their sub-agents working the Wiltshire markets.

A grisly tour was made of Wiltshire towns and villages in the autumn of 1605 by one Roger Cawdrey of London, yeoman, who ended up with a fat collection of indictments at the Exchequer Court when he got back in November. The crown was usually happy to split the fine with the informer, a 50% commission on the job, and Cawdrey had a long list of Wiltshire men and women whom he had discovered offending against the drink regulations: John Jaggard of Highworth had been selling claret and sack and allowing it to be drunk in his dwelling house, where he had no licence. Many Pembroke tenants and others were guilty: William Smith for the same offence, John Chamberlyn for the same offence, John Lewis, the same; William Barratt the same, John Bull the same, John Parry, John Holliday, Thomas Roffe, Robert Phipps, another John Chamberlyn, John Smith of Wilton, Christopher Whitacre, William Akklen, Robert Blackborne: every one of them had been selling a few drinks to their neighbours and passing travellers. Roger Cawdrey had presumably dropped in for a glass or two, got them chatting, discovered they had no licence and then dropped the bombshell.

Even straightforward attempts to make a commercial living fell foul of the rules and the informers. Cawdrey had trapped one Richard Crowder who had been 'engrossing' grain, that is buying up wheat at £3 an acre, barley at 40s an acre, peas at 30s per acre, in the hope that he might be able to sell it a little later at a profit. That was not allowed and he was to appear in front of the Exchequer Court unless he paid Cawdrey what was due.

People were summonsed for owning more than twenty acres of land and working as a clothmaker; for buying live oxen and other cattle and selling them in Westminster; for claiming to be a wheelwright without having been an apprentice; for buying wool and reselling it as raw wool instead of making it into yarn for the weavers; for buying and selling butter and cheese; for not going to church; for lending someone £50 at too high a rate of interest (19% when the usual rate was more like 8%); for selling loaves an ounce light, pints a drop or two beneath the king's standard or making a corner in firewood. Anyone found 'engrossing' foodstuffs would suffer two months' imprisonment at the first offence and forfeit the value of the goods; six months and a fine worth twice the value of the goods at the second offence; at the third, imprisonment at the king's pleasure and forfeiture of everything the would-be merchant owned. Cawdrey and many like him were still at work in 1611 but the government came to dislike the system and in 1624 it was made illegal. By then, there had been hundreds of cases every year since the mid-sixteenth century.

This strain, and the attempt to control behaviour which was bubbling up from the deepest levels of society, was symptomatic of a significant shift in the way the country was working: away from any kind of self-sufficiency and towards a growing reliance on the market. The closed world of the manor was coming apart but government control and the ideology which directed it were taking time to adapt to changing realities. Increasingly people were breaking the rules. At the Quarter Sessions in Salisbury in January 1634, several men including William Penny, who was one of the earl's copyhold tenants at Bower Chalke, near Broad Chalke, were 'presented' for marketing offences both in Wiltshire and in Dorset. They were trading in sheep, but what they were doing was described to the judge as if it were a sin against the Holy Ghost:

> They and every of them are great enemies to the woale publique of this county, in that they continually go from Faire to Faire, and from markett to markett, from Sheepefould to Sheepefould, from one man to another, where they buye continually great numbers of sheepe; as for example one Saterday to the markett at Blandford Forum, the Wensday following sell the same again at Wilton: Nay they and most of them will buye one day and sell the same the next, nay, buy and sell in one and the same day, insomuch that our Fayres and marketts, are generally and for the most part furnished by these sorts of jobbers and ingrossers who take up all the cobbs [a stall made with hurdles] and pens there that other men viz. Farmers and yeomen who doe not trade as they doe must sell their sheep in Common fields abroad in regard they cannot gett penns for them. Some of the before named have not been ashammed to brage and boast that they have sould this year last past 6,000, 5,000, 4,000 and 3,000 sheepe, some more some lesse, wch is contrarie to the lawes and statutes of this realme, wch wee desire by this Honble Court to be reformed and amended.

The court papers, as so often, have no record of what the justices decided but it is clear that the real wickedness for the seventeenth-century Englishman was working the market. Making a corner in wheat, or even failing to sell at a low price and waiting for a higher, was a criminal offence. 'Forestalling' – buying by private treaty before grain reached the market – and 'regrating', buying at one price and selling at another, the foundations, in other words, of simple market behaviour, were not only frowned upon but thought to be morally offensive. In 1630, all justices were sent a copy of a Book of Orders which described the price at which everything was to be sold. Those who hoarded 'pinched the guts of the poore to fill and extend their own courses, taking advantage by the dearth of corne to make it more deare'. The Book of Proverbs had made it clear: 'He that withholdeth corn, the people shall curse him; but blessing shall be upon the head of him that selleth it.' In case after case, informers told the justices of 'Private barnes', secret stores, places in which the spirit of communality was broken.

Among the commodities flooding on to the market was land itself. Sale of crown lands under Elizabeth had raised £817,359. In the first six years of his reign James I squeezed another £426,172 out of the royal estate, all of it pouring on to the land market. John Norden in 1607 had never known so much land passing from hand to hand, a symptom, it was thought, of the end of martial behaviour among gentlemen. 'The gentlemen which were wont to addict themselves to the warres,' Thomas Wilson wrote in 1600, 'are nowe for the most part grown to become good husbands [farmers] and knowe well howe to improve their lands to the uttermost as the farmer and countryman, so that they take their fermes into their handes as the leases expire, and eyther till themselves, or else lett them out to those who will give most.' That final phrase has the air of a death-knell about it. 'Those who will give most' are not those whose ancestors have tilled the ancestral acres, nor those whose first concern is the wellbeing of the community, but those for whom the relationship to the land is founded on money and the market.

It was all a cause for anxiety. Thomas Wilson found 'great alteracions almost every year, so mutable are worldly things and worldly mens affaires.' Those who were best sited to take advantage of the boom, particularly in the south of England, and particularly those who were sitting on a copyhold rent which had been fixed when prices were much lower, were outstripping those in the rest of the country who might have thought themselves socially superior.

A knight of Wales
A gentleman of Cales [Calais]
A laird of the north countree
A yeoman of Kent
Sitting on his penny rent
Can buy them out all three.

Everywhere there are signs of this world breaking down, of communality disintegrating and the authorities attempting, often brutally, to shore it up. The roads were awash with men, women and children who had fallen out of the social network of manor, village and town. The Vagrancy Statute of 1598 had ordained that any rogue, vagabond or sturdy beggar over the age of seven who was found 'begging, vagrant, wandering or misordering themselves' was to be whipped and sent back to the parish of his or her birth. Overpopulation, recurrent food crises, repeated cyclical collapses in businesses such as the cloth trade, which were dependent on fickle foreign markets, and the influx of the poor from the margins of the British Isles all put immense strain on the conventional distinction between the impotent or God's poor (the old, young or crippled) and the impudent or Devil's poor, who were considered capable but lazy. In a recession, or in a situation of chronic underemployment which lasted from decade to decade, there was little that whipping would do to address the real problem.

The scurf of unwanted humanity blew around the lanes and streets of Elizabethan and Jacobean England. Upright citizens, closely held within the confines of their customary manor or the chartered town, regarded this flotsam with disgust. They were masterless and ruleless. They 'have not particular wives, neither do they range themselves into Families: but consort together as beasts.' Sometimes a vagrant woman was spared punishment if expecting a child or if the body was crippled or ill. But the level and extent of punishment remain disturbing.

In Devizes, in April 1609, five men and a woman, charged with petty larceny, were sentenced to be publicly whipped in the market place 'till their backs do bleed and then discharged.' The next year Thomas Elye was 'burnt in the hand' with the letter F to mark him as a felon. A poor woman called Agnes Spender was whipped for deserting her child. Benjamin Salisbury was burned on his left shoulder with the letter R to mark him as 'an incorrigible Rogue'. In January 1617, William Farret and Elizabeth Longe were whipped 'by the Tythingman until their backs doe bleed, and this to be done at the comon metinge place under the Elme in Wylye neere the Church.'

The story of William Vennice, a husbandman or small farmer of Barford St Martin, just below the beautiful reaches of Grovely Wood, can stand as an example of how life could go wrong in the Arcadian valleys. 'Omitting and forgetting my prayers unto the Lord,' he told the justices in the spring of 1627, he

> became a prey unto the Devill who with his allurements and enticements fell into the terrible and fearful sin of adultery with one Joan Hibberd of the same parish, who being my wife by promise before God and ourselves in private, sithence being ruled or as it seemes, over ruled by her mother she utterly denies it.

Vennice brought the statement of his neighbours in Barford as witness that he and Joan – or Jane: the names were interchangeable – had even been to Salisbury to get themselves a marriage licence from a justice there. But he didn't win his case. Joan had given birth to a child, his, and the court told him he had to give her 9d a week until the child was ten. She refused to marry him and was sent to a House of Correction for a year. William 'shallbe well whipped on his naked back from his girdle upward until his body doe bleed and that the Tythingman of Barford do yt or cause yt to be done without delaye within a fortnight after Easter next.'

If anyone still imagines that cruel and unusual punishments were not a part of English life in the early seventeenth century, they should read the case of a widow called Katherine Peters brought before the Wiltshire justices in 1623. She and a woman named Alice King, whose sister Joan King also lived in Barford St Martin, were accused of stealing some washing, which had been laid out to dry on an orchard hedge on 16 July that year. Her accusers said she admitted to stealing the holland sheet and the tablecloth which they later found in her basket. She said she had found them lying under the rabbit warren fence. When it came to the trial, she refused to plead and so was sentenced to the punishment known as 'de peine forte et dure'. She was

> To be brought to a close room and there to be laid upon her back naked from the middle upward her legges and armes stretched out and fastened towards the fowr corners of the room, and upon her body to have so much waight and somewhat over then she is able to bear, the first day – she requiring food – to have three morsels of coarse bread and noe drink, the second day drinke of the next puddle of water, not running, next the place she lyeth and noe bread, soe every daye in like manner until she be dead.

Katherine Peters's infant son was taken from her before her punishment and death, and lived as a charge on the parish until 1641, when he was seventeen.

Bad behaviour, or at least behaviour which rubbed and worried at the tender edges of this fragile society, is what summoned the fiercest of reactions. At Broad Chalke in 1610, the leading men of the village decided they had put up with enough of 'the Manifold & Continualle Misdemeanors of one Robt Came of our sayed parish.' Obsequiously, and in the language which the world of hierarchy required, they approached the Justices of the Peace. Robert Came had, in seventeenth-century terms, gone half mad. Instead of living quietly with his neighbours, conforming to the custom and requirements of the manor, he was now

> wholy given to Contention & to raise strife & enmitye betweene Neighbour & Neighbour practisinge nothinge more then to breed brawlinge and discord Wherene hee imployethe all his time and his Whole endevores For havinge made away all his goodes and house & Nowe doth Idlely and in lasines he giveth himselfe altogether especially to this sayed trade of life as your Worships by our information followinge may Vnderstand.

They felt 'dayly Mollested disquieted & disturbed' and started to lay out some of the details of the case, 'Omittinge others to avoyde tediousnes of troublinge your Worshippes Which are these that Followe.' He had been accusing a woman of being a whore and a neighbour of wanting to sleep with his wife (who was said to have been complicit in this); making speeches which he hoped would start a riot; accusing another neighbour of theft; hitting his uncle in the village street with a flail; tearing up and then burning a hedge which belonged to old Bartholomew Dewe and fomenting arguments between neighbours. Worst of all he was the tithingman, the village policeman, and

> although it belonged to his office to see yat such thinges should be reformed and to complaine of such persones as vsed any vnlawfull games himself Would be the Chieff man to vse them most especially on the Saboathe day playinge out Eveninge Prayer most comonly and alsoe to fight and brawle to breake the king Maiesties peace Contrary to his office and the lawes of this Realme.

Was this madness in the Broad Chalke tithingman? Or was it simply the human spirit breaking out of the overwhelming supervision, the institutional control system of the English village?

There is another case, just over the down from Broad Chalke in the valley of the Nadder, from a couple of years before which makes much of this clearer. John Penruddock had heard this case too. Marie Butler, a young unmarried woman from Barford St Martin, courageously gave evidence about a terrifying night the previous winter. It was exactly the same time of year as the party in the mill at Broad Chalke,

> a boute St Iohn day att Christmas last, one Richard Hurst came vnto Bartfoord St Martin to her Masters house one Iohn Carpenter and there did solicite this examinate to haue the vse of her bodie, hauing formerly often promised her marriage and there vpon they coming from a dancing togeather wch was att Bartfoord aforesaid, hee perswaded her to goe home with him to her Masteres house, and when she was neare her Masteres house he desired her to goe in wth him into an out

house, where they vsualy tie there beast, wch she agreed vnto and there hee had to doe wth her, wch was the first tyme and after aboute a month befoore ouer Lady Day last, hee came to Bartfoord to her Masteres house, her saied Master and dame beeing from home, and there he had the vse of her bodie, and she verily bee leeueth that she was then beegotten wth child by the saied Richard Hurst, and she farther saieth that hee hath diueres times since promised her marriage and more she saieth not.

Cruelty to and exploitation of the poor and the weak appear again and again in the records, often with poignant clarity. There is an undated appeal in the Quarter Sessions records from a Ramsbury pauper, Thomas Seald: 'I am a pore man and have noe releufe out of the parrish of remsberie hether I come to have some relefe but I cane have none and I desire your worship that you wold helpe me to sume relefe Being I have noe munie.'

A note on Thomas Seald's appeal says: 'Recommended to the overseers [of the poor – smalltime parish officials] & on their neglect the next Justice to bynd them over.' Royal justice again ensures, or attempts to ensure, that the community looks after its own. But there is no hint that Seald would get any charity until his own parish gave it to him.

John Bevin of Brokenburroughe near Malmesbury came with an even more pathetic tale:

> Now the Church wardens & overseers have throwne yor peti-
> coner & his wife out of theire house & will not suffer them to
> rent that or any other, by reason of this their Tiranous dealinge
> your peticoner and his wife hath bin constrained to dwell in a
> hollow tree in the streete a moneth already to the great hazard
> of their lives they being anncient people.

Perhaps the elegant denizens of Sidney's Arcadia might have dreamt of living in the trees which seem to speak of love. Attempting to do so over a Wiltshire winter in the street at Brokenburroughe might have been a rather different proposition.

In 1631, John Dicke, a shepherd from Imber, had been thrown out of his house – the shepherd was not a copyholder and would have had no rights to any property once his employment had come to an end – and his 'landlord having use for the house he dwelt in hath taken it into his own hands to make him a stable by wc meanes yr por Supplyant is dismist of a house & could not get any roome nor house in ye parish.' The landlord had evicted the shepherd not because he wanted to live in the building himself, nor for another employee, but to house his horse. Again, the community had stepped in: 'the neighbours gave him a place to build a poor cottage but some enemies doth threaten to pull it down to the great spoyle and undoing of your Wor Supplyant.'

Inevitably the pressures of work and of coping with the stresses of the farming year would combine on occasions with sheer neighbourly vindictiveness. In 1633, Robert Feltham, a Pembroke tenant at Fovant, wrote to his friend and ally James Hill who was, at the time, with the Bishop of Salisbury on his visitation to the diocese, a regular tour to check that the people were behaving as they should. The visitation was, of course, another chance for informers to reveal to the authorities just what their enemies had been doing wrong.

Feltham had got behind with his ploughing, the weather having been bad, and had been caught doing the work on a saint's day by a couple of churchwardens from the village. They were under pressure themselves from a fourth villager, Hercules Candill, who had been thrown out of his own pew in the church, the so-called Maiden Seat, and he was angry about it:

> M[aster] James Hill I moste hartily com(m)end me unto you with many thankes for divers cortesees formerly receavid at your hands so now at this time presuming farther on your favoure somuch as to take note that if our Churchmen John Gervis & laurence Strong of Fovant doe present my self with others for goinge to plough uppon S[aint] Marks day which then being a time of grete necesite by reason of the weet wether & being much behind was the more pressious for husbandmen

nevertheles for my part I intend to make no coustome of it
nether did the lik in all my life for which matter I would intret
you to stande my frend it maybe staide untill I doe speake with
you next. For Hercules Candill hath thretned them if they doe
not present us he will present them for he doth it in mallis he
bears to John Gearvis for dismissing him his Mayden seat
wherein he had no right. This one busines shall reveng another
although it doe himselfe no good. So I leave you to gods moste
holy protettion.

Your loving Frend Robert Feltha(m)

To Mr James Hill his very
loving Frend now being at the
visitacion deliver
these I pray you.

This letter is a small model of the Wiltshire valleys at work. Church
and church obedience are central to the workings of the society.
Mutual supervision stimulates a habit of blackmail. The churchwardens would probably have let Feltham's indiscretion with the
plough go – he was not the only guilty one – but a malicious desire
for revenge in Hercules Candill disrupted the acceptance of failing
within the village. Favours were called in, grudges worked out,
obligations fulfilled and pleading was the substance of life. Arcadia?
Not exactly. This was undoubtedly an integrated society. These are
not the complaints of an atomised, individualised loneliness but the
social stress is palpable. Here is something of the reality which
Sidney's self-occluded gaze had drifted over in his daydream of
perfection. It was Arcadia, but Arcadia for real, with all the draw-
backs which real communality must inevitably impose.

10

Two Incomparable Brethren

The careers of William, Earl of Pembroke and Philip, Earl of Montgomery
1601–1630

PERHAPS BECAUSE of the threat of modernity, the double Arcadian idea was entrenched in the English mind. The inheritance of the copyhold manor represented liberty through community. It was not an idea but a practice, a habit of being, a communality. In an age of sometimes passionate antiquarianism, its time-honoured custom was valued for its ancient and organic connections to the land. It was part of the common law – law not ordained by the crown but evolved by the English people in common – on which the virtues of Englishness relied. Sir Edward Coke, the great and eloquent jurist, made the classic statement of the position in the course of a trial in 1608:

> We are but of yesterday (and therefore hath need of the wisdom of those that were before us) and had been ignorant if we had not received light and knowledge from our forefathers. Our days upon the earth are but a shadow, in respect of the old ancient days and times past, wherein the laws have been by the wisdom of the most excellent men, in many successions of ages, by long and continual experience, the trial of right and truth, fined and refined, which no one man, being of so short a time, albeit he had in his head the wisdom of all the men in the world in any one age, could ever have effected or attained to.

The community of wisdom stretched back into a time before the understanding of any individual and time itself had winnowed goodness from men's thoughts.

That idea had become allied in the minds of the cultural elite with a version of Arcadianism whose roots were in Virgilian Rome and which had been transmitted to England, not least through the agency of Philip Sidney, via the example and glamour of the Italian Renaissance. Culture thrives on hybridisation and the coming together of these two streams produced a moment in England of rich and deep vitality. Both the Italian and the native English forms depended for their vigour on a denial of the present. Whether through inherited English custom or an idealised Italianate antiquity, Arcadia was a refusal to accept that modern ways were best. Arcadia's role was to suggest that another finer and usually older alternative could and should be found.

This double inheritance was both courtly and anti-courtly. It existed in the paintings, masques and poetry written at court; but it was also driven by the idea that the court was an embodiment of the wickedness and corruption which Arcadia was bound to oppose. The two Herbert brothers straddled this double world, not in the form of a neat opposition to each other, but in differing emphases on this complex and subtle set of ideas. Both spent their lives at court but both would, in time, as successive Earls of Pembroke, come to champion the opposition to the court, to the king's favourites, to their policies and eventually to the king himself. The change to be measured between the sixteenth century and the seventeenth is the emergence of Arcadia, full-blown, into the political sphere.

The Herberts, like their contemporaries, were both entirely court and entirely country. The division was in their hearts and in their genes. No family was so identified with life at Whitehall, its entertainments and extravagances, its glory and honour; and no family carried in its sense of itself so powerful an inheritance of noble, aestheticised, principled independence from the crown. The two tendencies were folded in with each other, in their own family history, in their political and social assumptions, in their pride in themselves as great magnates in Wales and Wiltshire, and in their recognition that the crown, like it or not, was the source of virtually all modern wealth. They were lords dressed as foresters, Arcadianists of the real world, the incomparable brethren, the Earls of Paradise. These two currents in their lives ran at full bore for thirty years. To understand their Arcadianism, one must first understand the courtly world in which they lived and moved.

Philip Herbert, the younger, was the less burdened, the huntsman, the gambler, the charmer, the lightweight, the source of amusement and of the feeling, of vital importance to James, that after years in the barrens of Scotland, he had at last arrived in the Land of Promise. England for the king was a place of abundant and handsome young men who would like nothing more than to spend a week or two at play in the hunting fields of his newly acquired kingdom. Together, they lived out the images to be found on the tapestries which lined the royal apartments and the great canvases by Rubens and Snyders in which gentlemen, dressed in the most stripped-down of Arcadian clothes, acted the ritual of the hunt as a way of returning to the world of simplicity and honour. England, and nowhere more than Wilton, provided the backdrop of parks and downland where the hares would run, the hawks could fly, and fun, a holiday from care, could be had.

Although William Pembroke was also a regular member of those hunting parties, his role as the older brother became, increasingly, more serious, less spaniel-like, more dignified, driven by a growing awareness of his inheritance as the heir to the Sidney-Leicester-Essex connection, a militantly Protestant, Hispanophobic tradition which looked back to more glorious days under Elizabeth. Then, they told themselves, the great men of England had stood for a heroic Protestant clarity against the Spanish, and for ancient communal practices of hospitality, for the custom of the country, the law of the land and the ancient constitution, in a way that the modern world of James's court, disturbingly attracted to a foreign absolutism, seemed to be leaving behind.

William was already vastly rich from his Pembroke inheritance. Philip had to play the favourite to gain his fortune. In the summer of 1603, James made him a Knight of the Bath (which meant what it said: each candidate was given a purifying bath the evening he was knighted) and in Whitehall on 27 December 1604, Sir Philip was married to a girl he had fallen in love with, Susan de Vere, daughter of the Earl of Oxford and sister of the Bridget de Vere William had turned down in the 1590s. She was clearly a beautiful and entrancing person. Ben Jonson later fell in love with her and wrote her the most subtly erotic of poems. One of the shortest books of the Apocrypha describes the beautiful Susanna, as righteous as she was desirable, who liked to walk in her husband's garden. Two old judges, gazing on her face, had their 'lust inflamed toward her' and 'desired to have to do with her'. She refused them and in revenge they tried to have her executed, claiming they had seen her 'with a young man'. Only when the young prophet Daniel asked the two judges what sort of tree she had been lying under, 'companying together' with the young man, and one of the judges answered 'Under a mastick tree' and the other 'Under an holm tree' was she released and the two judges executed in her place. From the story – and Jonson's poem – emerges a world of irresistible desire and ineffable purity:

> Were they that nam'd you, prophets? Did they see,
> Euen in the dew of grace, what you would bee?
> Or did our times require it, to behold
> A new SVSANNA, equall to that old?
> Or, because some scarce thinke that storie true,
> To make those faithfull, did the *Fates* send you?

This was the entrancing woman Philip Herbert fell in love with. The king loved nothing more than the wedding of one of his chosen young men. A riotous party followed, at which 'many great ladies were made shorter by the skirts', whatever that might have meant. Silver and gold plate worth £2000 was given to the pair. The king gave them £10,000 worth of land at Shurland in Sheppey in Kent. The party rolled on deep into the night. Finally Philip and Susan were put to bed in the Council Chamber, where 'there was sewing into the sheet, casting of the bride's left hose, and twenty other petty sorceries'. First thing the next morning, 'the king gave them a *reveille matin* in his shirt and nightgown, and spent a good hour with them in the bed, or upon, choose which you will believe best.' The distance which Elizabeth had maintained from her court, her virginal horror at the marriage of any man or woman close to her, had shrunk to nothing. The king was now cuddling in public and in bed with his favourite and his favourite's bride.

A river of money now came the way of both the Herberts. William Pembroke was made Warden of the Stannaries in Cornwall, Steward of the Duchy of Cornwall and Lord Lieutenant of the county of Cornwall, every one of those appointments bringing patronage and payments in its train. Philip was given a half-share in a licence to export 30,000 undressed cloths duty free every year. In 1605, the doting king made him Earl of Montgomery, the title named after a castle and county in the Herbert heartlands in Wales.

William Pembroke had inherited the great estates garnered by his grandfather and had also married a hideous Talbot heiress with enormous riches, having, according to Clarendon, 'paid much too dear for his wife's fortune by taking her person into the bargain'. It was Philip, the happy beneficiary of a love-match with a beautiful and universally admired woman, who was in need of financial support. To the horror of royal Treasury officials, the king granted him a revenue from the crown of £2000 a year for sixty years, plus a pourboire of '200l. a year as our free gift'. This was favouritism in action, the draining away of crown assets into the pockets of the 'mignons' which would so radically threaten the wellbeing of the crown in the years to come.

The king paid off £44,000 of debts incurred by Montgomery and two other favourites. He was asked by the king to collect £20,000 due to the crown from lands that had been confiscated from Roman Catholics on which he was given a 50% commission. In the summer of 1612 a Roman Catholic, Sir Henry James, refused to swear the oath of allegiance to the king because it conflicted with his attachment to the Roman Church. Without a flicker, the Earl of Montgomery 'begged Sir Henry's goods and lands, worth 1,600l or 1,700l per an,' and received them. The mechanism was different from the way in which the first Earl of Pembroke had collected his estate, but the effect was the same: a redistribution of money and power into the hands of those who got themselves close to the body of the king.

Nor was William Pembroke immune to the gold-digging. In 1618, his mother-in-law, the ancient, widowed Countess of Shrewsbury, was said to be 'almost out of her mind, with a dread of being poisoned'. No thought was given to the old woman's mental health. More important was that Pembroke and her other powerful son-in-law, the Earl of Arundel, 'beg the protection of her estate' – meaning the control of her lands and money – 'and will enjoy the fruits of it if she do not mind', which in the seventeenth century meant 'if she does not notice'. A third, less important son-in-law, Lord Ruthin and his wife Elizabeth Talbot, were cut out of the arrangement.

No portrait survives of William, the third earl, as a young man, as Shakespeare fell in love with him, but there is a portrait of his brother, with the same reddish-brown hair, the same 'pritty sharpe-oval face' they inherited from the Sidneys, painted soon after Philip had become a Knight of the Garter on 23 April, St George's Day, 1608. In the painting, probably by William Larkin, Philip wears the badges of his recent elevation: the pearl-embroidered garter below his left knee, matched by the wide satin sash under the other. He wears the Garter collar around his shoulders, and hanging from it the enamelled jewel of George, wielding a sword, studded with diamonds, the green dragon crouching at his feet. His sword swings from a hanger around his waist, his cuffs and ruff are of lace, halfway between the Elizabethan cartwheel and the loose lace collars of the Cavaliers, and a beautiful coral bracelet circles his left wrist. His hand drops carelessly from the pommel of the sword behind him, the other hand held to his hip, holding a hat emblazoned with a cloud of ostrich feathers.

The broad scarlet riband and the scarlet velvet mantle of the Order of the Bath are laid over his doublet and hose of a satin that has been embroidered with silver thread in damascene stripes. Lace pompoms decorate his high-heeled shoes, his hair is loose and unaffected, his chestnut-reddish beard light, his lips feminine, his eyes intent and watching. There is no depth or complexity in his expression. There is even a kind of naivety in his face, as there is in this portrayal of worldly glory. This is the sort of materialist, enriched, pleasure-loving, world-enjoying figure against whom the Puritans railed. He is the Jacobean court personified. Everything here is new, so new in fact that the creases are still visible in the velvet and on the satin lining of the outer mantle. He is a bride dressed for a wedding, but what he has married here is no husband, but status, the Garter, riches, glory, himself.

This is perhaps the greatest portrait painted in Jacobean England and its beauty consists, at least in part, in its heightened worldliness, its frank enjoyment of the gifts the world has to offer. It is, perhaps, a portrait of luck. This is no ancient noble. His brother, not he, has inherited the ancient Pembroke title and the vast spread of lands in Wiltshire and Wales. But James has made him a peer too, simply because James loved the verve with which Philip went about his hunting and gambling, his life. It is a portrait of a man who has succeeded.

By the time William, the elder brother, first appears in a Daniel Mytens portrait of about 1616, he has left behind his wayward and passionate youth. He has become the noble politician, the patriot, the man who was maintaining the meaning of old England against the corruptions of court favourites. In the political and aesthetic ecology of the time, William, in his recessive patience, occupies the opposite niche to his brother's wonderful flamboyant display. In young Philip, at the peak of his courtly success, one sees the Jacobean courtier like a paeony in full bloom. He has done well by courting the sovereign. He can make no claim to independent power because he is the sovereign's creature. Without James, he would have been merely Mr Philip Herbert, not this jewelled, pearl-decked, coral-braceleted and gartered hero.

Against Philip's verve and risk-taking, William acted the judicious statesman. A famous incident occurred at court on 17 September 1608. He had been playing cards with Sir George Wharton, a wild young courtier, who was to die the following year at a duel in Islington with a young Scot who was also killed. On this occasion, Sir George, presumably losing at cards, also lost his temper, at which Pembroke told him, 'Sir George, I have loved you long and still desire to do so, but by your manner in playing, you lay it upon me either to leave [cease] to love you, or to leave to play with you. Wherefore, choosing to love you still, I will never play with you more.'

That is the voice of this tradition, looking back to Sidneyan sweetness of temper, a balanced composure, and an opting for long-term love over passing diversion. Wharton did his best to maintain the argument but Pembroke refused to be riled and tried to make peace. But Wharton was uncontrollable. Out hunting with the king in Surrey the next day,

> Sir George spurred his horse with all speed upon [Pembroke], which was observed by the earl of Montgomery who cried out, 'Brother, you will be stricken.' The earl thereupon received Sir George with a sound backward blow over the face which drove him almost back upon his horse's croop. But company being present, they galloped again till in the end the stag died in Bagshot town, where Sir George comes up to the Earl offering him a paper, protesting there was nothing in it unfit for his lordship to read. The earl said, 'Sir George, give me no papers here where all they may see us who know what hath passed; but tell me, is not the purport of it to challenge me.'
>
> 'Yes,' said Sir George.
>
> 'Well,' said the earl, 'this night you shall have answer.'

His answer was to send Wharton his sword by a messenger and ask him 'to take the measure of the Sword, for the earl would not take one hair's breadth of advantage at his hands.' They were to meet, alone, the following morning. William Pembroke's life might have ended there, but the king had heard of the argument and by his command no duel was fought.

Status anxiety, a man's honour endlessly under negotiation, a rivalry between Scots and English, a tense world in which tennis games, the hunting field, the racecourse, gambling, women, your relationship to the king, the chair one was given at dinner: all provided arenas in which offence might be taken and violence done. The king's habit of showering honours on his favourites and selling titles to the rich, whatever their background, served only to exacerbate the sense among the old aristocracy that the bonds of society, the old certainties, were under threat. A frenzy of duelling and gambling overtook the court, as though honour and luck had constantly to be re-demonstrated. Courtiers would bet on which of their footmen could run fastest from St Albans to London, on whether the King of Spain would turn Protestant (long odds there) and of course on horses, cocks and dogs. At every stage, offence waited in the wings. Of the two brothers, Philip, in the less established and more vulnerable position, was more likely to turn to violence. Even though he had a lifelong habit, which would finally erupt in a fateful contretemps on the eve of civil war, of hitting his fellow courtiers, he had no greater reputation for violence than any other. The culture had turned febrile.

Pembroke was rich enough and secure enough not to need to engage in this posturing. The illegitimacy in his ancestry had long been forgotten. Without any effort, he could act the easy dignified noble of ancient lineage and vast wealth, independent of the sometimes desperate market in favours and standing at court. He was known in particular for his generosity. When the Lieutenant of the Tower, Sir Gervas Elways or Elwes, was hanged for his part in the famous murder of Sir Thomas Overbury, the Elwes estate, worth more than £1000 a year, came to Pembroke. But without hesitation, he gave it away to Elwes's widow and children. Ben Jonson had described how his 'noblesse keeps one stature still,/And one true posture, though besieged with ill.' That dignified, unshowy self-possession appears in Mytens' painting and it is exactly the tone of Clarendon's later portrayal:

> As he spent and lived upon his own fortune, so he stood upon his own two feet, without any other support than of his proper virtue and merit; and lived toward the favourites with that decency, as would not suffer them to censure his master's judgement and election, but as with men of his own rank. He was exceedingly beloved by the court, because he never desired to get that for himself which others laboured for; but was still ready to promote the pretences of worthy men; and he was equally celebrated in the country for having received no obligations from the court, which might corrupt and sway his affection and judgement.

In that way, the two incomparable brethren were aligned on either side of the great cultural fault line of the age. William, the venerable earl, standing on his own dignity and ancient wealth, loved in the country, able to look the succession of favourites in the eye without fear or favour, a hero for passionate Protestants and intellectuals, a man of words; Philip, of no great intellectual dignity, delightful where his brother could be 'accounted melancholy', fascinated by the visual and physical aspects of culture, a creature of the very court milieu of which William remained at least in part sceptical and removed.

For both William, Earl of Pembroke and Philip, Earl of Montgomery, the tournaments or barriers that were held at court, and the dazzlingly expensive masques that were part of the same culture of courtly theatricality, were two of the principal stages on which this complex of attitudes could be displayed. Much of it derived from the Sidneyan world. The *Arcadia* itself is full of the fantasia of Elizabethan medievalism, knights in armour that was 'blew, like the heauen', shields showing 'a greyhound, which ouerrunning his fellow, and taking the hare, yet hurts it not when it takes it.' Others were 'armed in a white armour, which was al guilded ouer with knots of womans haire, which came downe from the crest of his head-peece, & spred it selfe in rich quantitie ouer all his armour'; some 'all in greene, both armour and furniture, it seemed a pleasant garden, wherein grew orange trees; which with their golden fruites, cunningly beaten in, and embrodered, greatly enriched the eye-pleasing colour of greene.' On his shield, the green knight had 'a sheep, feeding in a pleasant field, with this word, *Without feare, or enuie*. And therefore was called the Knight of the sheep.' His opponent 'was all in milke white, his attiring els, all cutte in stares'. Even now, one can sense the shudder of romance which these images of a purified, distant, idealised, meaning-drenched world sent through the Elizabethan and Jacobean imagination.

As descendants and carriers of that tradition, the Herbert brothers appeared in tournament after tournament and masque after masque. It was a world that was from the beginning deeply connected to the imagery of Arcadian and rural retreat. *The Masque of Blackness* in 1605, in which Susan de Vere and Pembroke's cousin (and mistress) Lady Mary Wroth both danced, opened with a curtain showing a hunt making its way through the woods. In that masque, as in the many that followed over the next thirty-five years, the pattern unfolded of disorder turning to order, or sometimes of order falling into disorder followed by an even more cosmic level of order. This was the story with which the court for decades and at quite enormous expense consoled itself. Everything would be all right in the end. There was a higher and a better reality, removed from the grubbiness of the everyday, and none were better qualified to embody it than these dancing nobles. Nobility was fineness and they were the vehicles for it. It could take any number of forms: medieval or classical, martial or pastoral, exotic or ancient, but the story was always the same: the lives they were leading, and the people they were, held within them the possibility of distinction.

So high were these ideals – the masques were not exactly stories, but glittering enactments of the nobility latent in this world – that money was irrelevant. In the wedding masque called *Hymenaei*, staged on 5 January 1606, in which both Susan, Countess of Montgomery and Philip, Earl of Montgomery danced their parts as masquers, one John Pory, a poor Greek scholar, looked on in amazement:

> The men were clad in Crimzon, and the women in white. They had every one a white plume of the richest herons feathers, and were so rich in jewels upon their heads as was most glorious. I think they hired and borrowed all the principal jewels and ropes of perle both in court or citty.

As citizens of Arcadia, their hair was 'carelessly (but yet with more art than if more affected) bound under the circle of a rare and rich coronet.' The sequins and silver thread sewn into their costumes glittered under the massed candlelight. The metal-thread lace – silver for the great, copper for the lesser masquers – chevroned all over the costumes, caught the highlights from the candelabra. All this combined with the glamour and exoticism of Inigo Jones's Italian-derived costumes to amaze the court audience among whom the masquers, at the climax of the performance, would descend to dance, blurring and even erasing any boundary between the imagined, perfect world of the masque and the world of the court itself.

Alongside the masquing came the tournaments, twenty-seven of them staged at court between 1604 and the moment when the tradition came to an end in 1622. Philip Montgomery was often the star. On 1 June 1606, four Knights Errant of the Fortunate Islands (the king's cousin the Duke of Lennox and the earls of Southampton, Pembroke and Montgomery) issued a universal challenge 'To all honourable Men at Arms, Knights Adventurers of hereditary note and exemplary nobleness, that for most maintainable actions do weild either sword or lances in the quest of glory.' They had 'four indisputable propositions' to defend:

1 That in the service of Ladies no knight have free will.
2 That it is Beauty maintains the world in Valour.

3 That no fair Lady was ever false.

4 That none can be perfectly wise but Lovers.

It was pure Philip Sidney, even if denuded of its political burden. At the barriers staged for the knighting of the young Protestant Henry, Prince of Wales on Twelfth Night 1610, Philip Montgomery won the prize. The show began against a Jonesian backdrop in which medieval and classical architectural elements were jumbled together, portraying 'the fallen House of Chivalry' where Chivalry was 'Possessed with sleep, dead as a lethargy.' Inevitably, the antics of Philip and the other young bloods of the court restored it to full life. No expense was spared. The skills of trumpeters, silk merchants, painters of the shields, chariot-makers, bit makers and cutlers were employed to work the silver velvet into caparisons for the horses, make dresses for pages and grooms, devise sub-classical, mannerist designs for the helmets descended from Cellini, with cumulus clouds of ostrich feathers above them, build tents like caves or castles, prepare lamp-bearers dressed as centurions and even at one point introduce an elephant covered in its own jewelled cloth and castle which trundled around the tiltyard too slowly for any sense of drama to survive.

The masques were, for all their materiality, an escaping of the material world. There was a bewitching fluency in Jones's designs, a sense for the first time in English draughtsmanship that the dross of existence was being left behind for a floating evanescence. These entertainments were not dramas, just as the almost obsessively repeated hunting expeditions were not acting out anything except reality. As the hunt was theatrical but not fictional, and as the park was a kind of dreamland but one that could be owned, the masque was a theatre of the real, a making visible of the highest of ideals.

The community of honour was not mere play-acting. It had its political dimension. A political and cultural grouping began even in the first decade of James's reign to form around the Pembrokes and the Sidneys, opposed to the cynical, passionless, unidealistic managerialism of the Cecils. It cherished, if perhaps underground, a resistance to autocracy and a belief in the possibilities of an Arcadian ideal. It was deeply retrospective. In the early years of James's reign, after his brief honeymoon was over, there was a feeling that the great moment of Englishness had gone. Sidney was dead, as were Leicester and Essex, his heirs. Elizabeth was gone, and who had they all been succeeded by but simpering 'mignons' and a Scots king, 'the cold northern breath', as the poet Michael Drayton, a Pembroke client, described him. For Drayton, only among people like Samuel Daniel and Sir William Alexander – both also Pembroke clients – was there any continuity, any hope for the virtue of England. There you could find 'men from base enuy and detraction free/of vpright harts and humble spirits'. The freewheeling materialism of Jacobean England, the vivid corruption of the court, the opening of the royal shopping centre, Britain's Bourse, on the Strand, drove these cultural conservatives into an embattled place where purity was longed for; much of the hope focused on the young Henry, Prince of Wales, who promised to be a martial champion of English virtue, unlike his soft, peace-obsessed, degenerate, mignon-dabbling father.

Pembroke might have become the natural leader of this party, but at least as a young man in his twenties he did not have the drive. 'For his person he was not effectual,' Francis Bacon said of him, and his political programme suffered from drift. Others claimed the centre of royal attention and policy. None was more successful than a young, Frenchified Scots page called Robert Carr, who managed to break his leg at a tilt in front of the king, was nursed to health by a solicitous James, who taught him Latin while lying on his sick bed. Carr soon climbed on to the escalator of Jacobean favour: a knighthood, the Viscountcy of Rochester, the Earldom of Somerset, manors, lands and the scattering of golden pennies which in the words of Thomas Dekker, the great satirist of the age, made 'spangle babies of them all'. Finally, in July 1614 the king made Somerset Lord Chamberlain, the man in charge of the royal household, the hinge between royal favour and royal favourites, 'because he would bestow a place so near himself on the friend whom he loved above all men living.'

The rise of Somerset was a defeat not only for Herbert interests – Montgomery was at the same time quietly eased out of the glow of royal kindness – but for the Protestant party as a whole. Carr was closer to the pro-Catholic, pro-Spanish interest at court. The fortunes of the Sidney-Herbert party were at a low ebb. But Robert Carr, Viscount Rochester, Earl of Somerset, was to experience a fall as rapid as his rise. He arranged with the king for Frances Howard, Countess of Essex, part of the fiercely pro-Spanish Howard family, with whom he had fallen in love, to be granted a divorce from her husband, the Earl of Essex, on the publicly humiliating grounds that the poor earl could not get an erection when in bed with her. The trial was fixed, the Earl of Essex exposed to ridicule and the divorce granted. Carr then married Frances himself. At their wedding she appeared with 'her hair long over her shoulders in brazen token of her virginity'.

At the very centre of national life, this kind of scandal did lasting damage to the prestige of the crown and court. It was everything Arcadia – not to speak of the enormous Puritan constituency and the knights of the shires – most deeply despised. The divorce and remarriage were scandal enough but the two Carrs then plotted the murder of Sir Thomas Overbury, who had been a close friend of Carr's, but had advised him not to marry Frances Howard. Overbury was a reproach and an annoyance and James sent a reluctant William Pembroke to persuade him to go abroad as an ambassador. Overbury refused and instead was sent to the Tower. There, Frances Howard arranged with the Lieutenant of the Tower, Sir Gervas Elwes, to send him poisoned tarts and jellies. He ate them and died an agonising death. Philip Montgomery, who had been accused a few years earlier of trying to seduce Frances Howard himself, was sent to her by James and she confessed all to him. Or so it is said:

no written version of the confession was ever produced. Both Carr and his wife were sentenced to death, but were pardoned by James and lived the rest of their lives in ruin, first in the Tower and later released to the country, where they lived, uncommunicating, in separate wings of the same Northamptonshire house.

In a recognition of moral crisis at the court, Pembroke, unstained by this scandal, was in December 1615 made Lord Chamberlain in Somerset's place. Ben Jonson dedicated his book of *Epigrams* to Pembroke, as 'THE GREAT EXAMPLE OF HONOUR AND VIRTUE' in a court which was as degenerate as the Roman court on which Martial's Latin epigrams, Jonson's model, had poured their 'wormwood and sulphur'. Among Jonson's barbs was Epigram XV, 'On Court-Worm':

> 'All men are worms:' but this no man. In silk
> 'Twas brought to court first wrapped, and white as milk;
> Where, afterwards, it grew a butterfly:
> Which was a caterpillar. So 'twill die.

The collapse of Carr's gilded wings was the moment for Pembroke to enter into what he might have considered his inheritance. He had already hatched a plot to insert a pliant and amenable favourite in the king's heart as a way of exerting even tighter control over the fount of all patronage. A 'great but private entertainment at supper' had been held the year before at the Pembrokes' London house, Baynard's Castle, attended by several Herberts and their friends and allies, including the brutally severe Archbishop of Canterbury, George Abbot. As heir-candidate for royal love, the Pembroke dinner party had settled on an impoverished but exceptionally beautiful twenty-two-year-old Northamptonshire man, who had travelled to Italy, was cultured charm itself and a master of the dance and the hunting field: George Villiers. In August 1614, he was a guest, not by chance, at a house party in Northamptonshire where the king's eye fell on him. By April 1615, Villiers had arrived, appointed Gentleman of the Bedchamber, knighted by James and given an annual pension of £1000. By August, the plan had succeeded beyond all possible dreams: Villiers and the king slept in the same bed at Farnham Castle, then in Hampshire, where the king was on progress. This, in itself, did not necessarily mean that their relationship was sexual but Buckingham's own later description – of 'the time which I shall never forget at Farnham, where the bed's head could not be found between the master and his dog' – can leave little doubt.

The prizes came rolling in: the Order of the Garter, a barony and a viscountcy, an earldom, a marquisate and eventually a dukedom, all of Buckingham, a title which it was suggested at the time, even by the king, carried some sexual implication. Lands, manors and appointments all followed, not only for himself but for almost everyone he knew. His mother became Countess of Buckingham, his lunatic elder brother, John, Viscount Purbeck, his younger brother, Christopher, Earl of Anglesey, his brother-in-law Earl of Denbigh and for his half-brother, Edward, a knighthood and the vastly profitable post of Comptroller of the Court of Wards. 'He loved Buckingham,' James told his Privy Council, gravely sitting around their table in Whitehall, with Buckingham himself on his chair among them, 'more than any other man.' James liked to call his favourite Steenie, short for Stephen, as it was said of St Stephen in the Acts of the Apostles that 'all that sat in the council, looking stedfastly on him, saw his face as it had been the face of an angel.' This love was only appropriate for a king, James insisted. 'Jesus Christ had done the same as he was doing . . . for Christ had his John and he had his George.'

The Herberts were left in the wake of this Villiers coup. Philip Montgomery kept up a friendship with him, based on their joint enjoyment of courtly pleasures. They danced together in the masques (performing in January 1617 to an audience which included Pocahontas, the Indian Queen) and hunted together with the king. In 1618, Buckingham became godfather to Montgomery's son. But a growing distance developed between Pembroke and Buckingham.

Although part of a single court, they represented two sides of the great cultural divide opening up in early seventeenth-century England: the old aristocracy against the new; a Protestant inheritance against Spanish-loving modernity; propriety against glamour; integrity against corruption; chivalric medievalism against self-promoting, money-gathering absolutism. To some extent, Buckingham simply made Pembroke look old-fashioned. Pembroke's attachment to his tradition, to the Elizabethan-revivalist 'patriot party', as it was called, the party in effect of the country, which saw England not as a crown and a people but as a patchwork of manorial estates, with a deep suspicion of courts and their favourites – all of that seemed out of date in the context of Buckingham's high-glamour internationalist, ineffably charming appeal. For Buckingham, the old aristocracy with its fantasies of goodness rooted in the old social structures was an irrelevance. But to that ancient aristocracy, of which Pembroke was the leader, Villiers himself, the archangel of beauty and power, the smooth facilitator in the market for titles, monopolies and office, was the embodiment of wickedness. Philip Montgomery hung uncertainly between the two of them.

The coming of Villiers polarised the Arcadian inheritance. Around Pembroke clustered a group of writers, poets and playwrights who maintained a steady and constant stream of nostalgic, Arcadian, anti-court literature, dreaming of a better time when England was whole. In those fantasies, lords were always kind to their people, and friendship, unlike the bitter rivalries of court, described the relationship between men. 'Friendship on earth we may as easily find,' Sir Benjamin Rudyerd, a Pembroke client, wrote,

> As he the North-East passage, that is blind.
> Sophisticate affection is the best
> This age affords, no friend abides the test.
> They make a glorious shew, a little space
> But tarnish in the rain like copper lace.
> So by degrees, when we embrace so many,
> We courted are like whores, not lov'd of any.

The world was in decline, and only in Arcadia, the place not of cheap copper but of real silver lace, not of show but of truth, not of whoring but of love, did any virtue remain. Eclogues, pastorals and Arcadias poured from the pens of these poets. *The Shepheards Pipe, The Faithful Shepherdess*, the *Queen's Arcadia, The Shepherds Hunting, Shepherds Calendars, Shepherd's Pastorals*, the *Shepheards Sirena*: one after another they emerged to imply or state the wickedness of modernity. English pastoral Protestant comedy, Italianate pastoral tragicomedy, ancient British pastoral tragedy, Italianate English romantic pastoral comedy, Virgilian Georgian civic pastoral romance, native pastoral satire: Arcadianism surged out of England in response to the modern wickedness of courts.

William Browne, in residence at Wilton and the author in 1616 of *Britannia's Pastorals*, wrote bitterly and angrily on the differences between the reality of Buckingham's Britain and the dream of pastoral. There had been enclosure riots, poverty, famine. The lords, for their own pleasure, were destroying the ancient landscape of custom. Copyholders who had been in their houses and lands for years were being dispossessed.

> The country gentleman, from's neighbours hand
> Forceth th'inheritance, ioynes land to land,
> And (most insatiate) seekes vnder his rent
> To bring the world's most spacious continent.

This was in a poem dedicated, with permission, to William Herbert, Earl of Pembroke. The upstart alien Stuarts were irrelevant compared with the profoundly British Welshness of his patron: 'Cambria is a land from whence have come / Worthies well worth the race of Ilium.'

Next to that rooted heroism, the court, which should have been the source of such life and goodness, was nothing but a sink of iniquity and the home of sterility and desolation.

> What wreck of *Noblesse*, and what *rape* of *honor*,
> Hath laboring Tyme brought forth (to humane dearth)

Whose Womb, a Tomb; whose Byrth a liveles Earth.
What *Howse*, or rather hospitable *Court*
(Erewhile a Receptable for resort
Of all Estate) is that which seemes so vast
With desolation, emptiness, and wast?

In the mind of this school of poets gathered around the Pembroke interest, England was a wasteland of wrongness, and to that wrongness one name could be attached: Buckingham.

The tensions between Pembroke and Buckingham were those which would break into civil war in the 1640s. Was the crown to show respect for the ancient habits and practices of England, for its deep structure of manors and lords, whose relationship was one of head and limbs, equivalent to the relationship of king and parliament? Or was the crown to abandon that organic structure and set up instead an effective, authoritarian government, much as was happening all over Europe, which treated the country as a whole much as a landlord would be treating a manor if he abandoned the copyhold system and turned it all over to leases and commercial rents?

Pembroke's relationship with Buckingham had for many years been brewing for a crisis. It was not merely a matter of two court grandees manoeuvring for advantage. They had squabbled over the appointment of minor functionaries at court, Pembroke asserting his right as Lord Chamberlain, Buckingham his influence as the king's favourite. But large-scale ideological differences came between them too. Buckingham had no inheritance; even though originally promoted by Pembroke, he was a creature of the court and of the moment; the glamour of Spanish prestige, sophistication and style attracted him; his interest was in monopolising and extending royal power in England. Pembroke was his opposite: acutely aware of his place at the head of a powerful, half-nostalgic, half-subversive movement in England which needed to protect the 'pattern of manors' against the depredations of a hungry court and state. His task was to defend that world against greed and corruption. He was the heir to the Sidney inheritance: the independence of a self-respecting nobility; the location of that nobility's meaning and source of significance in the land over which it held sway; the sense that in that connection there was an authenticity and value which the world of the court would erode; fixedly Protestant and anti-Spanish, always looking for the ways in which the royal administration was either drifting towards Rome and Catholicism or simply failing to defend the Protestant interest in Europe; highly literate and with a high-minded view of its destiny; a patriotic position which could contemplate the possibility of civil war. There was nothing contradictory in its close service to the crown over several generations and the possibility that one day, if the crown failed to uphold the custom of the manor, the way in which England had always regulated itself as a form of balance, it might desert the crown in favour of the health of the country.

Pembroke had long cultivated a position in parliament, which he could use to fight his battles at court. At least twenty MPs, and on occasions half as many again, including Benjamin Rudyerd and the young Edward Hyde, later to be Earl of Clarendon, depended on his patronage and could be expected to speak out in favour of this agenda. He also controlled the proxy votes of several peers. On one occasion, under the great new Palladian coffered ceiling of Inigo Jones's redesigned chamber for the House of Lords, Pembroke was reported by the letter-writer John Chamberlain to have cast four votes on one side of a question and four on the other, an act of supreme, patriotic nonchalance. Unfortunately, this marvellous story cannot be true because Pembroke only ever controlled five proxies in the House of Lords, but it is a signal of the role he played in England's political imagination in the 1620s: a man of power because he was a man of balance.

Pembroke's programme always insisted on unity, on making the king responsive to parliament and vice versa. The wellbeing of the body required the head and limbs to be in balance. The surging ambition and power control of the Duke of Buckingham was like a hectic in the blood. Unfortunately, the power struggle on the mainland of Europe between the Catholic Habsburg empire and the new Protestant states could not provide an environment of calm and ease. Throughout the 1620s, English domestic politics were riven by the unsolvably difficult questions of alliance and aggression within that shifting European political-military-religious storm.

England in the 1620s became embroiled first in marriage proposals with Spain and then with France; first in war with Spain and then with France. All four of those policies were more or less catastrophically handled. The prestige and financial position of the crown and of Buckingham in particular crashed under the impact of expensive failure and national humiliation. This was not how it had been in the great days of Elizabeth when England, the Protestant hero country, had defeated the great Spanish Armada.

Pembroke played around the edges of these catastrophes, never dictating policy but working consistently to maintain a position that was anti-Spanish, anti-Catholic and anti-Buckingham. His freedom of manoeuvre was severely restricted by the deep affection which both James and Charles had for their favourite. If Pembroke was to maintain his own position at court, he could not attack Buckingham openly. When a Privy Council vote was taken in the summer of 1623 to approve Charles's proposed marriage to a Spanish princess, Pembroke was unaccountably ill with the stone in Wilton. His brother Montgomery stood in for him. But he had not been that unwell. Three weeks later, the king was down at Wilton for some hunting.

When James died in March 1625, Buckingham was so distraught that he took to his bed. The new young king took Montgomery and Pembroke along with him to Buckingham's sickbed and the four of them spent three hours talking together. But the underlying differences between them were too powerful for such palliatives to work. Pembroke told the Venetian ambassador, who had begged him to be reconciled to Buckingham for the sake of European Protestantism, that internal enemies must be dealt with before external ones and that the cause they both had at heart would be better served without Buckingham than with him.

Buckingham was the enemy within and by the spring of 1626 Pembroke was ready to make his attack on the favourite. Through his network of patronage spread across the whole of the west country, Pembroke, in alliance with the fiercely Calvinist George Abbot, Archbishop of Canterbury, had assembled his team of MPs. As the parliament gathered that year, the Pembroke party had Buckingham in its sights. A disastrous attack on Cadiz of which Buckingham had been in charge as the Lord Admiral, a recent revelation of his sympathy for Roman Catholics in his own family and beyond, a growing disgust at his self-enrichment and his singular intimacy with the late king: all were weapons in Pembroke's hands. 'Affairs are not guided by the public counsel,' it was said in parliament. 'Was it good for the state that all things should be guided by the Duke's single counsel?' No money would be granted by the parliament before these worries had been addressed.

Leading the charge, Dr Turnour, the member for Shaftesbury, Pembroke's nominee in one of the constituencies his grandfather the first earl had acquired and where most of the people voting would have been Pembroke's tenants, asked whether,

> by common fame, the general cause of evils in the kingdom was the Lord Admiral, whether his being Admiral was the cause of the King's loss of his control of the Channel, whether unreasonable gifts to the Duke and his kindred were the cause of impairing the king's revenue, whether the multiplicity of offices held by the Duke and his dependents was the cause of the ill government of the kingdom, whether recusants were increased because his mother-in-law and father-in-law were known papists, whether he was a cause of scandal through sale of offices and whether his being lord Admiral was the cause of the ill success of the Cadiz action.

It was a bruising list, perhaps drawn up by Pembroke himself in the form of attacking questions which he often used. It was undoubtedly designed to destroy the duke. The crown was desperate for money from parliament with which to wage war on the French. But Charles would not surrender his beloved Steenie and instead dissolved parliament. Moneyless, divided from the kingdom and with a war to fight, but with his favourite at his side, Charles now turned to the solution which, perhaps more than any other single act, pushed England on the road to civil war.

He decided to demand directly from the people the money which their representatives in parliament had refused to grant. In July, letters went out to all the justices of the peace requiring the men of property 'lovingly, freely, and voluntarily' to subsidise the war. The request was greeted with a silence and that summer, almost no one in England paid up. In September, the king decided to levy a 'Forced Loan'. This was a euphemism for a compulsory tax, for which there were rare and extraordinary precedents but never on the scale now required nor in such bubblingly dangerous political circumstances. Under threat of being summoned to the Privy Council, the gentry of the country paid £250,000 into the royal coffers. Some refused and 'very many gentlemen of prime quality', in Clarendon's words, were imprisoned for that refusal to pay, one of them Sir William Coryton, a Cornish MP who was one of Pembroke's key clients. In a famous case, Coryton and four other knights challenged the legality of what the crown had done to them. To the shock and surprise of the ancient constitutionalists in England, they lost the case and were returned to prison. The gap between the two tendencies in English life represented by Pembroke and Buckingham, between a government based on balance and consent and an authoritarian government, had grown wider and angrier than it had ever been. 'Could it be imagined,' Clarendon wrote, 'that these men would meet again in a free convention of parliament, without a sharp and severe expostulation and inquisition into their own right, and the power that had imposed upon that right?' Writing in the 1650s, on the far side of a terrible civil war, Clarendon thought that this Forced Loan and the imprisoning of the gentlemen was the source 'from whence these waters of bitterness we now taste have flowed'.

In June 1626, perhaps at the prompting of the king and perhaps drawing on some earlier approaches, Buckingham and Pembroke started to be reconciled. Pembroke would not have wanted a rupture in the state. The entire foundation of his life was a belief in organic unity and he began to make arrangements with Buckingham which would restore that unity. Pembroke was to become Lord Steward of the Household, a post he had long desired, the linchpin of any administration, controlling and auditing the king's finances. His brother Montgomery would replace him as Lord Chamberlain, the officer who organised the running of the household. In an era of personal monarchy, these offices were at the centre of the political nation. As a balancing gesture for Buckingham, his own allies, the earls of Carlisle and Holland, became Gentlemen of the King's Bedchamber and the earls of Salisbury, Dorset and Bridgewater became Privy Councillors. It was an attempt to re-integrate the fissure which was opening in the court and which the events that year in parliament had been widening. Both sides benefited, the Pembrokes establishing themselves at the heart of the administration, Buckingham drawing legitimacy from his connection with the leader of the patriot party. The Venetian ambassador put it succinctly: Buckingham had gone in for the arrangement 'to gain the Lord Chamberlain's faction'. The seal was to be put on it with money and marriage between the two families, Buckingham's daughter Mary to marry Montgomery's son Charles.

The deal was done and the legal documents settled and signed on 3 August 1626. The two children, who were seven and four, 'played together before the King, calling one another Husband and Wife. My lord Montgomery is promised great things to raise his House and Fortunes.' The same day, Pembroke became Lord Steward and Montgomery Lord Chamberlain. And on the same day the queen's French attendants were suddenly commanded to depart, Samuel Pepys's future father-in-law among them. This no doubt was also part of the deal to reduce the influence of Catholicism on the court. In less than ten days, Pembroke was moving to assert real physical control. On 12 August 1626 he wrote to William Boneman, the King's Locksmith:

> Too much liberty having been given for making keys of his Majesty's Privy Lodgings at Whitehall, he is to take off the locks and make them in such sort that the former double keys may be quite shut out, but without interfering with the King's, Queen's and Lord Chamberlain's treble keys.

In the next session of parliament in 1628, Pembroke called off the attack on Buckingham, but affairs went no better for the duke. The disastrous campaign at La Rochelle and the Ile de Ré had blackened his name still further. The commons then called on the king to consider 'whether, in respect the said Duke hath so abused his power, it be safe for your majesty and your kingdom to continue him either in his great offices or in his place of nearness and counsel about your sacred person.' But Charles would not abandon him and again the session of parliament was brought to a close. Buckingham equipped himself with a bodyguard. His personal astrologer was torn to pieces in a London street. Finally, in August 1628, in Portsmouth, an enraged ex-soldier called John Felton murdered him, stabbing him from behind. Buckingham was able to shout 'Villain!' and pull the knife from the wound before staggering back dead. Felton said later, when asked for a motive, that he thought by 'killing the Duke he should do his country great service'. It was one conclusion of the long debate between court and country, custom and corruption, Pembroke and Buckingham which had held England in its grip for so long.

For all the elaborate alliances, Pembroke had remained hostile to his old enemy. After the assassination, he wrote to the elegant self-indulgent old courtier and diplomat, the Earl of Carlisle (a man who had spent 'over £400,000 in a very jovial life'), that 'the king our master begins to shine already. And I hope this next session to see a happy agreement between him and his people.' Every element of Pembroke's statement – a dawn-like glowing of the light, happiness, agreement, an Edenic togetherness in the nation – reflects a kind of Arcadian optimism, the conclusion of the sort of plot on which masque after masque had relied for decades.

But it was a hope without foundation. England, in the words of Izaak Walton, had changed from what they thought it used to be, 'that garden of piety, of pleasure, of peace, and a sweet conversation', into 'the thorny wilderness of a busy world.' Demons had been loosed at every level. The trust in the ancient constitution was eroded. The anxiety about the lack of commitment to the manor courts, the failure of individuals to join their sheep to the communal flock or provide their hurdles for the communal fold was the same political instinct as the MPs' distrust of the royal government increasingly dominated by favourites. The joint enterprise was under threat. To those seekers for themselves, the making of parliaments or the communal flock no longer seemed like an essential part of the fabric of England. Parliament even accused Buckingham of poisoning James I to get rid of him, as if he were a witch casting spells on the prize bull of the manor. The parliamentarianism that emerged in response was not radical; it was defensive against the power-acquiring, independence-enjoying instincts of the new crown and its new counsels. England would have loathed Buckingham whether Pembroke had encouraged the country in that or not. But his orchestrating of the campaign against him and his championing of the anti-Buckingham cause had done nothing to diminish the hatred. Felton's downward strike with the knife at Portsmouth was in that sense an intimate part of this long story, a blow for the country.

William Pembroke did not long survive his great rival. He 'departed this mortall life at Baynard's Castle, the 10th of April 1630.' He was fifty years old, the victim of an apoplexy 'after a full and cheerful supper' and £80,000 in debt, much of it to his own household officers. One of them, his steward, Sir Thomas Morgan, the seventh son of a Welsh squire, who had been knighted at Wilton in 1623, built for himself what remains William Pembroke's most poignant memorial: a great Jacobean house, posing as a toy castle and bearing the Pembroke arms, at Ruperra in Glamorgan, the centre of the ancient Herbert estates. Morgan, as steward and controller of the Herbert household, had acted for Pembroke in the function Pembroke had acted for the king. What Wilton had been to Whitehall, Ruperra was to Wilton. Now burnt and in collapse, Ruperra's toy towers and mock battlements are one of the last remaining vestiges of that honourable and chivalric ideal to which William Pembroke had devoted his life, an image of late-medieval perfection brought into a modern world which would neglect and ruin it. Clarendon called him 'the most universally loved and esteemed of any man of that age.' He was buried in Salisbury Cathedral where, in 1644, a royalist trooper, Richard Symonds, quartered in the town that 'wett, cold, and wyndy' October, saw his memorial:

> Upon the south pillar next the lower steps of the altar hang the atchements [a coat of arms in a black lozenge-shaped frame which would previously have hung over the great door at Wilton], sword, and golden gauntlets of William earle of Pembroke . . .

That sword and those golden gauntlets, perhaps from the tournaments and barriers in which he had fought as a young man forty years before, were the relics from another age.

11

Elizian Fields and Ayery Paradises

The perfecting of Wilton
1630–1640

AFTER WILLIAM PEMBROKE'S DEATH, Wilton and its world became the property of his brother Philip, Earl of Montgomery, who also inherited from him the Pembroke title. In the eyes of many, Philip scarcely measured up to the Pembroke tradition. He may have been named after Philip Sidney, but he was no poet, no politician and no speaker. He had the genetic background, he could certainly be charming, but did he have the moral backbone? Was he not an indulger of physical and material passions?

For all that, he had his own virtues and in his hands Wilton came to glow with enhanced beauty. It is thanks to this earl – widely disparaged at the time and never admired by historians – that Wilton acquired the fame it now has. The 1630s became the finest moment in its history, when the fantasy of perfection was burnished to a deeper sheen. With every aspect of courtly glamour he could summon, Philip, a great aesthete and collector, turned it into something new. Earlier, in the sixteenth and early seventeenth centuries, the best collections had all been kept in London houses. It may well be that here, in Philip's fusing of the Italianate art palace with the hunting lodge, the great rural English treasure house was invented. In bringing this exquisite courtliness to the country, Philip was not following an Italian or French model. He had made a new and English discovery, the English Country House as it has been known ever since, the Palace in the Trees.

A sermon was delivered at Baynard's Castle in late April 1630, preached on the life and legacy of the earl who had just died. It was the work of a Jacobean divine called Thomas Chaffinge, born in about 1581, of whom little else is known. The words of his sermon, 'The Iust Mans Memoriall', ring out like a summons to seriousness, a sudden revelation, under the surface of court intrigue, money and manipulation, of an intense and radical Protestant agenda. It was a pointer to the fact that this family was not merely, like the Earl of Carlisle, let alone the Duke of Buckingham, engaged in self-enrichment and self-promotion. The Protestant inheritance from the time of Philip Sidney remained a moral imperative for them. Chaffinge's sermon, in magnificent, old-fashioned, Jacobean language, reads like the voice of their conscience speaking.

In the printed version, Chaffinge began with an 'Epistle Dedicatory', addressed to Philip, the first Earl of Montgomery and now the fourth or twenty-third Earl of Pembroke. Seventeenth-century England sanctioned truth-telling, whether from the dwarf fools who played at court and who even went on diplomatic missions, or from preachers, whom divine authority allowed to step beyond the bounds of deference. Chaffinge addressed Philip directly:

> My Lord, let me take the boldenesse to tell you, that the eyes of the world are fastned on you; you cannot bee hid, your actions are not done in a corner, notice will be taken of all your Counsels, and your Counsellors, men are big with the expectation of you; and blame them not that they should be so, especially of you, who (besides others of your illustrious stock and linage well known) have had so pious and religious an *Aeneas* to your Brother, and so famous and valiant a *Hector* to your Vnckle.

This was the burden of inheritance: to have William Pembroke as a brother and Philip Sidney as an uncle was both a spur and a goad. 'Let the Piety and goodness of the one, and the valour and Cheualry of the other, serue as so many siluer watch-bels in your eares, to waken you to all Honourable and Noble atchieuements.'

There was an implication here, not stated, but clearly under-

Inigo Jones's drawing of a backdrop for *The Shepherd's Paradise*, (*above*) performed by the Queen and her ladies in 1633, may well be a sketch of the new Wilton then being designed by his associate and pupil, Isaac de Caus. De Caus's huge new garden at Wilton (*below*) appears lightly drawn in Inigo Jones's design, occupying the middle ground between the sinuous colonnade of parkland trees and the formality of the Palladian villa in the distance.

The great wedding portrait of the Pembrokes at Wilton, painted by van Dyck in late 1634 or early 1635. At the top left, the dead children of the family float on clouds. Below them, the three youngest brothers, William, John and James, look up to that heaven. In the centre, Lady Mary Villiers, the bride in white. Two steps above her, the boy she is marrying, Charles Lord Herbert, and his younger brother Philip, with whom she is in love.

Holding centre stage, Philip, earl of Pembroke and Montgomery, and his wife, Lady Anne
Clifford. On the right, the earl's daughter Anna Sophia and her husband, the high glamour
cavalier figure of Robert Dormer, earl of Carnarvon. Life for the Pembrokes would never
again seem as complete.

OPPOSITE The 50-year-old earl, looking tired and run-down, and Lady Anne Clifford his wife, aged 44. His left hand loosely holds the Lord Chamberlain's staff of office. Her gesture may signify that she cradles the ghost of a dead child in her arms.

The two young Herberts, Philip aged 13 and Charles 15, (*above*) both about to embark on a grand tour to Italy, dazzle in silks, a balanced pair of assertion and withdrawal.

The 12-year-old heiress, Lady Mary Villiers, daughter of the assassinated Duke of Buckingham , brought a £25,000 dowry to the marriage, the equivalent of 2,000 years of a Wiltshire shepherd's wages.

OPPOSITE Anna Sophia Herbert and her husband Robert Dormer, Earl of Carnarvon, both aged about 44. Anna Sophia holds the pearl of a living son, their heir Charles Dormer, between the fingers of her hand. He openly dabbles his fingers with hers.

The second earl of Carnarvon, aged about 12 in 1644 when painted by the young Peter Lely, a year or so after his father's death in the first battle of Newbury. Lely gives the boy clothes and a stance which echo his father's in the van Dyck wedding portrait. Behind him, what were once Arcadian boughs are now shattered by war.

stated, that Philip was not quite up to the mark. Was he not an indulger of physical and material passions?

> You liue in the face of a glorious Court, where your eyes are daily fill'd, as with Magnificence, so with Vanity; yet you shall doe well, otherwise, to cast them aside from such Gorgeous Spectacles, and sticke them in the shrowds and winding-sheetes of the dead. Nothing shall more humble you then this, and so nothing lift you neere Heauen then this . . .

That was the Puritan paradox: never more elevated than when self-abasing, and the paradox was never more heightened than when dealing with the great of the world, whose elevation was exceptionally fragile:

> None is your Peere now, but your Peere; yet the time shall come, when you and I shall be fellows; in the common bag of mortality, the Rooke in Checke-mate with the King.

> The theatres and scaffolds of the greatest eminency, whereon you great Potentates, and Grandees act your seuerall parts, either stand leaning and reeling on the quick-sand of Mutability, and Inconstancie, or else lie open and obnoxious to the wind of Disfauour, and Disgrace.

Anyone listening to this, with the memory in their mind of what happened to the Duke of Buckingham, would have experienced a shimmer of schadenfreude, a form of aesthetic and moral pleasure at the conventions of courtly life being so ruthlessly stripped away. The life of worldliness at court would always be anxious at its own instability; both God and Arcadia provided a refuge from it. That elision of categories is exactly what Chaffinge then embraced, drawing on the botany of the Bible, looking around him at the next generation of Herberts gathered in Baynard's Castle and, from the sound of it, knowing exactly the look and atmosphere of Wilton. William, the dead earl, was not dead.

He seems to liue (as it were) multiplied in an Honorable Brother, and many a sweet Nephew; and O may the dew of Heauen still lodge vpon those branches; let them spread forth as the Vallies, as Gardens by the Riuers side, as the Trees of Lign-aloes, which the Lord hath planted, and as Cedar trees besides the waters.

Gardens by the river's side, planted by these lords, and cedar trees beside the waters: that exactly and curiously describes the great south lawn at Wilton, where giant cedars still grow beside the clear, shallow waters of the Nadder. One of these cedars, which was felled in 1874, was found by the gardener Mr Challis to have 236 rings; it had been planted in 1638, certainly the oldest cedar tree in England. How had it got there? Edward Pococke, professor of Arabic at Oxford, the first great Arabic scholar in England, whose son later became chaplain to the Earls of Pembroke, had gone to Aleppo, to be the chaplain of the Levant Company, in the autumn of 1630. He returned to England, to Oxford, in 1636. In his baggage, he brought back seeds from the Cedars of Lebanon, kept some for himself and gave some to Philip, Earl of Pembroke. The dates fit exactly: are the vast looping limbs of the Wilton cedars William Pembroke's memorial, prefigured in Thomas Chaffinge's sermon, commissioned from Edward Pococke, brought back from the Lebanon, and planted by Philip to remember his brother and dignify Wilton's riverside lawns?

Chaffinge, once he had opened this vein of Arcadian Protestantism in his sermon, went on to explore and exploit it. England was anxious. It was like a 'darke, cold, stormy tempestuous night.' Wouldn't anyone envy William the dead man his peace? He was like a man 'a-bed and asleepe', while the rest of us were 'vp and awake', suffering the storms and troubles of existence. There was a possibility that 'the abomination of desolation, the idol of the Masse' would appear again in England. There was even the prospect of civil war again in England, 'of Ensigne borne against Ensigne, and Crosse against Crosse.' But William, lucky man, would see none of it.

We dreame of rest here, and contemplate vpon I know not what Elizian Fields, and Ayery Paradises vpon earth, whereas God knows, we haue here nought else but *desiderium quietis,* a desire to rest; onely in Heauen *quietum desideriorum,* rest to all our desires!

All worldly treasure is but mere beggary, all the pompe and glory of this earth, but dung and darknesse, all pleasures what-soeuer but nauseous and lothsome; in a word, All flesh is grasse, and the glory of it as the flower of that grasse, not *gramen* but *faenum,* withered grasse; withered before it be plucked up.

The whole Herbert family would have been in the congregation listening to Chaffinge's magnificent words. Surrounded by the pomp and glory of Baynard's Castle, they would have believed and also disbelieved what he had to say. They would have loved and not despised the 'Elizian Fields and Ayery Paradises' at Wilton, and would scarcely have considered the dazzling collection of paintings which Philip Pembroke was then already gathering as 'dung and darknesse'. All flesh may have been grass, but this world was also a real, if pale, reflection of a higher and more beautiful world. A painting, like a masque or a poem, could cross that boundary, could be both worldly and unworldly at the same time.

Chaffinge's congregation only had to look round them to see how, in the great infusion of Italianate beauty flooding into England in the 1620s and 30s, that high, delicate tentativeness of the beautiful could be captured on canvas. At some time in the 1630s, the pictures were probably moved to Wilton and then with the coming of the civil war to the Pembrokes' other London palace, Durham House on the Strand, but in 1630 Baynard's Castle was the great treasury of Italianate taste: Correggios, both oil paintings and sketches by Titian, including a particularly prized 'head of an old man', four or five figures said to be 'by Giorgione', a painting of the Four Seasons by Bassano, a 'ritratto of a Venetian looking sidewaise & showing a full body by Tintoretto il filio', a portrait of 'ye King of Spayne at length by Tizian as big as the life', and many others. These, with the van Dycks, were to create the Wilton atmosphere.

Philip's upbringing meant that his frame of mind had been formed in the rumbustious atmosphere of James's court and, at least according to Clarendon, something of that manner persisted in him. Clarendon – his enemy in the civil war – saw him as a clumsy oaf, a man left over from an earlier age, who got away with his rudeness and stupidity because he was rich and influential. He would make himself look more significant than he was by

> discoursing highly of justice and of the protestant religion, inveighing bitterly against Popery, and telling what he used to say to the King, and speaking frankly of the oversights of the court that he might not be thought a slave to it. He had been bred from his cradle in the Court, and had that perfection of a courtier, that, as he was not wary enough in offending men, so he was forward in acknowledging, even to his inferiors, and to impute it to his passion, and ask pardon for it; which made him to be thought a well-natured man. Besides, he had a choleric office, which entitled him to the exercise of some rudenesses, and the good order of the Court had some dependence on his incivilities.

This bitter and grudging description of one courtier by another was written by Clarendon many years afterwards from the despondency of failure and exile. But others wrote of Philip's kindness and grace. When opening deliveries of paintings from his agents in Italy, Charles chose to have Philip alongside him (with Inigo Jones and others) to judge the quality, something he had never done with William Pembroke. Even Clarendon, in a passage of his manuscript which he struck out of the published history, confessed that he felt 'great kindness for him and was never without a desire to serve him, having been formerly beholding to him for many civilities when there was so great a distance between their conditions.' He was in fact 'a man to be relied on in point of honour and fidelity.' Something of the complexity of Philip Herbert's real character emerges from that cancelled aside. He was both a civilised and an angry man.

The court over which as Lord Chamberlain he presided was a far more refined and controlled place than anything James I's courtiers would have known. Charles was an intensely pious person. He never went hunting in the morning before he had been at public prayers and would not tolerate even the lightest and wittiest of jokes about religion in his presence. A certain chillness had come about the court when he succeeded his father. 'He was not in his nature very bountiful,' even the hyper-loyal Clarendon later admitted. 'He paused too long in the giving, which made those to whom he gave, less sensible of the benefit.' He was insistent on a precision and orderliness at court. He liked quiet. He didn't enjoy the company of strangers nor of very confident men. Presumptuousness was the ultimate source of failure at the Caroline court, largely perhaps because Charles himself was not intellectually confident. There was a sense of inner weakness about him, which showed itself as a stiffness, a rigidity. He was, in fact, a cultural Puritan, disliking excess or even gaiety, once saying that the victory in a drinking contest of a particular earl – unspecified in Clarendon's story – was nothing to be proud of, and 'that he deserved to be hanged'. Soon afterwards, when the earl came 'into the room where his Majesty was, in some gayety, to shew how unhurt he was from the battle, the king sent one to bid him withdraw from his Majesty's presence; nor did he in some days after appear before him.'

The ramshackle warren of the old palace at Whitehall, where some 2000 rooms, many of them not redecorated since the 1550s, were surrounded by a labyrinth of closets, garrets and kitchens, would not have appealed to a king who required clarity, order, propriety and calm. Nor would the unfailingly public nature of his own existence have satisfied him. One instruction issued by Charles reveals the habits of a Jacobean court he hoped to reform: 'None of our bedchamber whatsoever are to follow us into our secret or privy room when we go to ease Ourself, but only our Groom of the Stool.'

A half-jokiness had hung about Arcadia in the world of *As You Like It*. By the 1630s, that had been replaced by an earnest sense of its perfections. The withdrawal from court to a life of – imagined – Arcadian purity, a return to the goodness of the old world, was something embraced by the court itself. The anti-courtly drive of Arcadianism was itself a courtly phenomenon, never more central to courtliness than in the pre-war years of Charles's reign. Throughout the early seventeenth century, proclamations had been made, 'commanding the repaire of Noblemen, knights and gentlemen of qualitie, unto their mansion houses in the Country, there to attend their services, and keepe Hospitalitie.' Just as the coherence of the kingdom depended on the largesse of the king, the workings of the country required the hospitality of the great lords in what was called their 'countries'. The urgency of these appeals heightened under Charles.

Whitehall 28 November 1627

> The Kings most excellent Majestie, taking unto his royall consideration the present state of the times, together with the great decay of Hospitality & good house-keeping, which in former ages was the honour of this nation, the too frequent resort, and ordinary residence of Lords spirituall and temporall, Knights and gentlemen of quality, unto cities and townes, especially into, or neare about the Cities of London and Westminster, and manifold inconveniences which ensue by the absence of so many persons of quality and authority from their countreys, whereby those parts are left destitute of both relief and government, hath thought fit hereby to renew the course formerly begun by his dear father of blessed memorie.

That was repeated in June 1632 and those lords who refused to obey it and remained in London for the summer were prosecuted and fined in 1634, 1635 and again in 1637. These are precisely the years when Wilton was transformed from a Tudor to a Palladian house. As Lord Chamberlain, Pembroke would have needed to be more responsive to this idea than any other. More than that, though, the courtly-Arcadian fusion, the creation of an Italianate pleasure house in the midst of the Elysian beauties of his chalkland estates, would have seemed by the early 1630s an inevitability. To make a palace in the trees was almost the only possible response to his inheritance.

John Aubrey's description of the new Wilton's origins is full of clues. 'King Charles the first did love Wilton above all places,' Aubrey wrote, 'and came thither every summer. It was he that did put Philip first [*sic*] Earle of Pembroke upon making this magnificent garden and grotto, and to new build that side of the house that fronts the garden, with two stately pavilions at each end, all "al Italiano".' Philip's remaking of Wilton was not as a classical building but Italian, urged on by the king, part of the same cultural world as Titian and Tintoretto, even as Sannazaro's original Italian *Arcadia*. The old Tudor palace, larded with Henry's elaborate armorial glass and escutcheons, was hopelessly out of date, a remnant of the faux-chivalric world to which they had all subscribed twenty years before but which now seemed flat-footed and unsophisticated. The king's suggestion was first of all a summer idea: the new Wilton was not to be a pompous prodigy house of the kind which the earlier generation had built, but a light and elegant thing. And the first element was to be the garden and grotto.

The scheme devised and installed by the Fleming Isaac de Caus – 'the fat Dutch keeper hereof, a rare Artist,' according to Lieutenant Hammond on his 1635 visit – was huge, stretching a thousand feet from the house, but for all its scale, the garden was playful. De Caus was an associate of Inigo Jones. He had already worked on the Banqueting House in Whitehall and had built a grotto in the undercroft there. His work on the Wilton garden began in 1632 and peaked in 1634. There were long gravel walks with pots of flowers, embroidered platts, and marble fountains, marble statues standing within the fountains, long covered arbours and raised terraces from which the plan could be viewed. Female deities, a statue of Susanna, perhaps in memory of Philip's dead wife, and the pair of Bacchus and Flora, the deities of fullness and fruitiness, loomed over the beds. At the far end a huge bronze Roman gladiator stood surrounded by cherry trees. Beyond him was a vaulted grotto in which the passage of the water through pipes could be made to imitate the singing of nightingales and 'Monsieur de Caus' could somehow, by a secret he never shared, make rainbows appear to the visitors. Elaborate underground and underwater machinery could make stone swans swim and stone balls float. No expense was spared but gaiety rather than grandeur was the effect, a realm of delight through which the Nadder flowed. In the 1690s, when Celia Fiennes visited, the sequence of gardens was still 'very fine with many gravel walkes with grass squaires, set with fine brass and stone statues – fish ponds and basons with Figures in ye middle spouting out water – dwarfe trees of all sorts and a fine flower garden – much wall fruite.'

If all of this seems like the background to a masque made real, that is an effect which was also apparent at the time. This family had appeared in one performance after another at Whitehall. In 1631 Pembroke had played the 'Judicious Lover' and his son-in-law the Earl of Carnarvon the 'Valiant' in Ben Jonson's *Love's Triumph*; the earl's two eldest sons, Charles, Lord Herbert and Philip Herbert, had come on in *Tempe Restored* in February 1632, as two of the children portraying 'the influences of the stars on divine beauty'.

Right in the middle of the garden's construction period in the early 1630s, one of the most expensive masques ever staged, *The Shepherd's Paradise*, was designed by Inigo Jones and performed by the queen and her ladies in Somerset House on Twelfth Night in 1633. The masque lasted an interminable seven or eight hours, was largely inaudible and was celebrated as one of the most boring explorations of Platonic purity ever devised, but two of its back-drops, for which drawings survive at Chatsworth, seem to bear an extraordinary relationship to Wilton. The first is labelled by Jones 'The Shepherds Paradise'. Behind the dancing masquers, the courtly audience would have seen a colonnade of park-like trunks receding from them. The trees are loose and easily flowing. They provide a frame for the view of the great house in the way that a formal colonnade would have done – and did in other masques designed by Jones – but here the lines have become sinuous, and seductive. This is order so orderly that it can afford to let any stiffness go. The trees have about them that elegant, relaxed poise of *sprezzatura*, a form of disdain or carelessness, the grace that comes from inner nobility, the charm of effortlessness. This cultivated wildness approaches to within hailing distance of the great house. Beyond the trees, and within their embrace, one sees the palace itself as a model of classical restraint, of exactness and overt order, with an elegant and neatly laid-out garden in front of it. Jones drew this as de Caus was building the great Renaissance garden but probably before any work had begun to transform the house. The house he has drawn is not as Wilton would emerge in a few years' time, but it is not unconnected to it, with its two terminal pavilions and central emphasis, but the relationship of house, garden, hill and park is identical. It seems at least possible that in this sketch of paradise, the form to be taken by the new Wilton first emerged. Before anything had appeared in stone or mortar, the image of Wilton had already floated before the eyes of the court as part of a shepherd's paradise.

Inigo Jones was certainly involved from the start. As the royal architect, for a rebuilding which was the king's idea, he was the natural choice. He certainly knew the Herberts. There is a remote chance that he may have travelled to Italy with William Pembroke as a very young man, but in later life he certainly knew both brothers well. As successive Lords Chamberlain, they would have dealt with him regularly over his masques. He had also been to Wilton long before, when in 1620 James I had been staying there and their conversation had turned to Stonehenge, ten miles north of Wilton on the edge of Salisbury Plain. William Pembroke had sent for Jones to investigate the monument. He soon realised it was Roman. The Ancient Britons had been incapable of art. It was the Romans who 'gave first rise to civility in this island' and so Stonehenge could not be druidical, nor an emanation of the soil, but was clearly the imposing on a wild, ancient country of an imperial idea. It was not recognisably Roman in its decorations, but that was deliberate. The Romans chose a form of architecture, the Tuscan Order, 'best agreeing with the rude, plain, simple nature of those they intended to instruct. [And] of this *Tuscan Order*, a plain, grave, and humble manner of *Building*, very solid and strong, Stoneheng principally consists.'

Jones's analysis of the Bronze Age monument reveals his cast of mind: civilisation came from abroad, in fact from Italy. There was no point in looking for home-grown models for architecture, but the classical system could, nevertheless, happily adapt itself to local circumstances. The massively-eaved barn of a church he built in Covent Garden was chunky and Tuscan in its style, deliberately avoiding the kind of finesse which in the early 1630s might have smelled of Roman Catholicism. And the great south front of Wilton also chooses a simplicity and lack of show, an external sobriety, which is more suitable to a palace in the trees than enrichment and elaboration. A drawing does survive of a much grander elevation for Wilton, 400 feet long, double its present length and with a large central portico and pediment. There is no evidence that it was ever seriously considered, although that greater length of façade would have aligned itself more easily with the scale of the de Caus garden.

Work on the house probably began in 1635, even as the garden was being finished. An entry in the Pembroke household accounts for 1634–5 mentions a contractor, Antony Hinton, gentleman, who was paid £1200, 'for works building the new garden and the lord Earl's house at Wilton by order of the lord Earl.' Inigo Jones himself was busy completing the Queen's House at Greenwich and so de Caus was instructed to 'take downe the side of Wilton House which is towards the garden & such other parts as shall be necessary & rebuild it anew with additions according to ye Plott which is agreed.' A Mr Brookes was told first 'to remove all the stuffe in ye roomes & Lodgeings of that side of the house which is to bee pulled down and rebuilt.'

Beyond that, the actual building history of Wilton remains fairly obscure. A catastrophic fire in 1647, which began, according to Aubrey, after fires had been lit 'for airing of the roomes', destroyed this part of the house. If you climb into the attics above the Single and Double Cubes, you will find alongside the massive adzed carpentry of the new 1640s roofs signs of the catastrophe: burnt bricks, sooted plaster and the stub ends of the oak joists still in the walls. The joists have turned to charcoal where they met the air, but you can dig them out and still find, where the brick protected them, the clean sawn 1630s estate oak. But there is no telling if the rooms as they were rebuilt in the late 1640s and 1650s resembled what had been here before the fire. On top of that, major alterations to Wilton were made in the eighteenth and nineteenth centuries and it is no longer possible to be sure that Wilton's great rooms are real Stuart interiors or later pastiches.

Nevertheless, Inigo Jones was certainly involved in the 1640s rebuilding, which was largely done by his pupil and nephew, John Webb, and there is no doubt that if not in detail at least in atmosphere Wilton still reeks of that moment in English taste and sensibility. It remains the central Arcadian statement in England, a masque made real.

Philip Pembroke enriched the house with every picture he could. There were many inherited from his father and perhaps his grandfather: ministers and heroes from Queen Elizabeth's time, some of King Henry the Eighth, the Earl of Essex. But to them he added a great Italianate upper storey: Charles I on horseback by van Dyck and a lifesize picture of Peacock, his favourite white racehorse, 'to both of which Sir Anthony gave many master touches'. Perhaps among the first collectors in England to do so, he also brought the great modern pictures by Titian, van Dyck and Giorgione down from London.

An inventory made of the house in November 1683, on the death of the seventh earl, and preserved among the Pembroke papers, gives some sense of the enormous riches gathered at Wilton. The inventory roams through 158 separate apartments laden with goods and tapestry hangings, pictures and furniture, which if nothing else marks the oceanic gulf between the life-conditions of this family and those scratching their existence in the chalkland valleys they could see from their windows. If there is a certain boniness and paucity in the copyholders' possessions, here you can scarcely move for material goods: 'a Ffustian quilt', 'a blew damask carpet', pair after pair of silk tapestry hangings, chairs covered in black damask, a Purple Room with a purple damask bed, a silver table and looking-glass, cloth-of-silver curtains and a headcloth to the bed embroidered with gold, a close stool and three pads for it, Turkey carpets and warming pans, an Indian quilt, a crimson velvet sideboard cloth, cloth-of-gold cushions with gold fringes, maps, folios and volumes, 'rich China bowls tippt and bottomed with silver', one Book of Common Prayer and one Bible, both embossed with the family arms in silver, one Japan China teapot and enormous quantities of wine in the barrel. Among it all, part of the 'Goods belonging to the Dyning Room', alongside '1 set of Elbow chairs' and '4 stools of shaggy purple', was 'The picture of the family & other pictures in ye Dining Roome', together thought to be worth £1200, by far the most valuable thing in the house. It was by van Dyck and is the greatest painting of a family ever made in England. It represents the climax of this family's fortunes, of this book and of the Arcadian story it has pursued.

If this was the exquisite frame, its vital contents were the family itself. As much as for Shakespeare in the early sonnets addressed to Will Herbert, there could be no meaning in riches if there were no heirs to enjoy them. Philip had been careful to assemble his family. Three children had died young, with great sorrow for the parents, in the years before 1620. But many others had survived. His daughter Anna Sophia had married his ward, the enormously rich Robert Dormer, who in 1628 had become the Earl of Carnarvon. Charles, Lord Herbert, and his brothers Philip, William, James and John, were the boys Thomas Chaffinge had referred to so encouragingly in his sermon. After the Duke of Buckingham was assassinated, his daughter Mary Villiers and her brothers had come to live with the Herberts, as her mother had married a wild Irish Roman Catholic lord and the king did not want the Villiers children brought up Catholic.

To this ensemble, after the death of his first wife Susan, Philip added one of the most intriguing figures of Stuart England: Lady Anne Clifford, the Dowager Countess of Dorset. By the time she married Philip, in June 1630, only two weeks after William had finally been buried in Salisbury Cathedral, she had suffered years of bullying and denial by her first husband, her relations, by the king and by the court in general. She was a product of the greatest of English families, her mother a Russell, her cousin the Earl of Bedford and her father the Elizabethan buccaneer, George Clifford, Earl of Cumberland, tournament champion, captain of the *Bonadventure* against the Spanish Armada in 1588, conqueror of the Spanish at Puerto Rico and the winner of the golden prize Henry Pembroke had offered for his first horse race on the Wilton downs in the 1590s.

The Clifford earls of Cumberland had been the great medieval magnates of the north-west, one generation after another dying in battle. They controlled vast estates in the Pennines and the Lake District. Those lands always descended to the 'heir of the body' of the current earl, regardless of the heir's sex. Anne Clifford's father died 'of a bloody flux' without a son in 1605. He left his lands to his brother.

For decades, Anne and her mother waged a legal battle to recover them, gathering stupendous piles of ancient documents by which to prove her rights to them, compiling biographies of those noble ancestors, becoming an authority on the ancient constitution by which the great magnates of medieval England had maintained their independence of the crown. In 1609, she married the spendthrift rake, Richard Sackville, Earl of Dorset, who sided with her enemies in trying to coerce her into surrendering her claim on lands that were rightfully hers. Dorset tried every way he could to make her conform to his and her uncle's patriarchal dominance: threats of separation, refusal to sleep with her when she knew she was fertile, shaming her in public by flirting with his mistress Lady Penniston, cancelling her jointure – the income from the lands to which she would have a right if he died before her – terrorising her servants, and taking away from her the daughter on whom she doted.

She was tiny, 4 feet 10 inches tall, but indomitable. James's Queen Anne gave her 'warning not to trust my matters absolutely to the King lest he should deceive me', and when confronted with the demands of the Cumberlands as voiced by the king himself in 1617, she stood up to him with a courage that is astonishing for a twenty-seven-year-old woman, even more so with the court largely ranged against her. 'I beseech'd his Majesty to pardon me for that I would never part from Westmorland while I lived upon any condition whatsoever.'

Unsurprisingly, her spirits had often sunk under the relentless pressure and lack of respect. Retreating towards the comfort of a diary, she was often 'sad to see things go so ill with me'. She bore Dorset five children, two girls who survived, and three sons all of whom 'dyed young at Knowle in Kent, where they were born'. After Dorset himself died in 1624, she came into her jointure of £2000 a year, but Dorset's own heir and brother continued to persecute her and her troubles deepened when she suffered a violent attack of smallpox 'which disease did so marter my face that it Confirmed more and more my mynd never to marrie againe.'

This was the woman Philip Herbert married at the Bedford house of Chenies on 1 June 1630. There were many surprised that he married her at all: a forty-year-old, ravaged by smallpox, with the reputation for independence of mind and pugnacity of spirit. And why should she, a woman perfectly well provided for, enter into a marriage with a man whose own reputation was not entirely sweet-smelling? Partly, there were material considerations: her income from the Sackville lands, his enormous wealth (an income of perhaps £20,000 a year) and his position at court. Gossip was against them: 'nor did there want divers malitious illwillers to Blow and foment the Coals of discontent betwixt us,' she wrote much later. But there were also many aspects of their two backgrounds which would have brought them together. Both would have considered they came from the ancient, not the modern, court aristocracy. Both had been tutored by the poet Samuel Daniel in their youths. The works of Edmund Spenser, Sir Philip Sidney and Michael Drayton – all of them part of the Pembroke circle of patronage, all of them Arcadianists – were in her library. She even erected and paid for a monument in Westminster Abbey to Spenser, who had been her mother's protégé. Both families had longstanding connections to John Donne, who enjoyed her company. She could talk of anything, Donne once said, 'from slea-silk to predestination', the whole range of existence from God's mind to the kind of fluffy silk which would ball up like cotton wool. It is not inconceivable that this marriage was more than a corporate alliance and that these two battle-scarred veterans of the court world saw in each other the possibilities of happiness.

This is the family portrayed in the great van Dyck portrait. In 1634, the long-laid plans for the wedding of Mary Villiers and Charles Herbert had come into focus. The convoluted, debt-ridden Buckingham estate was finally to be granted probate in March 1635 and the prospect of that tangle being resolved may have prompted the earl into action. Equally, his fifteen-year-old-son Charles was approaching the age when he would be sent abroad with a tutor to visit Italy. In July 1634, Mary's mother the Duchess of Buckingham settled on the heads of an agreement with the earl. Swaths of Pembroke lands in Dorset, Glamorgan, Monmouth and Wiltshire were to be transferred to the young couple in return for the £25,000 Mary would bring in her wake. Then, very nearly, disaster struck. Mary began to fall in love not with the intended heir, Charles, but with his younger brother. 'The young lady began to affect the younger brother Philip Herbert,' George Garrard, a court gossip, wrote, 'and of herself warned the Chamberlain, that she might marry him, saying he did apply himself to her more than my lord Herbert did; but the dutchess chid her out of that humour, and now she is marrid that affection will vanish.'

Although Anne Clifford's daughter would later refuse the hand of a younger Herbert, this particular twelve-year-old girl was not going to shipwreck the elaborate corporate deal. The ceremony was eventually conducted at the end of Christmas 1634 'by the Archbishop of Canterbury in the closet at Whitehall. It was done privately, and few invited, and sooner than was intended.'

The financial details had not been settled and were not to be until the following May when a huge vellum document, with four blobs of sealing wax, each the size of a squash ball and deeply impressed with the seals of the participating parties, was finally signed: Mary's mother and stepfather, the Earl of Antrim, the Earl of Northampton (a courtier), Pembroke himself, Sir Thomas Morgan of Wilton and Ruperra and Sir John Thorowgood of London (a government official) all witnessed the transfer and commitment of lands and money 'in consideration of a marriage heretofore had and solemnized.'

The money flows were enormous. The earl was to assign all his lands in Wiltshire, Dorset, Somerset, Monmouth and Glamorgan to his son, keeping for himself only an interest in them for the rest of his life. There could, in other words, be no going back on what he now agreed to give to the new couple. The duchess, for her part, agreed to give her daughter 'twentie thousand pounds of lawfull money of England'. She would pay it in instalments of £4000 a year for five years, beginning at Michaelmas 1634. In addition, Lady Mary was to hand over £5000 from another inheritance, her grandfather's, which she had already received. The earl agreed to spend this money, plus an additional £15,000 of his own, on lands which he was going to give to the children and which would provide Lady Mary with the £4000 a year jointure after Charles died. If either of them died 'after the said intended marriage and before cohabitation or before the said Lady Mary shall atteyne the age of sixteene yeares', then the whole deal was off. All money was to be repaid to the duchess and the earl was free of his obligations to either his son or Lady Mary. The deal was to be concluded 'by making of conveyances and assurances by Counsell learned on both sides before Xmas next, as convenientlie as may be done.' There was no thought whatsoever that these two people, aged fifteen and twelve, would sleep together until they were substantially older, perhaps not for the next four years.

One other development had occurred in these busy months: Pembroke's marriage to Lady Anne Clifford had collapsed. She had resisted his claims over her lands in the north. He had refused the claim she would traditionally have made over a third of his lands after he died and together they signed a document, in which each stated their position:

> Wee are content to referre the consideration of the reason-ablenss of theis propositions, & what may be fitt to be done thereupon, unto the Rt Honble the Lord Priuy seale [a judge, the Earl of Manchester], & the Earle of Bedford [Anne's cousin and longstanding ally] & what they shall advise wee will per-forme and obsirue
>
> > Pembroke Montgomery
> > Anne Pembroke

But this was only a symptom of a deeper underlying malaise. Anne Clifford had been shaped by her sufferings. It is no coincidence that she became a diarist, because her life had turned into one of withdrawal and privacy. 'I stay'd much in the Country,' she had written when with Lord Dorset at Knole, 'having many times a sorrowfull & heavy heart, and being condemn'd by most folks because I would not consent to the agreement [with her husband], so as I may truly say I am like an owl in the desert.' It would turn out no better with Pembroke.

> The marble pillars of Knowle in Kentt and Wilton in Wiltshire were to me often times but the gay Harbours of Anguish. Insomuch as a Wiseman that knew the inside of my fortune

would often say that I lived in both those my Lordes great familyes as the river Roan [Rhone] or Rodamus runs thorow the Lake of Geneva, without mingleinge anie part of its streames with that Lake; For I gave myselfe wholly to Retyredness, as much as I could, in both those great families, and made good Bookes and verteous thoughts my Companions.

She had retired not into widowhood but into diaryhood, an exceptionally rare condition in the early seventeenth century, a river running unmingled through the waters of a family. Two further levels of unhappiness should be added to this picture. At some time in December 1634, in the days before the wedding between his son, Charles, and Mary Villiers, Pembroke ejected Anne Clifford from his lodgings at Whitehall. From then on, at least for the next fifteen years, she was to live in one of his houses in Wiltshire or London, but only rarely with him. The immediate cause is unknown, but the context is more pitiable still. Anne became pregnant twice with Philip Herbert, bearing 'two sons that were born both before their time while I lived at Whitehall'. Both premature sons died at birth.

It is sometimes assumed that the frequent death of children in pre-modern England caused no grief in their parents. That is untrue. No explicit record remains of Anne's reaction to the death of these Herbert sons, but there is a letter from her mother, the Countess of Cumberland, written on the death of a son and heir of her own, Robert Clifford. Half-coherent with grief, it is addressed to the family chaplain and translator of the King James Bible, Dr John Layfield:

Oh miserable woman wretched in the hope of my Life, to loose a Child of that hope, of that Love, to mee a Rose, that sweet Robin pulled before the tyme, the only sonne of his Mother, tormented with sicknesse, so many weeks before. Oh troubles come in by floods my deare Lord in dangers unknown for number myself sonneless, my honnour brought down, my poverty increased my misfortunes to my enemy's laid open they gain, when I loose.

It does not take much to extend that heartfelt grief to the daughter.

These are the circumstances in which, as the 1652 list of the pictures described it, the 'mighty large piece of the Ea of Pembrooke and all his family by Vandyke' was made. Everything in this long history can be seen to contribute to its meaning. Its strange and enigmatic qualities become clearer in the light of the family's story.

The painting is a drama of fertility, time and death, much of its meaning carried by a subtle ballet of the hands which moves across the whole surface of the picture. The Earl and Countess of Carnarvon, on the right, are already the parents of a young heir, Charles, born two years before. They glow with sexuality and health: Anna Sophia's bosom is deeply revealed and between her fingers she holds a single pearl, standing for the precious heir which she and her husband have conceived. Their hands dabble together in an unmistakably sexual way, the only sign of human contact in the painting. Theirs is the realm of fecundity and fullness. But still their eyes do not meet. No member of the family, in fact, looks at any other. Each is alone in his glorious world and none is more glorious than her husband, Robert Dormer, Earl of Carnarvon, at this stage in his life a traveller and gambler, a notorious womaniser and rake, and a man filled with the vigour of an active life.

Next to that fertile and engaging pair is its opposite: the hands of the countess are folded together in a way that is repeated nowhere else in the entire body of van Dyck's work: an explicit gesture of enclosure and melancholy, shut off from those around her. The marriage of the Earl and Countess of Pembroke, both of them shadowed and pushed back within the picture, is barren. Her sons have died and their relationship has failed. Her averted eyes and her folded hands are the gestures of a woman who is no longer 'mingleinge anie part of [her] streames' with this family. She is central but absent, her gaze indirect, her relationship with everyone around her cut away and inarticulate.

Beside her, but not touching her, the earl, Lord Chamberlain, the high official who ran the royal household, holds his white staff of office easily in the relaxed and lengthened fingers of his left hand. With his other hand, he reaches forward to the virginal promise of Mary Villiers, gesturing openly and generously towards the heart of the young woman, who is to marry his son. These are the signs of power. She, however, holds a closed hand to her womb, a self-preservation even as she is to be married. In the picture space she is nearly but not quite connected to Charles, Lord Herbert, in red, who holds his left arm out as if in love, an openness to the world, but the hand itself is reflexed and withdrawn, perhaps also a sign of his virginity.

These three pairs make a diagrammatic set: fertility achieved, barrenness accepted, breeding promised. The younger brother Philip, sharing with his brother the reddish-brown hair which had come down through the generations, hangs back on the edge of this group of six, not part of it and not quite distinct. Is it too much to see in his portrayal the story recounted by George Garrard, of love disappointed, of his place in Mary Villiers's heart usurped by his older brother not because love required it but simply because their father and her mother insisted? And is there an element, in Mary Villiers's own look of disdain, of a discontent with this marriage which was forced upon her for dynastic reasons?

The final elements are the two sets of three children on the left of the painting. The three young Herbert boys on the ground are gloriously alive with their hounds and their books. The three young Herberts who died as children are here above them as angels, throwing roses into the wedding party. The painting as a whole flickers between content and discontent, between a celebration of the beauty of existence and a recognition of its sorrows and travails. As a whole it is not unlike Thomas Chaffinge's sermon on mutability, time, beauty, inheritance and grief. Behind them all, Arcadia recedes into an inscrutable perfection.

The painter was a man of the world, ambitious, rich and realistic, and this painting is also part of that urban, entrepreneurial world. If a sitter could not pay for his portrait – van Dyck usually charged

£50 to £60 for a full-length (three years' stipend for a country vicar), £30 for a half-length and £20 for a head and shoulders; the Wilton group portrait cost more than £500 – he would quite happily sell it to someone else. Those who required portraits from him had to book a series of appointments in advance. He would never paint a sitter for longer than an hour at a time and would usually have assistants complete the painting once the head and hands were done. Sitters sent their clothes to the studio where hired models posed in them and Flemish specialists, employed by van Dyck, painted the sumptuous cloths. There was something of a factory about it, but during the precious hours in which the master's eye was engaged with his subject, van Dyck's easy manners and self-possession encouraged in those who stood before him what was called at the time 'an eloquence of the body', a poise, a form of bodily control which implied spiritual and social distinction.

As they stood within the lit circle, van Dyck charmed them as a photographer might. The way these people appear in his paintings was the way he encouraged them to appear in that discriminating atmosphere. Preliminary sketches of the two Carnarvons have survived: between those sketches and the finished oil painting, van Dyck simplified some details of clothing, loosening and romanticising it, but he did not change substantially the way the people stood or looked. These are portraits not inventions, even if what they portray was as much an aspiration as a reality.

Here then, consciously drawing on roots which dive many generations and many decades back into the English past, is the climax of this Arcadian civilisation. Its regal air intersects with a subtle, individualised psychology. Its subject is nobility, but its method questions the simplicity of that word. For all the charm of its presentation, its alluring surface, this is not a trivial or decorative object. It is about power and vulnerability and its dressing of that power in these silks is itself an Arcadian act. Its governing paradox is that the man at the centre, the ageing earl, the most weakly portrayed figure on the canvas, is the man who is making all the decisions. Time is conquering him. Van Dyck would paint him again, two or three years later, worn down, sitting heavily within the frame, the vitality of hope ebbed out of him.

Overall, the atmosphere of the painting is not quite secure. There is nothing cruel in it, nor even unkind, but it is full of uncertainty, hesitation and even surprise, a tentativeness which makes complacency impossible. Where are they? Not in a comfortable interior, as they would have been in both the sixteenth century and the eighteenth, but half inside and half out, half in a theatre, half in the margins of a palace. Nor is there a settled middle to it. What seems to be central flickers from the earl and countess to the young Mary Villiers who stands before them. The geometrical centre in fact hovers in the awkward space between her head and the body of Charles, the young lord in red, a charged absence at the heart of the painting.

Once you become alert to this sense of insecurity in the painting, it seems pervasive. Look at Philip, the younger of the two glamorous young Herberts, wearing the colour called 'carnation' in the seventeenth century. There is no ease in him. His pose is uncertain and his face unsure. A little less edgily, his elder brother stands beside him, performing it seems to nothing but the air. Only the three young boys at the left-hand side, framed by their dogs, a greyhound and a setter, are immune to this atmosphere, yet to enter the world of knowingness, sophistication and uncertainty inhabited by their elders. (But even the dogs carry a signal: the ownership of setters and greyhounds was made illegal by a royal proclamation in 1638. Any greyhound found within ten miles of the court was to be hanged. Their presence here could also be taken as a statement of lordly independence from royal autocracy.)

Each of their hands in turn gives, blesses, meets, contains, promises, protects, challenges and suggests. There is a play here to do with love, family, selfhood, engagement and distance, between closedness and openness, intimacy and removal, spread across the whole width of the picture. They are the signals fitted to this particular moment, a marriage but not yet a sexual union, which will have to wait until both bride and groom are older.

Van Dyck had a famous and treasured ability to give a scene the sense that it was a caught moment, to imply from his nearly mobile figures that within a second their perfect arrangement would change and collapse. It is a stilled dance. Transience was at the centre of his art and here it is set against its opposite. Behind the figures, two enormous certainties preside: the landscape of perfection on the left, receding into deep-shadowed calm, and in the centre-right, the vast coat of arms on the cloth which hangs behind them all, the inheritance of nobility, an assertion of the permanence from which they come. But do those certainties transmit themselves to the anxious figures in the foreground? Or do they serve to throw those figures into question? How do the two glorious young men really compare to the solidity and fixity of the two fluted columns behind them? They seem momentary beings by comparison, balanced on the balls of their feet, no more lasting or substantial than the clouds or the putti or the fading of the sunset.

The beauty and allure of this picture lie in its central acknowledgement that complacency and fineness cannot co-exist. The highest condition, it seems to say, is one of uncertainty and doubt. Questioning forms of irony and intelligence are applied here to a conventional ideal. The sense of movement and of the contingent in van Dyck's baroque masterpieces is the embodiment of that uncertainty. A body that hesitates between the steps of a platform, that makes a gesture which is at the same time withheld, that displays a sense of grace but does so in shadow: these are the ambivalent qualities to which one instinctively still responds. Look beneath the surface of this painting and you see in it not a story of worldly glory but of transience and fragility, of failure and disconnection, of the place of death and the erosion of time even in the most perfect circumstances. This is a painting which might be entitled 'Et in Arcadia Ego'. But that poignancy of decline and infertility is not the only meaning here. Its light falls not on a tomb but on the beautiful, pale, glowing optimism of the young faces for whom the future holds out buoyant promise.

The portrait was probably finished by the end of May 1635. By then, Pembroke had arranged that 'Lord Charles Herbert of Cardiff and his brother Philip Herbert Esquire sons of the Earl of Pembroke and Montgomery are by His Majesty's Licence going into France to travel.'

The commander of the fleet in the Channel was instructed by the Lords of the Admiralty 'to cause some of the ships of the fleet to transport the Lord Chamberlain's sons to Dieppe' and on 6 June 1635, the *Swallow* carried them there. They were on their way to Italy, the heartland of the civilization with which their father was in love.

In the middle of March 1636, nine months after the two boys had left England for the continent, the news reached London. They had been staying in Venice. Philip wrote a 'thank you' letter to Lord Feilding, Buckingham's nephew and the English ambassador, for the 'excessive courtesies and great civilitie' he had shown to his boys when they were there. They had moved on to Florence and in that city, just after Christmas, Charles, Lord Herbert died of smallpox. The earl 'took the news most grievously' and did not emerge from his rooms in the Cockpit at Whitehall for more than a week. Van Dyck's painting of a wedding had become an epitaph.

It has often been said that the death of Charles ruined the earl's financial prospects because the great £25,000 Villiers dowry was withdrawn on his death. But that misunderstands the nature of the marriage agreement, which was designed to be equal on both sides. Mary Villiers's mother would no longer have to produce the money but Philip, Earl of Pembroke would no longer have to give the jointure of £4000 a year to his widowed daughter-in-law. The deal had been balanced and works at Wilton did not stop at Charles's death. The earl's annual income, including the £6000 a year from his deranged sister-in-law, was now about £30,000 (at a time when it was possible to build a perfectly good manor house for £150).

There is, in fact, a slight and poignant memorial at Wilton to Charles's disappearance from the scene. In the hunting room, decorated with painted panels derived from Antonio Tempesta's scenes of different forms of hunt around the world – the bludgeoning of crocodiles and the sticking of ostriches, men hiding from their prey dressed as cows, or underwater wearing rock-like hats to trick the wild duck – the painter Edward Pierce inserted here and there images of the fourth earl and his heir. The boy who is represented was not Charles, but the younger brother Philip, who had risen to take his place.

Mary Villiers was still at Wilton and van Dyck painted her in 1636 as a fourteen-year-old widow, low in the picture space, black bows on her bosom and at her waist for her dead husband, a rose in her hand as a sign she would marry again. The king wanted her back at court but Mary was refusing, even as early as March 1636, to succumb. Within eighteen months, she had married the king's cousin, James Stuart, Duke of Lennox, a young and naive Scotsman, 'of small experience in affairs', fiercely loyal to the crown – Clarendon would later write of his 'unspotted fidelity' and 'entire resignation of himself to the King'. Mary brought him her £25,000 dowry, and in doing that this high-spirited and strong-willed woman swam out of the Pembrokes' lives.

12

The most I can look for is to scape undoing

The break-up of Arcadian England
1640–1650

THE GREAT van Dyck portrait was the high tidemark of the Pembroke Arcadia. At least on the surface, the 1630s had been a moment of contentment. England then, Lord Clarendon would later write in his silky Augustan phrase-making, had been 'the garden of the world', blessed with 'the greatest calm and the fullest measure of felicity that any people in any age, for so long time together, have been blessed with', enjoying 'a full, entire undisturbed peace', glowing in 'the general composure of men's minds'. Compared with the situation in Europe, where Germany in the Thirty Years War was 'weltering in its own blood', Great Britain was a haven of civility. Scotland was at peace, Ireland had been 'reduced to profitable husbandry', England was rich, 'flourishing with learned and extraordinary men', where government revenue was higher than ever, the navy stronger, the king 'the greatest example of sobriety, chastity and mercy that any prince hath been endowed with'. England was 'a pleasant promontory' from which the general grief of Europe could be surveyed.

But there were undercurrents, the calm was illusory and at the end of the decade profound discontents broke into the open. The integration of court and country on which the Pembrokes had based their lives for so long, and of which Wilton was the symbol as the Palace in the Trees, now began to fall apart. At the parliaments which Charles was forced to call in 1640 in order to fund his wars against the Scottish Presbyterians, Philip Pembroke, who was natur-

ally sympathetic to the Scots, re-assembled much of the old parliamentary grouping, perhaps a dozen MPs, which his brother had
used against Buckingham in the 1620s. Now, along with the radical
party in the House of Commons, they turned against two ministers,
the Earl of Strafford and Archbishop Laud, the executives of court
power and of the anti-Puritan church, both loved by the king, both
feared and hated by the country. The king's personal rule through
these ministers had begun to feel like the betrayal of a contract.

All over England the old arrangements began to break up. In
May 1640, Pembroke's son-in-law Robert Dormer, the Earl of
Carnarvon, was trying to raise the militia in Buckinghamshire for
the Scottish war, but was meeting with little but reluctance from a
gentry who had been subjected to forced loans and 'new unheard-of
taxes' and were not now interested in paying for the king's desire to
spread a Laudian church to Scotland.

> Concerning our soldiers, I make no question they will be
> forewith very well clothed, but I do not see a possibility of
> procuring the draught horses, the country is so averse to paying
> ready money. I have sent out my warrants twice, and met the
> country twice, but they will part with no money.

In Wiltshire it was worse. Pembroke and his sons accompanied the
king to the north but other Wiltshire gentry sent money at best.
Some refused to do that. In the summer of 1640, soldiers were
pressed from all across the county. John Nicholas, successor to Sir
Thomas Morgan as steward of the Pembroke estates, wrote to his
son Edward, clerk to the Privy Council in Whitehall. John was in
the family house at Winterbourne Earls in the beautiful valley of
the Bourne just north of Salisbury. 'It begins to be bad enough
here,' he wrote on 1 June 1640.

> Yesterday, being Sunday, a company of soldiers which were
> pressed [for the war against the Scots], about Martin and
> Damerham, in Wilts., [on the southern slope of the downs
> south of Broad Chalke] passing through our parish towards
> Marlborough, where the rendezvous is appointed, took all they

could catch in their way, and being resisted by the owners of such poultry and other provisions as they took, they beat many very sorely and at Idminston [Idmiston, a couple of miles up the valley from Winterbourne Earls] cut off the hand of one Nott, and hurt another very dangerously . . . There were but five soldiers, they came by my house as I was at dinner, and asked for victuals, and your mother sent them a piece of beef and beer enough, wherewith they were well pleased; yet after this they did the mischief. It is an ill beginning . . . I wish you would take more time to stay with us than you have done heretofore.

That image of the hand of the poor chalkland farmer Robert Nott – he died in 1660 – being sliced off by a small platoon of passing soldiers introduces the 1640s, as if the gentleness and expressiveness of the hands in the Pembroke family portrait, the linking gestures between them, had turned instead to this.

The world had darkened. The king's use of his prerogative powers in the 1630s had thrown the entire basis of the state into question. 'We must not only sweep the house clean below,' John Pym, the leader of the radical party in the House of Commons, told Edward Hyde, one of the old Pembroke adherents, that summer. 'We must pull down all the cobwebs which hang in the top and corners, that they might not breed dust, and so make a foul house hereafter; we now have the opportunity to make our country happy, by removing all grievances, and pulling up the causes of them by the roots.'

This was the deepest possible change. The cluttered ancient arrangements which were the essence of custom no longer seemed adequate. The great jurist Sir Edward Coke had repeatedly quoted an old saw: 'out of the old fields, as men saith, cometh new corne fro yere to yere'. That was a frame of mind which to Pym and his allies no longer seemed valid. It had been betrayed by a crown which had ruled without a parliament for a decade, had imposed illegal taxes, had imprisoned people wrongfully, had suborned the judiciary and was steering the Church away from the purity of its Protestant reformation towards the sinks of Roman Catholic iniquity.

If the lord had betrayed the copyholders of the manor, the copyholders no longer owed him any allegiance. The mutuality had gone. Instead, for Pym and his followers, a kind of brutal clarity was needed, a sweeping away of the unreliable superstructure of monopolies, forced loans, income from the sale of wards and all the other baggage of inheritance. The ancient constitution had failed. The king and his ministers had failed England and England needed to move on to a more enlightened and clarified future. The king saw all this clearly enough. The idea of Pym's party in parliament, he said, was 'to erect a universal over-swaying power to themselves'.

The deep disenchantment of England soon focused on the most powerful and uncompromising minister of the crown, Sir Thomas Wentworth, Earl of Strafford. He was not only guilty, Pym thought, 'of vanity and amours' but as President of the Council both in Ireland and in the north of England had tried to 'subvert the ancient fundamental laws of these realms of England and Ireland and to introduce an arbitrary and tyrannical government, against law.'

That spring, as the Bill for the condemnation of Strafford was being debated in parliament and in the council chamber, mobs gathered at Westminster and even within the precincts of Whitehall Palace:

> As any lord passed by [they] called *Justice, justice*! And with great rudeness and insolence, pressing upon and thrusting those lords whom they suspected not to favour that bill; professing aloud 'that they would be governed and disposed by the honourable House of Commons and would defend their privileges'. This unheard of act of insolence and sedition continued so many days, till so many lords grew so really apprehensive of having their brains beaten out, that they absented themselves from the house.

Eighty or so lords had heard the arguments for Strafford and against, but in the end only forty-six dared attend on the crucial day, thirty-five voting for his death, Pembroke among them, a mere eleven daring to defend him. In all this Pembroke had moved still further against the king, on 3 May 1641 telling that angry anti-Strafford crowd jostling outside Westminster Hall that 'His Majesty had promised they should have speedy execution of justice to their desires', a set of words which reached the ears of Charles and his queen and condemned Pembroke in their minds.

On 12 May 1641, after the king had reluctantly given his authority for the act, Strafford was executed on Tower Hill for treachery against the English nation. A crowd of 200,000 exulted in his death; the king would never recover from what he thought of as his betrayal of a loyal servant. The king was clear in his mind: Pembroke, even if acting in defence of the ancient constitution, had himself betrayed his sovereign and his duty. It was the conflict of idealisms which would lead to war.

The tension at Westminster in that hot and close-pressing summer would finally burst and destroy Pembroke's career in July. The trigger for the crisis was trivial but symptomatic of this complex, involuted world. As part of his wife's dowry, Philip, now the earl's eldest surviving son and heir, had come into the possession of some lands in Sutton Marsh in the south Lincolnshire fens. It was one of the most contested pieces of ground in England. The rights of commoners, who had been accustomed to living off the wildfowl and fuel from the marshes, had been extinguished by a set of aristocratic landlords who had drained, improved and privatised their property. Along with other drained fens, it had become the scene of regular riot and destruction.

On top of that, Herbert's title to these fenlands was in dispute, amongst others, with the king's cousin the Duke of Lennox, now the husband of the very Mary Villiers with whom Philip Lord Herbert had once been in love and on whom Pembroke had once been relying for her dowry. As yet another ingredient in this tangle, Lennox's sister, Elizabeth Stuart, was married to Henry Howard, Lord Mowbray and Maltravers, the heir to the Earl of Arundel, part of the Howard family which had been longstanding rivals and enemies of the Herberts. Maltravers, of enormous wealth himself, and one of the major investors in fen drainage, had in 1626 married this girl against the king's wishes. William Pembroke and Philip Montgomery, as Privy Councillors, had both been part of the decision to commit him to the Tower.

Now in the fiercely heightened atmosphere of the summer of 1641, polarised by the trial and execution of the Earl of Strafford in May, amid whispers of an army plot to take over parliament in the king's name and the presence of the bellowing crowds outside the parliament house, this angry confusion of aristocratic enmities and rivalries came to a head. Lennox, Pembroke and Maltravers, as well as Lord Seymour, an old rival of Pembroke for local influence in Wiltshire, were all members of a small committee of the House of Lords whose task it was to consider the petitions of the people. The young Philip Herbert was also in attendance himself, acting as a messenger between the House of Lords and the House of Commons. Pembroke had voted for the execution of Strafford; Maltravers had made himself conveniently absent for the day; Lennox had voted to save him. The summer was hot and overpowering. Smallpox and the plague were spreading in the city. One Puritan MP had proposed a bill 'for the gelding of Jesuits'. According to a document in the papers of the House of Lords, taken down from witnesses the following day, the tension burst at a meeting of the committee on 19 July 1641.

It began with a pedantic discussion about an ancient statute from the time of Henry IV which had been dragged up by one of the lawyers in one of the Sutton Marsh cases. The Duke of Lennox arrived late at the committee, heard the phrase 'Sutton Marsh' and asked what they had been discussing. Pembroke, looking across the table and pointing towards Maltravers, said, 'No man named Sutton Marsh till you named it.'

> To which my Lord Matravers replyed I never named it till you named it first, and I appeale to the Committee. To which my Lord Chamberlayne sayd – But you did. The other answered –

I did not; and so twise or thrise to and fro. Then said my Lord Chamberlayne – My Yea is as good as your No, to which my Lord Matravers – And my No as your Yea, and further sayd that he would maintayne that he had named it twenty tymes this day. To which my Lord Chamberlayne sayd that he durst not maintayne it out of that place. Then my Lord Matravers sayd, That he would maintayne it in any place, for it was true; To which my Lord Chamberlayne replyed that it was false. My Lord Matravers sayd, You lye. Whereupon my Lord Chamberlayne reached out his white staff and over the table strok him on the head. Then my Lord Matravers took up the Standesh [a stand for pen and ink] that was on the table before him, and my lord Chamberlayne goinge farther from him, he threw it after him but misst him. Then my Lord Chamberlayne came towards him agayne and over the table gave him a second blow with his white staffe.

It was a catastrophe. Pembroke had lost his temper often enough before and had even hit people with the staff of office which van Dyck had shown resting so elegantly in his fingers. But he was not to get away with it this time. His hurried, draft apology, written the same day as the incident itself, survives among the papers of the House of Lords, scratchy and no more than half legible:

at the committee for
am fallen into the dishonour of
this House
for my offence I am greatly sorry for that offence
of your Lopps
of that House
to be most iust. So I in all   humility
submit my selfe thereunto

Both he and Maltravers were sent to the Tower. On 21 July, Pembroke made his apology to the House of Lords for his 'miscarriage towards your lordships'. The opportunity was too good for the king to miss. He had long been exasperated by Pembroke's rough and uncourtly behaviour and took the chance to 'send to him by a gentleman usher for his staff'. The symbol of authority was removed from him and his career at court had ended in humiliation. Efforts by parliament to have him appointed Lord Steward of the Household were rebuffed by the king. Pembroke, as the inheritance from his grandfather the first earl, from Philip Sidney and from his brother might all have suggested, was being pushed into the arms of those who were opposed to the king when the king had betrayed the constitution on which the health of England relied.

It was utterly humiliating. Pembroke could not 'choose but think forty-four years' service ill requited to be thus disgracefully dismissed.' As the crisis deepened, it became increasingly clear that Pembroke, no longer Lord Chamberlain, would side with parliament against the king. The atmosphere at Westminster was filled with anxiety and threat. At the end of October an anonymous gentleman on horseback gave a porter a letter for Pym, with 12d to deliver it. When Pym opened it in the chamber of the House of Commons, a filthy and bloody rag which had been drawn through a plague sore fell from his hands. The letter said: 'Do not think a guard of men can protect you if you persist in your traitorous courses and wicked designs . . . If this do not touch your heart, a dagger shall.'

Early in January 1642, after word had reached the king that parliament would try to impeach his Catholic queen, Charles went with a party of a hundred troopers to the House of Commons to arrest the leaders of the anti-Stuart faction. They had escaped before he arrived, but the military intervention was an irrevocable and disastrous step. He had become a king who was prepared to threaten the nation gathered in parliament with military force. On 10 January Charles left London and gradually made his way north, attempting to persuade the country that his task was to defend the liberties of England against the prospect of an increasingly tyrannical parliamentary government. The body of England was pulling apart into head and limbs, each claiming they were the true heirs of the integrated whole. After parliament decided to raise its own army in March 1642, war was inevitable. By May the king was in York and from there on 30 May 1642 he wrote to Pembroke. That letter, a folded foolscap sheet, has survived. It is the fulcrum of this story, the point at which this family's long double commitment to king and country splits apart.

> To our rt trusty & right wellbeloved Cosin & Councillor Philip Earle of Pembroke & Montgomery
>
> Wee greet you well. Whereas Wee have some occasions of importance highly concerning our person, honor, & Service, wherein Wee are very desirous to recieve your advise and assistance, having had experience of your Affection, Wisdome and Integrity, Our express Pleasure therefore is, And Wee doe hereby will and command you all delayes and excuses sett apart, to make your immediate repaire hither to vs, When you shall understand the particular & urgent causes of this our sending for you: Of wch you may in no wise faile, as you value the good of Vs & our Service. And for so doing this our letter shall be your sufficient Warr[ant]. Given at Our Court at York the 30th day of May 1642.

'Charles R.': the king had signed this letter, with its ominous mixture of command and entreaty, by putting his large feathery signature, the pen scarcely touching the paper, at the head of the secretary's text. But Pembroke ignored it and the letter remains today in the House of Lords where it had arrived that spring day. England was en route to civil war. The two sides were gathering their troops all over England. In August, after the harvest had been taken in and men could turn their thoughts to war, Charles raised his standard at Nottingham and began to collect his army around him. Robert Dormer, Earl of Carnarvon, was with him. The Earl of Pembroke, his father-in-law, was not.

The discontent had surfaced and in Clarendon's words 'every man [became] troubled and perplexed'. Sir Benjamin Rudyerd, the Pembroke client, had said to the House of Commons in July 1642 that 'If blood once again begins to touch blood, we shall presently fall into a certain misery and must attain an uncertain success.' The sense of the community of England, of a single organism connecting crown and people through the ancient constitution, had broken down and for the next decade, as they repeatedly expressed it, it was as if the body of the country was at war with itself. It was 'an intestinal war', 'the troubles', the 'unnaturall war', 'the late unhappie difference'. For Philip Skippon, the Roundhead commander at Marlborough in December 1642, the royalists were 'a race of vipers, that would eat the passage to their ambitions through the entrails of their mother, the Commonwealth.' The favourite term used by parliamentarians for royalists was 'malignant', as if they were an infection of the body. If they had possessed anything like the frame of mind which could produce this expression, they would have recognised the civil war as a form of auto-immune disease, the tissues of the body filled with its own hostile antibodies, a war in which not only liberty but the entire constitution of the body – a word which in its political and physical senses still preserves this ancient analogy – was endangered.

The war was brutal, not only in its battles where the proportion of dead in infantry units could at times reach 75%, usually under the swords of the cavalry, or in the aftermath of sieges whether of towns or fortified manor houses, where rage and revenge exacted a terrifying price from the defenders. A man emerged from one of these sieges with his mind so destroyed that he spent the rest of his life walking around on all fours, hoping to be mistaken for a dog. Nor only in the dreadful weather, the cold and rain, which beat almost ceaselessly, winter and summer, in the early 1640s. Nor in the disastrous harvests, particularly in the middle of the decade, which left swaths of England hungry and weakened. Nor in the attacks of the plague that ravaged the hungry villages. Wilton, Bemerton and Fugglestone were all devastated by the disease, which not only killed the people but kept others shut up so that they could not work but 'during wch tyme they were inforced to waste and consume yt small pparcon of estate wch they formerly had gotten by their hard labour to ye utter impoverishinge of them and theire families,' so that 'as they have died in the plauge so now will they dye with famen also.' Village after village made 'a miserable cry to the magistrates' imploring the authorities for aid.

More than that, the civil war was a brutal eruption of anarchy, rape, theft and violence, of gang dominance and gang attack, a pervasive lawlessness which spread across the country, terrified the ordinary people, gave free rein to thugs and thieves and turned the roads through the Arcadian valleys of Wiltshire into routes no ordinary man or woman would dare travel. Everything which six-teenth and seventeenth-century England had feared, against which the idea of Arcadia had been set, became a reality in the 1640s: a breakdown of order and even of meaning, a sense that no one knew any more what mattered or what they believed in. The only constant, becoming ever more urgent as the years of war and turmoil rolled on, was a desire for a better time, a time in the past, an increasingly Golden Age of peace and happiness.

Wiltshire was turned over time and again. Already by March 1643 'the ways are now very dangerous to travel in by reason of the interruption of soldiers.' Pembroke abandoned Wilton for his London houses and sent his estranged wife Lady Anne Clifford to live in Baynard's Castle where she could look after his paintings and treasures. Detachments from both sides camped from time to time in the great rooms at Wilton and at Ramsbury, the troopers quar-tered in the stables, the household servants providing meals for the officers. His son-in-law the Earl of Carnarvon, on the enemy side, spent a night in the house with other Cavalier commanders in late May 1643. The king himself spent a few nights at Ramsbury and at the very end of the war his daughter Princess Elizabeth held court with one or two of the Wiltshire Cavaliers for a few days at Wilton. Around these passing wartime ironies, the county became a battle zone, controlled by parliament to begin with, then taken by the royalists making raids from Oxford, full of country houses which became armoured hardpoints in the war, besieged and stormed, first by one side then the other, often sacked with astonishing and terrible ferocity, the women raped, the children abused, while armies marched across the ravaged lands between them.

The men and women of the county found themselves in a labyrinth of contradiction, not sure how or why the country had come to this, nor what their part in it should be. Where they had known before what their rights and restrictions had been, now they were to answer to strange masters on strange grounds. Arguments they were only faintly familiar with had erupted into their lives. 'Do you not thinke the condition of the poor Countryeman hath not suffered a sad alteration,' one anonymous Wiltshireman asked at the end of 1642, 'from a state wherein he knew what was his owne, and was not capable of any violence for which he was not sure of a remedy and reparation, to this, where he receives commands under the penalty of plundering and hanging from persons of whom he never heard, for horses, for money, for personall attendance, for which he can find no ground?'

Few sights are more pathetic than the marks of illiterate Wiltshiremen from these villages, perhaps related to the symbols with which they identified their sheep in the common flocks, put at the end of the hundreds of petitions and complaints to the justices that detail the damage and destruction done to their lives in these years.

A selection of marks made by Wiltshiremen
on Civil War presentments and petitions

'Tis indeed a sad and miserable condition we are fallen into,' the anonymous Wiltshireman wrote. He was addressing his friend, an MP at Westminster. Why, he asked, had the war even begun? They were 'weltering in one anothers bloud before we know why we are angry, and to see our houses and towns fired and our Neighbours and Friends taken prisoners, by men who do not onely speake the same language with us, but are of our owne families and of the same (or seeme to be of the same) Religion.' Violence and viciousness had erupted in precisely the way the whole culture had been designed to prevent.

There was 'a strange dejection in the spirits of the people,' this Marlborough man continued, '& if I am not cozened, an inquisi-tivenesse, by questions they did not use to aske. Who raised armies first? Why they did it? What the Commonwealth wanted? Whether the King hath denyed anything was not in his lawful power to deny?' And was the prize worth the grief that would inevitably come?

> That so many widowes must be made, so many children fatherlesse, and such a desolation brought upon the whole kingdome? With the like questions which in a little time may raise such a storm as the cunning and power of both houses cannot allay.

All certainty had gone, all trust and assurance. On Monday 19 December 1642, when the country was deep into the first bloody phase of civil war, when the forces of king and parliament had already shed each other's blood, Pembroke made a speech in the House of Lords. On the instigation of the queen, he had been shut out of the king's councils and the anarchy which he sensed around him, both social and political, made him defensive. He did not feel that his allies in the House of Commons would remain allies for long. It was, as he said, the speech of an honest man and all he was looking for was 'an accommodation' between the warring sides. In its straightforwardness, its lack of guile, its deeply conservative conception of himself as a grandee and its fearful, honest pleading with his peers, it might stand as his credo, his apology for himself and the decisions of his life. It was the statement of a man whose only intention was 'to scape undoing'.

The earl clearly liked what he had said, as he had the speech printed and distributed. The words of his enemy and rival, the fearsomely godly Lord Brooke, were then also printed in response. In their two speeches, one can see, in fierce confrontation, the revolutionary opposed to the man for whom revolution is a greater disaster than the ills it aims to cure. It is the meeting of radicalism and gradualism, between the ferocity of first principles and the beliefs of someone like the Earl of Pembroke, for whom continuity between past and future was more important than anything which might be put in its place.

The Earl of Pembroke's Speech for an Accommodation
Munday 19 Dec. 1642

My Lords,

I have not used to trouble you with long Speeches, I know I am an ill Speaker, but though I am no Scholler, I am an honest man, and have a good heart to my King and Country.

I have more to loose then many of those who so hotly oppose an Accommodation. I will not forfeit mine estate to satisfie their humour or ambitions. My Lords, 'tis time to look about us, and not suffer ourselves to be fooled out of our Lives, our Honours and our fortunes, to help those men, who when their turns are served, will dispise us; and begin to laugh at us already.

A fellow here of the Town, an ordinary scurvy fellow, told me the other day to my face, that he cared not if I left them to morrow; nay if all the Lords went to the King, they should do their businesse the better: yet my Lords, I think we have helped them. Now nothing will content them, but no Bishop, no Book of Common Prayer, and shortly it will be no Lords, no Gentlemen, and no Books at all.

My Lords, I wonder what we shall get by this war. We venture more then other men, I am sure I venture more then five hundred of them, and the most I can look for is, to scape undoing; we have but a narrow way to walk in: we hear every base fellow say in the street as we passe by in our Coaches, that they hope to see us a-foot shortly, and to be as good men as the Lords themselves; and I think they will be as good as their words.

My Lords, I am no Scholler, but I understand men. I have served the Kings Father, and Himself, and though I have been so unhappy to fall into His displeasure, no body shall perswade me to turn Traytor, I have too much to loose.

Lord Brooke then replied with a speech like a sword, a denial of every Arcadian principle of accommodation, gentleness, hierarchy, love and custom:

My Lords,

His Lordship tells you much of what he has to lose, and into what great contempt the Nobility will grow, if there be not a speedy accommodation; and I fear some of these vile Considerations have hung Plummets [small lead weights] on some of our wings, which by this time would have mounted far higher; but these are the baits the enemy of godlinesse and true holinesse flings in the way, to discourage worldly mindes from fighting the good Fight of the Lord.

They who are transported with naturall affection to their Fathers and Brothers, kindred, friends, will not keep us Companie; yet this troubles me the lesse, whilst I see those Noble Lords in my eye (upon whom I can never look enough) who, banishing those womanish and effeminate fancies, cheerfully undertook to serve against that Armie, wherein they knew their own fathers were; and on my conscience (I speak it to their honour) had they met alone, would piously have sacrificed them to the commands of both Houses.

The Laws of the Land (being but mans invention) must not check Gods children in doing the work of their heavenlie Father. Let us proceed to shed the blood of the ungodlie.

All the ingredients were here of the destruction that would unroll across the country for the next eleven years, founded on the idea that any damage, the killing of fathers by sons, the destruction of estates, was good and strong if done in the service of the word of God. Any doubts were effeminate fancies, any law a tissue of worldly invention. The custom of the manor had lost all authority.

The result of such sweeping certainty on both sides was that for the next few years a harrow would be dragged across the body of England. No part of the country suffered more than Wiltshire and its surrounding counties, the borderlands of royalist influence both around Oxford and to the west, with parliamentary control in the country around London.

There was a pervasive feeling that wickedness was loose in the land, and in its wake came an unprecedented level of hatred: parliamentary prisoners taken in the first months of the war were forced by their royalist guards in Oxford to drink the water in which the guards had previously washed. Nothing was safe from the thieving of the armies. The wonderful Quarter Sessions Rolls on which much of this book relies for its evidence were only preserved because in January 1643 the Wiltshire justices, wondering how the 'sessions records may be preserved in this time of danger', ordered 'a strong chest with two locks and keys for that purpose be provided and kept in the vestry house of Warminster church.'

Rough gangs of pressed soldiers roamed the valleys. 'When service happens,' one recruiting sergeant boasted, 'we disburden the prisons of thieves, we rob the taverns and alehouses of tosspots and ruffians, we scour both town and country of rogues and vagabonds.' War legitimised violence and theft. Soldiers staying in Salisbury in the spring of 1643 set fire to the beds they had slept on. Others raided a butcher's shop and threw the pig carcasses into the Avon. In the small chalkland village of West Lavington, about eighteen miles north of Wilton on Salisbury Plain, one of these savage gangs broke into the house where the young Henry Penruddock of Compton Chamberlayne, whose father was famous as a Catholic and royalist sympathiser, was staying, exhausted after days in the saddle. He was asleep in a chair in the house and woke to find the troopers in the parlour, armed, the women shrieking and fluttering around them. One of the men pulled him up by the hair, knocked him down and 'broke two pistols over his head, without so much as tendering him quarter'. Another, said to have been 'a collier', perhaps a charcoal maker, famously independent men of the woods, 'swore that he should die for his father's sake, and putting a pistol to his belly shot him dead'.

A steady stream of casual death, theft and violence overwhelmed the ordinary people. Abraham Hale of the House of Correction at Devizes was forced 'to entertayne the Prest souldiers & to make pvision for them wch came to Seven pounds fifteene shillings & Seaven pence,' never paid. In 1644 in Warminster, on 25 March, a young mother, at home alone with her child, was surprised to hear a man called George Long knock on her door,

> 'and two soldiers in Armes with him and the said Long and one of the souldiers required the peticoner to open her dore who answered she would not unless he was an officer. Then the said Long said he was as good as any officer whatsoever and ymediately by force broke downe a windowe leafe wch fell into the house upon a paile of water whereby both window leafe and paile of water fell on yor peticoner and her child wch did so bruise the child that it fell sick and shortly after dyed. Yet not being contented they also brake up the dore and enterd the house by force and then the said Long fel to byting pinching and scratching of yor peticoner saying & swearing in most execrable and ignominious manner shee was a witch and therefore hee would have her blood wch he drawed from her in great abundance.'

There is no explanation in the records of why Long and his armed friends attacked her and killed her child. At the same time, George Reynolds was asked to be high constable of the hundred but declared himself incapable 'haveing byn by souldiers soe heavily abused & beaten yt he is not able to ride nor travel.'

Carriers had 'corne and malt taken from them by a turbulent multitude by reason whereof they cannot travel with the said comodities and therefore many poore people in those parts are in great distresse for want of the same.' Widows were robbed, villages burned and attacks made on hedges and other enclosures. The chance was taken to carry out revenge killings under the cover of ideological difference. After the war, the courts were full of cases trying to decide whether individual deaths were murders or occurred in the cause of duty.

All over Wiltshire, parks were broken into and deer chased with greyhounds and shot. Incidents of sheep-stealing peaked, and any attempt to gather them back ran the risk of gangs of men coming to find you. Thomas Astill of Peasemore recovered sixteen of his sheep and was driving them home when he 'was overtook by a man on horse back with dogges & other men wth Clubbes who took the sheep away from him.' The gang then menaced Astill and the posse of neighbours with him, threatened to take him to Devizes '& have them tyed neck to heels together & afterwards hanged for demanding and medling with the sheepe.'

The people of Horningsham, Maiden Bradley and Kingston Deverill, three villages at the far western end of the Wiltshire chalk, applied to the justices for permission to take the law into their own hands. The war had left them plagued by thieves:

> the number of Ffelons have greatly multiplied in and about our pishe by whom we are dayly robbed of our cattell (especially our sheepe) wth much bouldnesse not spareinge sometimes our very howses to our great discouragement in the buildinge and keepinge of sheepe the over throwe of tillage and soe to the generall damage of the whole Comonwealth.

They wanted a warrant from the court which would allow the villagers to attack and arrest their enemies. But the court, which had worked only intermittently during the war, did not trust this vigilante law. The petition of the three villages is signed by the justices: 'Noe order.'

If that is a signal that some fragment of the system of law was still operating, many other places suffered from the ebb and flow of armies to which the whole county was subject, attacked in turn, plundered in turn, taxed in turn and then, for many, 'barbarously burned'. Gentry like the Penruddocks would receive the familiar imploring-cum-threatening letters, demanding '£100 for our necessary support and maintenance of our army' – this was from the king's camp – 'And of this service we cannot doubt since if you should refuse to give us this testimony of your affection you will give us too great a cause to suspect your duty and inclination both to our person and the peace.' Lesser folk were simply bullied into the provision of goods and services. Thomas White of Potterne near Devizes had taken from him 'as much Beare, Stronge water and Sack as came to the Sume of xii li or neare thereabouts and carried the same to a place called Rundwayehill [Roundway hill] with promise to pay,' which of course was not honoured. The armies took food and carriage on tick but had moved on by the time payment was due. A mason from Meere, for the want of building work, took to buying and selling cheeses. He was told to take 200 Wiltshire cheeses to Oxford 'for his Majesty's provision there', half of the payment on credit. But he was never paid the sixteen shillings he was owed for the cheeses, nor the shilling a day for himself and his three horses for eight days.

Worse still was when an army detachment took up residence where you were living. There was no avoiding what was called 'free quartering'. The landowners simply had to provide. Thomas Randoll of Fisherton Anger between Bemerton and Salisbury in Easter week 1645 had quartered on him 'of Sir William Walers Army six men for eleven dayes viz until the twentieth of April aforesaid whereof three were Ensigns, one Chirugion a quartermaster and a Marshall 3li 6s.'

In the previous November, the mayor and aldermen of Salisbury had been ordered to provide 'upon sight' twenty bushels of wheat, twenty quarters of oats, twenty dozen candles, twenty bushels of salt, twenty flitches of bacon and twenty quarters of meat 'whereof we shall exact a punctuall account off yow as yow will answer to the Contrary.' The Pembroke's old steward John Nicholas of Winterbourne Earls was 'never free from billeting of soldiers of both sides, some times thirty, forty or fifty men and as many horses three or four days and nights together.' He took to hiding in his pigeon loft when army detachments were seen coming down the road.

No side was better than the other. When Lord Percy's soldiers were quartered in the village of Odstock on the Ebble in 1644, they scribbled in the parish register, drawing wild, looping carefree scrawls all over one page and an irreverent rhyme, now partly blodged out, on another: 'God mad[e] man and man mad[e] [money] / God mad[e]bees and bees mad[e]hone[y].' When Cromwell's troopers entered Winchester in 1645, they used the priceless medieval documents in the cathedral's muniment room to make kites.

The royalists who descended on Salisbury in December 1644 were particularly destructive. On a series of ninety-eight little torn notes and scraps of paper the citizens of Salisbury recorded their losses to the troopers of Sir Marmaduke Langdale's famously aggressive Cavaliers: shops broken up and plundered, widows robbed, a man deprived of his doublet, hose and shoes, blankets and a carpet taken, gloves, stockings and hats. One man, John Russell, a cobbler, had everything stolen and then found he had 'a poore sick soldier lieth uppon my hands and I am not able to release him'. William Philipps had a hat taken off his head, all his clothes stolen, both wool and linen, and 'they kame a kene aftere word & had a plondeare a kene'. Richard Durnford had his wife's petticoat taken, Bennet Eastman £4 'taken out of his pockets in money', Hugh Smith his Bible.

The other side was no better. An old man made a pitiable list of the goods in his house, all of which had been taken by parliamentarian soldiers:

7 pairs of sheets, 3 brass kettles, 2 brass pots, 5 pewter dishes, 4 shirts, 4 smocks, 2 coats, 1 cloak, 1 waistcoat, 7 dozen candles, 1 frying pan, 1 spit, 2 pairs of pot hooks, 1 peck of wheat, 4 bags, some oatmeal, some salt, a basketful of eggs, bowls, dishes, spoons, ladles, drinking pots, and whatsoever else they could lay their hands on.

The violence left the country littered with victims: men who had been pressed for service with one or other of the armies, who had deserted, been imprisoned and driven into penury; men falling sick 'with a disease called the Mesells' after being exposed to the unprecedented wartime movement of people; and many men claiming pensions for the injuries they had received in the war. Richard Rickette was 'a poor lame mayned man a carpenter at worke at Ridge' – a Pembroke possession to the west of Chilmark – who had been 'dangerously wounded crippled & disabled for all future service or labour whereby both himself and a small child is left wholly to the Charitie of his neighbours for their releefe & sustenance.' The justices decided that the parish itself was 'to releeve him according to the necessity of the party.' There were men who had been shot in the back and were unable to work, a man blinded 'having lost the sight of both eyes by a cut across his face and left for dead' in Salisbury. Hundreds were left homeless and destitute in the towns which had been stormed and burned, filled with 'heaps of rubbish [and] consumed houses, a multitude of which are raked in their own ashes. Here a poor forsaken chimney and there a little fragment of a wall that have escaped to tell what barbarous and monstrous wretches there have been.'

Under the strain of such levels of violence and invasive theft, the social fabric stretched and broke. Men in the villages refused to play their part as tithingmen, the essential keepers of order. Those who had been chosen tithingman before the war found no one willing to take the duty on from them. Parishioners in Lacock were presented to the justices in July 1641 for failing to do their communal work, the essential mechanism for the workings of the village:

John Pountney, Martin Gass, for not doing his six hours service
Ambros Browne came not in with his plow to do his six days
worke (same John Rumsey and Nicolas Barett)
John Banks for doing but 3 dayes service (same Richard Ashly,
William Frie)
John Bush for not scowring his ditch along Nash way
John Davis for not clensing his ditch along Nash way

Others would not or could not contribute their share of the taxes
and rates levied by both sides. Village by village, Wiltshiremen
complained that they were being forced to carry the burdens of
war alone. Many individuals refused 'to pay their rates with their
neighbors towards the charge of the prest souldiers.'

Robert Locke, the tithingman at Wylye, and Anthony Ballard,
the constable, had

> disbursed and layd out of their owne purses divers sums of
> money for the setting out of soldiers for his Majesties service
> this last summer out of the Tythinge of Wily aforesaid

> Whereupon a rate hath bin there made by the said Tything for
> the collecting of such summes of money as were to be paid
> out of the said Tythinge

> Roberte Greene, Henry Patient and John David doe refuse to
> pay the severall rates imposed upon them by the said Tything
> whereby your said peticioners are likely to pay the said monyes
> out of their owne purses beside all their great travaile and
> chardges already in the premises by them expended.

The rest of the village needed 'to beare their burthen with their
neighbours'. It may be significant that both Locke and Ballard were
members of longstanding Wylye families, who had maintained the
workings of the village over several generations. (The Ballards had
the inn, the Green Dragon.) None of the three men named – Greene,
Patient and David – appear in the survey of the village made in
June 1631. They were newcomers, perhaps parliamentarians, not
prepared to contribute to the general fund or to the royalist cause.

Communal payment for communal goods was the customary

expectation of the manor, but war meant that neighbourliness itself was under threat. Villages became even less tolerant of difference than they had been before. Vicars such as Thomas Lawrence at Bemerton had clearly drifted into un-Puritan churchmanship and it was reported by his neighbours 'That he do & did usually ducke and make obaysance to the communion table at the entering in to the church and at the goinge forthe and did always bowe at the name of Jesus.' Anyone who stepped outside the norm, who was said 'to have conveyed armour into Scotland, who had spoken treason or done felonie', was reported to the authorities. Edward Williams of Marlborough was presented in 1641 for saying 'there was base rogery in that book', when talking about the Book of Common Prayer. Increasingly confident Puritan ministers campaigned against dancing, music, games and drink. John Newman, minister of Upavon on the north side of the plain, addressed the justices as though he were their moral physician, giving them a sermon on the good and healthy life:

> There is a greate complaint of bastardies, sheep-stealers, hedg-breakers, quarrellers and ye like. Would you be eased of these diseases? Believe it, they gather into Alehouses as humers doe into ye stomach. Doe you but drive them thence with som strong Physick, and you hele our towne and villages of infinite distempers.

People were beginning to pursue their private ends and neglect the needs of the community. The inhabitants of Tippett found their sheep dying of foot-rot after 'Henry White gent' neglected the water channels on his own land and allowed their common meadow to remain flooded. The royalist Lord Seymour was presented 'for flotting his meadowe called long Meadowe for destrowing the Kings high way.' Susan Long of Warminster 'delivered to one Henry Garratt, blacksmith, a fire pan to have the same mended, but the said Garratt deteyneth it and telleth yor peticoner she shall come by her pan as she can for (saith hee) there is noe law.' *There is noe law*: that might have been the motto inscribed over 1640s Wiltshire. War had dissolved the bonds of custom.

The ground was slipping under old meanings and structures. An intriguing petition came in to the justices in 1646 from the villagers of West Knoyle on the very edge of the chalk, about sixteen miles west of Wilton. It was against 'William Willoughby Esq, Lord of the said Mannour of Westknoyle concerning Rates and payments for the service of the king & Parliament.' Willoughby was a royalist, who would be implicated in a futile royalist Wiltshire rebellion in 1655 led by the Penruddocks against the Commonwealth, and this petition is a moment of revolution against him. In a small Wiltshire village, the ordinary copyholders make a requirement that the future should be fair, that the lord of the manor should not ride in on the deference of his tenants but that he too should pay his way and should be no burden on the common man. Before the war, Willoughby had paid only a third of the parish rates or taxes although his demesne lands represented far more than a third of the productive land in the parish. Previously, the parishioners had submitted to this unfairness, 'hee being their landlord, and these payments then but small in respect of the tymes now.' But times had changed; the amount which the villages had to contribute to war expenses on both sides, 'daiely and weekly', was so great, that the men and women of West Knoyle felt this was no longer fair.

> Therefore we most humbly do peticion you to soe order this busynes that hee may now beare and pay equall share with us according to his and our estates, which he refuseth to doe, although his demains be worth 300 li per annum besides the parsonage there, worth 60 li per annum which wee heare to fore never questioned in making our rates

Willoughby refused to budge: 'hee will pay but according to his former rate, which comes but to 26 shillings 7 pence a weeke and some of his said Tennaunts doe pay 9 shillings 10 pence halfpenny which is verie unreasonable and unconscionable that hee should

soe free himself and lay the burthen upon his country who pay
more payments as fines [on entering a copyhold], heriots [on the
death of a copyholder] and yearly rents.'

There is even a suggestion that, at the most internalised of levels,
the power of authority had evaporated. In 1647, Grace Stokes, the
wife of Henry Stokes, a glazier from Fisherton Anger just on the
edge of Salisbury, came to the justices to complain about a girl
called Susanna Candby who was the daughter-in-law of William
Locke, the husbandman from Wylye. Grace had taken Susanna on
as her apprentice for three years. Susanna had, at least in the past,
suffered from scrofula, a disease of the lymph nodes in the neck,
which was severely debilitating and erupted in rough, raw pustules.
Since the early Middle Ages, it had been known as the King's Evil
and was thought to be curable by the touch of the monarch. When
Susanna first came into Grace's employment, she was 'extreamely
troubled with a disease called the Evill Which when yor peticoner
perceived asked her how long she had bin troubled with it, as also
whither she was cured of it. she answered that she had bin with the
King and was cured and did amend.'

Grace took her on but in the circumstances of the war the magic
no longer worked. Grace found herself with a girl so sick she was
useless as an apprentice and she wanted to be rid of her. Susanna,
it turned out, 'hath bin and nowe is soe vehemently troubled with
ye said disease that she is not able to helpe herselfe and is almost
redy to perish for want of Cure, to ye greate griefe and damadge of
yor poor petr.'

As usual, the records have nothing to say about the outcome of
the case, nor whether it was thought reasonable that a sick girl could
be dispensed with in this way, nor any reason why the king's cure
no longer worked.

Alongside this erosion of old meanings, there was a longing for
peace and for a return to the conditions before the war. As early as
October 1642, the leading Wiltshire gentry petitioned the king for
peace, as did the burghers of Salisbury. For the first time in the

world of seventeenth-century politics, women began to make their voices heard in these petitions for peace, but as the damage, taxation, violence and – increasingly – disease and hunger took their toll, a fiercer and more directed reaction emerged from these villages. Each side was taking more than £700 a week out of Wiltshire at the height of the war. From the spring of 1645 onwards, the men of Wiltshire, combining with their counterparts from Somerset and Gloucestershire, gathered themselves into the bands known as the Clubmen, opposed to all armies, all incursions and all taxations, whether for the king or the parliament. The Clubmen were attempting, in fact, to restore locally the peace which national politics had denied them.

In July 1645, the parliamentarian general Sir Thomas Fairfax told his masters in London what he had heard about the Clubmen. 'They pretended only the Defence of themselves from Plunderers, but not to side either with the King's Forces or the Parliament's, but to give Free Quarter to both: They list themselves under several Officers daily, and meet in great Bodies at their Rendezvous, and boast they can have Twenty Thousand Men at Four and Twenty Hours Warning for assembling them together.' It was Wiltshire gathering its own power. They were, at least apparently, well organized, sending messages throughout the valleys and summoning the men from the fields by ringing the church bells.

> For Distinction of themselves from other Men, they wear a White Ribbon, to shew, as they say, their Desires of Peace. They meet with Drums, flying Colours, and for Arms they have Muskets, Fowling-pieces, Pikes, Halberts, great Clubs, and such like. They take upon them to interpose betwixt the Garrisons of either Side.

Salisbury itself provided 700 Clubmen 'some with Pikes and Muskets, and others with Carbines and Pistols' and in mid-July they and others from all over the Pembroke estates and from further afield gathered at a rendezvous in the great Saxon forest of Grovely on the ridge above Wilton, where Philip Sidney had loved to ride.

About 4000 men gathered there to hear 'certain Articles read and proposed to them, which they all assented to by giving a Shout.'

It must have been a moment of self-reassurance, the reassertion of self-defence against the inroads of anarchy and alien ideas. The leaders of the Wiltshire Clubmen included two Pembroke tenants: Thomas Bennett of Broad Chalke and William Gould of Alvediston. Both of them signed petitions sent by the Clubmen to both king and parliament, 'for procuring a Peace'. They told them of their woes.

> More deeply than many other Parts of this Kingdom [they had] tasted the Miseries of this unnatural intestine War, which have been the more extremely embittered unto them by the Pressures of many Garrisons both here and in the neighbour Counties, and the opposite Armies continually drawn upon them by the reason thereof.

They had given up hope of a negotiated peace and had been forced to take the future into their own hands. All they wanted was 'the true Reformed Protestant Religion; and next, as free-born *English*, not degenerating from the Virtues of their Fathers, by all possible and lawful Means to preserve and uphold the native Inheritance of their Laws, their Liberties, and Properties, which they equally hold in Esteem even with Life itself.' They were asking for a restoration of the custom of the manor. The very instinct which had led Englishmen to war in 1642 – a defence of the ancient – now led them in their desire for peace.

> Immesurable Taxes, continual Free Quarter, and uncessant Plunderings [they told the king] have scarcely left Your poor Suppliants sufficient for the Support of Life. Our purses have bin exhausted, corn eaten up, cattell plundered, persons frighted from our habitacons and by reason of the violence of the soldiers our lives are not safe.

The simple desire for certainty, for structures by which they could pay their rents, have their debts honoured, make their living and maintain their wives and families 'from utter ruin and decay' was all that drove them. They wanted 'peaceably [to] return to their wonted habitations and to the obedience of the established laws.'

But it was a fantasy. The reality of the Clubmen's impotence and posturing was made apparent on 4 August 1645 when Cromwell at the head of the New Model Army brushed them aside. The brief engagement was at the Iron Age fort on Hambledon Hill, just over the county border in Dorset, where the Clubmen had gathered, shouting taunts at Cromwell's disciplined Ironsides. 'I believe we killed not twelve of them,' Cromwell wrote to Fairfax that evening, 'but cut very many and put them all to flight. We have taken about three hundred; many of which are poor silly creatures, whom if you please to let send home, they promise to be very dutiful for time to come, and will be hanged before they come out again.'

It was a 1640s version of the long story this book has described: the meeting of a retrospective idealism with the overwhelming facts of power.

This is the background to Pembroke's own involvement in the war. He behaved in a way that was little different from the thousands of Wiltshiremen who were first uncertain which way to turn, felt perplexed at the catastrophic outcome of events, wavered one way and then another, and felt deeply attached both to the ancient constitution and to the king who had betrayed it. But the 1640s were not a time for understanding and Pembroke was ridiculed and despised for his flickering and uncertain behaviour. Clarendon claimed that Pembroke became a parliamentarian because he wanted to protect Wilton and thought parliament was simply the stronger side. Others thought his rivalry with the Seymours, the great family from the north of the county with whom the Herberts had sparred since the 1540s, who became ardent royalists, explained what Pembroke had done. Neither was right and the explanation is simpler. The tradition of which he was a part, and which this book has described, could only have led him towards parliament. The 'life of loyalty' which one satire attributed to him was a loyalty to what? Perhaps to himself, to Wilton, to his family's culture, to a true reformed Church and to the Scots Covenanting, to the hunting he had loved since he was a boy and to a world that was lost, destroyed from both ends, by an increasingly authoritarian crown and an increasingly radical parliament and army.

Nevertheless, he became something of a joke to his contemporaries. The royalist Earl of Dorset, in a letter to his son-in-law, a parliamentarian, wrote sarcastically that: 'You cannott suffer, while you have soe sure and constant a man amongst you as the earl of Pembroke ... Paraselsus himselfe [the great sixteenth-century German alchemist and pharmacologist] cowld never have fixed the mercuriall spirit thatt predominates in his breast: if hee weere alive to practise on him.' The brilliant satirist Samuel Butler published the definitive verdict:

> Pembroke's a Covenanting Lord
> That ne'er with God or men kept word
> One day he swore he'd serve the King
> The next was quite another thing
> Still changing with the Wind or Tide
> That he might keep the Stronger Side
> His Hawks and Hounds were all his Gaze
> For them he made his daily Prayers
> And scarce would lose a hunting Season
> E'en for the sake of darling Treason.

Parliament sent him out to gather the militia on their behalf. In 1642 he was appointed 'Generall for the Western part of the Kingdom' and Lord Lieutenant in Wiltshire, Somerset, Hampshire, Dorset, Devon, Cornwall and the Isle of Wight. If it looked for a moment as if his grandfather's Tudor fiefdom had somehow reappeared a century late, that was mere illusion. Pembroke had no military expertise and was too old at nearly sixty to be an active soldier. He soon withdrew to the comfort of his rooms in the Cockpit at Whitehall, taking part in the increasingly unreal debates in the House of

Lords, where at times in the 1640s Pembroke and two or three other peers were the only figures on the empty benches under Inigo Jones's vaulted ceiling.

Repeatedly, parliament sent him as one of their commissioners to negotiate with the king. But that too came with its humiliations as parliament would not allow the commissioners freedom to negotiate without reference back to Westminster. Late one night, in the very cold January of 1645 at the negotiations between the two sides at Uxbridge, Pembroke came to pour his heart out to his old friend and client Edward Hyde, later to be Lord Clarendon, who was one of the king's commissioners at the negotiations. Pembroke sat with Hyde for many hours, trying to persuade him that the king should consent to parliament's demands. Hyde was adamant that the crown could not submit, as the only outcome of that submission would be tyranny in England. Pembroke then confessed that he too thought 'there was never such a pack of knaves and villains as they who now governed in the parliament.' Pembroke was 'of the moderate party' and they needed this treaty to work. Otherwise there would be a coup and England would become a republic. Hyde 'told him if he believed that, it was high time for the Lords to look about them, who would be then no less concerned than the King. [Pembroke] confessed it, and that they were now sensible that they had brought this mischieve upon themselves, and did heartily repent it, though too late, and when they were in no degree able to prevent the general destruction which they foresaw.' Only if the king agreed to their demands would they be able 'to recover all for him that he now parted with, and to drive those wicked men who would destroy monarchy out of the kingdom, and then his majesty would be greater than ever.'

Hyde thought Pembroke and his fellow parliamentary commissioners both contemptible and ridiculous, 'so broken were they in their spirits, and so corrupted in their understanding, even when they had their own ruin in view.' Pembroke left him late in the evening, a pitiable sight, scarcely the same man who had posed for

William Larkin with his ostrich feathers and his coral bracelet so long before.

The family had fallen apart. Pembroke's sons had stayed with him. Two of them, Philip and James, became members of parliament. But his glamorous son-in-law Robert, Earl of Carnarvon had become a leading and courageous cavalry commander on the other side and had been killed, casually, in the evening of the first Battle of Newbury in 1643, when a parliamentary trooper recognised him after the battle was over and ran him through with his sword. Carnarvon's wife Anna Sophia had very nearly died of smallpox the same year. Their son, Charles, the young boy born in 1632 and represented by the pearl between Anna Sophia's fingers in the great van Dyck portrait, was painted by his successor the young Lely perhaps in that year. The young boy's pose looks as if it deliberately reflects his father's in the family portrait, one foot raised on a step, his head turned to look, the colour and manner of his clothes also a form of inheritance from his father. In the background, the Arcadian trees were painted by Lely as withered and broken under the blast of war. It is just possible that this painting was made for Pembroke, the boy's grandfather, a sign that his love for his daughter's son spread across any ideological divide. Among the executors' accounts preserved at Hatfield, there is an item: 'Paid to Mr Lilly painter for severall pictures made for the late earle of Pembroke the sume of £85.'

After the defeat of the king and the fall of his headquarters at Oxford in January 1647, Pembroke was sent to Newcastle with parliament's propositions to the king. Charles had been given a copy privately some time before. He asked Pembroke and the other commissioners

> whether they had powers to treat with him on the Propositions or in any way discuss them. On their answering that they had no such powers, and had only to request his Majesty's *Ay* or *No* as they stood, 'Then, but for the honour of the business,' said the King testily, 'an honest trumpeter might have done as much.'

It was a good remark but symptomatic of the collapse of any authority Pembroke might have had. Pembroke stayed with the king as he was moved under house arrest to the giant Elizabethan palace of Holdenby in Northamptonshire, walking with him on 'the Long Gravel-Walk' of the garden there, maintaining a fond and 'mirthful' relationship with a man who had known him all his life 'and not without some difficulty held pace with him, his Majesty being quick and lively in his Motion.' When, on 3 June 1647, the king was kidnapped by the army officer George Joyce, on Cromwell's orders, arriving at Holdenby at dawn, with 500 armed troopers behind him and 'a cockt pistol in his hand', Pembroke went with the king in the coach to Cambridge, Newmarket and eventually to Hampton Court.

In these years of disaster and dissolution, Pembroke's affection for the king grew and flowered. The king was not allowed his old Gentlemen of the Bedchamber to attend him and Pembroke arranged for his cousin Thomas Herbert to play that role. Herbert watched the two of them carefully. 'The earl of Pembroke (let others say what they will) loved the King in his Heart, and had certainly never separated from him, had he not (by the Procurement of some ill-willers) been committed to the Tower, and his White Staff taken from him, only by reason of a sudden and unhappy falling out.'

Thomas Herbert also recorded the most poignant of all tales to do with Pembroke at the very end of Charles's life, a prisoner in the unhappy, Orwellian world of Westminster in 1648, with its whisperings and deceits, its sense of unbridled power lurking an inch or two beneath the surface of life, the air of mutual treachery. Herbert had at times been failing to wake up in the morning and the king had tried through the offices of the Earl of Pembroke to get him a repeating watch with an alarm. Herbert, in the third person, described a visit to Pembroke's rooms in the Cockpit at Whitehall. Pembroke

> then as at sundry other times enquired how his Majesty did, and gave him his humble Duty to him, and withal ask'd [Herbert], if his majesty had the Gold Watch he sent for, and how

he liked it. Mr Herbert assured his Lordship, the King had not yet received it. The earl fell presently into a Passion, marvelling thereat; being the more troubled, lest his Majesty should think him careless in observing his Command; and told Mr Herbert, at the King's coming to St James's, as he was sitting under the great Elm-Tree, near Sir Benjamin Ruddier's Lodge in the Park, seeing a considerable Military-Officer of the Army pass towards St James's, he went to meet him, and demanding of him if he knew his cousin Tom Herbert, that waited on the King? The Officer said, he did, and was going to St James's. The Earl then delivered to him the Gold Watch that had the Alarm, desiring him to give it Mr Herbert, to present it to the King. The Officer promised the earl he would immediately do it.

But neither king nor Herbert had seen anything of the watch.

My lord, (said Mr Herbert) I have sundry times seen and pass'd by that Officer since, and do assure your Lordship he hath not delivered it me according to your Order and his Promise, nor said anything to me concerning it, nor has the King it I am certain.

What were they to do? Could they accuse this military high-up of theft from the king? Not then. 'But such was the Severity of the times, that it was then judged dangerous to reflect upon such a person, being a Favourite of the time so as no notice was taken of it.'

Herbert did of course tell the king this story. 'Ah,' he said. 'Had he not told the Officer it was for me, it would probably have been delivered; he will know how short a time I could enjoy it.'

In January 1649 Pembroke was appointed by parliamentary ordinance to the court that was to try the king. But Pembroke could not bring himself to attend and remained in his beautiful rooms in the Cockpit, from where he 'swore he loved not to meddle with businesses of life and death and (for his part) hee would neither speake against the ordinance nor consent to it.' He had not signed the king's death warrant but he had done nothing to save him.

The king was executed on 30 January 1649. One of his last acts before he stepped out from the Banqueting House window on to the wintry scaffold was to give Thomas Herbert his own gold watch. Pembroke, with his old friend the Earl of Salisbury, watched the execution, quite dispassionately, from his lodgings in the Cockpit. On the scaffold Charles I prayed to God: 'Look upon my misery with Thine eye of mercy and let Thine infinite power vouchsafe to limit out some proportion of deliverance unto me.' John Milton would reveal in *Eikonoklastes* that this prayer was not the king's own but a quotation from *Arcadia*. By doing so, Milton maintained, the king had polluted 'prayer itself, by borrowing to a Christian use prayers offered to a heathen god, a prayer stolen word for word from the mouth of a heathen fiction praying to a heathen God; and that in no serious book, but the vain amatorious poem of Sir Philip Sidney's *Arcadia*.' For Milton, it was symptom of everything that was wrong with royalism: no access to the divinely revealed truth, no belief in liberty, no pride in what a free-born God-fearing Englishman should take pride in. And Milton had no trouble binding together the two Arcadias. Anyone who still longed for this crown-dominated, Arcadian world, Milton wrote, showed

> themselves to be by nature slaves and arrant beasts – not fit for that liberty which they cried out and bellowed for, but fitter to be led back again into their old servitude like a sort of clamoring and fighting brutes, broke loose from their copy-holds, that know not how to use or possess the liberty which they fought for, but with the fair words and promises of an old exasperated foe are ready to be stroked and tamed again into the wonted and well-pleasing state of their true Norman villeinage, to them best agreeable.

This was probably true. The English could not bear too much liberty, nor the fear of tyranny which came in its wake. *Eikon basilike*, the king's own (ghosted) justification of his life and kingship, went through thirty-six editions in 1649 alone. Hunger for a Restoration had surged on the execution of the king.

Pembroke himself would be dead within a year, one in which the new regime would continue to humiliate him. The Council of State discussed whether they should demolish his castle in Cardiff, whether his art treasures should be sold along with the king's for the good of the country, whether soldiers should or should not be quartered in Durham House, his London residence since 1640, whether he should be allowed to keep the keys to the doors and gates into St James's Park, or whether they would be better off in the hands of Colonel Pride. On 19 March 1649, the House of Lords was abolished by an Act of Parliament, which declared that 'The Commons of England [consider] by too long experience that the House of Lords is useless and dangerous to the people of England.' Although there had been talk the year before of making Pembroke a duke, he now became a member of the House of Commons, sitting alongside his sons, as the member for Berkshire, a move ridiculed in the London broadsheets as 'an ascent downwards'.

He was not well. He was seriously ill in May, again in June and again in July, running up apothecaries' bills for £122 over the summer. His digestion was failing him and the painful affliction returned in the autumn. Mr Metcalfe, the apothecary, was paid ten shillings a day for attendance, making large quantities of 'alterative ale, issue powder and deobstructive electuary' to get the bowel working. The most expensive was sweet powders containing musk and amber which aided the digestion and 'intestinal elimination'. Everything known to seventeenth-century medicine was thrown at him:

> Sweet fenall seeds, liquorice and coriander seeds, acqua cardiata, acqua cinnamon, syrup of roses, Syrup of citrons with Rhubarb, Syrupe of dryed roses, Syrupe of Limons, Syrupe of the Juice of Citrons, Syrupe of raspberries, Syrupe of Corrall, Two Ivory Clyster pipes prepared, Maiestry of pearle, Maiestry of Corrall, Crabbs eyes, Salt of Wormwood, Salt of scurvie grass, Confectio de Hyacinth, Conserve of Red Roses, Conserve of Rosemarie flowers, Chymicall oyle of wormwood, White sugar candy, Sweetes with musk and amber, purging potion

with rhubarb and a cordiall julipp with syrupe of pome-
grannutts.

On Christmas Day he had a 'syrupe of marsh mallows with liquorice
and maydenhaire' followed by conserve of bugloss and borage, a
mysterious 'Box of tabletts' along with Syrupe of jujubes. On and
on the treatments went until 28 January 1650 when he had a posset,
a gargarism with syrup, a cataplasm and finally 'a cooling Julipp'
which would cost his estate 2s 8d and after which he died. The sum
total for all of this was another £177 17s 10d, the price of a good house.
The executors were having none of that and reduced the bill by £65.

On Pembroke's death, bitter, spoof accounts by secret royalists
of his last hours were quickly printed and published on the streets
of London, the ranting visions of a man guilty of killing his king, of
pursuing nothing but his own appetites. 'Dam' me,' Pembroke is
meant to have muttered on his deathbed, 'there 'tis againe, a man
without a Head, beckoning me with his Hand, and bending his fist
at me; what a pox art thou? Speake, if thou art a man, speake;
speake, speake; zblood, canst thou not speake without a Head?'
Then, after his guilt, his desires:

> O mistress May. Come to bed Sweet-heart, come, my Duck,
> my Birds-nye; Zblood I must go to Salisbury tomorrow, bring
> me my Boots quickly; Zounds will not the Rogues bring me
> more Money; zblood that Cock's worth a Kings Ransome, a
> runs, a runs, a thousand pound to a Hobby Horse; Rub, Rub,
> Rub, a pox. Rub a whole hundred Tubs. Tell them I'll restore
> those *Pictures* and *Modells* I had from S. Iamses; the seiling of
> the banquety-House at White-Hall, tell them is as fit for my
> parlor in Ramesbury mannor as can be. I come, I come, good
> Devill lead the way. When Rebells dye Hell makes a Holly-day.

The long arc which the Pembrokes had traced from the 1520s
had now returned to earth. Their status had gone and the family
was deep in debt; the fourth earl's horribly involved estate took five
year to sort out. The executors' accounts survive at Hatfield. Friends,
neighbours and relations all came crawling out of the woodwork,

with promissory notes and obligations at dice or cards. The bills came in. Most of the earl's London pictures were sold to pay off the creditors. Connoisseurs toured the rooms to inspect them. Lands were mortgaged and jewels pawned. Valuers picked their way through the great rooms in Durham House, the Cockpit at White-hall, Baynard's Castle, Wilton and Ramsbury.

But this was more than a personal catastrophe. The world had changed and the central place in the workings of England which the Pembrokes had occupied for so long was no longer available to them. The England they had known was now broken. Their conservative revolt against the crown had in turn released huge revolutionary energies in the country which had swept away their old dreams of a renewed and potent nobility. England, infused with these dreams of radical and universal freedom, was now for ten years to be subjected to a brutal military dictatorship which that threat of freedom had summoned from the Republican authorities.

In this fierce and polarised world, the balance and organic integrity of Arcadia could be little but a forgotten memory. Only the ex-royalists, savagely fined by the new regime, and creeping back to their damaged and neglected estates in the depths of the country, could turn to the consolations of poetry and the beautiful, quiet life, a wan and defeated ghost of what Arcadianism had once been.

Arcadia had been the dream of power. Only the powerful could indulge in its fantasy of wholeness, because it relied in the end on an imposition of authority. It was everything which the world of Adam Smith, and of the triumphant and beneficent market, would not approve. It was, in that sense, also the dream of illiberal beauty, of a calm and richness which emerged not because individuals had been allowed to pursue their individual ends but because they had submitted to a protective authority.

Our modern nostrils quiver and bristle at this idea. Can happiness and contentment really come from such radical limitations of individual freedoms? Can the system really be justified when so few seem to benefit in their silks and gilded rooms and so many were condemned to a life of poverty and drudgery in their small poor houses on the edges of their damp river meadows?

But if one looks at what happened to these villages in the course of the eighteenth century, and the condition to which their inhabitants had sunk by the time Cobbett came to see them, then is that not some kind of justification for a social system based not on the exclusive power of the individual – which has a tendency towards dominance by the few and pauperisation of the many – but on the coherence of the community and the ecological balance which Philip Sidney saw in the grasses growing equally together in an Arcadian lawn?

Another question emerges from that: was the vitality of the chalkland valley communities dependent on a powerful overlord? Or could anything resembling the vivid communal life embodied in 'the custom of the manor' have survived in a system that did not depend on hierarchy and dominance? Maybe not. Communities need to obey agreed laws and those laws need to be imposed.

This, in the end, is surely the moral of the Pembrokes and their Wiltshire valleys. As individuals, they were clearly fallible, corrupt, self-seeking, vacillating, irresolute, irascible and at times less than articulate. But their story is not about individualism: it is about their joint belief in a version of the communal, Arcadian idea, in which principles both of hierarchy and of mutuality were deeply embedded. That is a strange pairing to modern minds. We think that hierarchy is bound to be domineering; and that mutuality cannot have hierarchy as one of its elements. The virtue of the Arcadianism this book has described was that, in an evolved and balanced way, it had understood how to accommodate these contradictory principles.

It is important, of course, to recognise that those who were most energetic in promoting this system were those who benefited most from it. Did the poor really like the stasis and exclusion of the copyhold manor? Probably not. The eruption of popular anger and violence in the Civil War might well be seen as the expression of a rage whose origins were in generations of oppression and denial which the old sytem had imposed.

Nor is it likely that the elite rural idyll was something the Pembrokes' tenants wholly subscribed to. George Herbert's description of his parishioners as a dumb and sullen lot, scarcely dancing their way to the fields or church, must have some truth in it. Arcadianism didn't always feel Arcadian if you were a member of the cast. Nor, importantly, were the people of these valleys unreconstructed rustics, as Herbert and others were tempted to describe them. The streets of Salisbury, until controlled and cleared by the city authorities, were as chaotic and frightening and as full of importuning and sometimes quite aggressive beggars as the streets of Calcutta. Much of the valley of the Nadder to the west of the city was busy with traffic and distinctly suburban in character by the early part of the seventeenth century.

So, for all the communal ideology, there is a divergence between the wish-fulfilment ideals of the Pembrokes and the reality of ordinary lives. The examples towards the end of this book of all the stresses and strains in the run up to the Civil War, the seeking for market solutions to chronic poverty, the disobedience of communal laws and the ever-present sense of violence and abuse: all that may well have occurred earlier, but the evidence has not survived. Documents from the Tudor decades are much thinner on the ground than from the early seventeenth century, particularly the Quarter Sessions records, which survive in quantity only from the beginning of the reign of James I. The dream of perfection undoubtedly sheltered in its heart both a systematic limit placed on the individual and his liberties and a natural human effort to escape and resist that limitation.

It was certainly an exploitative world: how, except by exploitation, could the earls have paid for their luxuries from the rents and fines of their copyhold tenants? But it was also a world which in its ideals and practice was alive with a sense of jointness, of a joint enterprise between the different connected parts of the social organism. It lived above all in its gathering: at the village courts, at the masques and tournaments, at the hay harvest and the wheat harvest, at the plays in the candlelit halls, at the great funerals and eventually at the desperate hilltop meetings during the civil war. It is a world that has entirely disappeared, but one whose virtues disappeared with its faults.

13

Hear this, O ye that swallow up the needy

The destruction of the downland communities
1650–1830

THE CROWN was restored in 1660, but not everything was restored with it. England could scarcely go back to the system or the mentality on which the pre-war country had once relied. The war itself had been too deep and disturbing a rupture. There was no going back. The Earls of Pembroke each in turn became the man of his moment: Restoration rakes (one a multiple murderer), eighteenth-century connoisseurs, army officers and Conservative politicians. But around them, in the chalkland valleys they owned, as elsewhere, a disaster unfolded.

The Anglican divine, Richard Baxter, wrote a homily in 1691 on *The condition of poor farm tenants*. 'The old custom was,' Baxter wrote nostalgically, 'to let lands by lease for lives or for a long term of years, and to take a fine at first and a small yearly rent afterward, and so when a man, with his marriage portion, had taken a lease he lived comfortably afterward and got somewhat for his children.' That is the air of retrospective regret for a land of lost content. The pattern of human relationships had been folded into the habits of the country. The wife's dowry had paid the fine with which the couple entered into the copyhold and the man's life's labour prepared for his children to do the same.

'But now in most countries,' Baxter continued, meaning in most parts of England, 'the custom is changed into yearly rack-rents,' meaning not only that custom itself was over and done with, but that the new annual rents were equal or nearly equal to the value of what the land could produce in the year. His subtext went far deeper into moral outrage. The new rents had been racked, bent, stretched and strained to the point where they were no longer morally legitimate.

'The poor tenants are glad of a piece of hanged bacon once a week,' Baxter told his gentlemanly audience, the grandsons of those who had read John Norden's treatise on mutuality as the essence of estate management at the beginning of the century,

> and some few that can kill a bull eat now and then a bit of hanged beef, enough to try the stomach of an ostrich. He is a rich man that can afford to eat a joint of fresh meat (beef, mutton or veal) once in a month or fortnight. If their sow pig or their hens breed chickens, they cannot afford to eat them, but must sell them to make their rent. They cannot afford to eat the eggs that their hens lay, nor the apples or pears that grow on their trees (save some that are not vendible) but must make money of all. All the best of their butter and cheese they must sell and feed themselves, and children, and servants with skimmed cheese and skimmed milk and whey curds.

The change from copyhold to leasehold and rack-rent, which began in earnest in the seventeenth century and would continue far into the nineteenth century, (copyhold was not finally abolished until 1925) was the deepest possible transformation of the social fabric of England. Where people before had, as Baxter implies, eaten their own produce, now their produce amounted to a single thing: money. The yeomen copyholders became what Baxter was already calling in the 1690s 'the poor enslaved husbandmen' of England.

Few landlords, he said, 'scruple raising rents to as much as they can get, when poor men, rather than beg and have no dwelling, will promise more than they can pay; and then, with care and toil, make shift as long as they can.' The idea of a balanced community, of mutuality in rights and obligations, in a control of the government of the manor through the custom of the manor: all that had been collapsed into a simple cash deal. If you could pay the rent, you could stay on the land. If you couldn't, you couldn't. The natural drift of such a system was the replacement of an integrated copyhold community with a monopolistic landlord and a gang of rightless, dependent, impoverished tenants. Huge, non-communal farms would have on their margins scatterings of paupers' cottages, precisely the pattern which developed in these valleys in the nineteenth century.

Jump to the end of August 1826 and William Cobbett is riding through the green and gold chalkstream valleys of the Wiltshire downs. He cannot believe that he is seeing a place of such unparalleled and dreamlike beauty.

> This is certainly the most delightful farming in the world. No ditches, no water-furrows, no drains, hardly any hedges, no dirt and mire, even in the wettest seasons of the year: and though the downs are naked and cold, the valleys are snugness itself. They are, as to the downs, what *ah-ahs* are in parks or lawns. When you are going over the downs, you look *over* the valleys, as in the case of the *ah-ah*; and if you be not acquainted with the country, your surprise, when you come to the edge of the hill, is very great. The shelter in these valleys, and particularly where the downs are steep and lofty on the sides, is very complete. Then the trees are everywhere lofty. They are generally elms, with some ashes, which delight in the soil that they find here. There are, almost always, two or three large clumps of trees in every parish, and a rookery or two (not *rag*-rookery) to every parish. By the water's edge there are willows; and to almost every farm there is a fine orchard, the trees being, in general, very fine, and this year they are, in general, well loaded with fruit. So that, all taken together, it seems impossible to find a more beautiful and pleasant country than this, or to imagine any life more easy and happy than men might here lead.

It is difficult to think of two people in English history more different than Philip Sidney and William Cobbett, but here they are as one. 'During the day I crossed the river about fifteen or sixteen times, and in such hot weather it was very pleasant to be so much amongst meadows and water.' Cobbett's wonderfully expert eye ranged over the stack yards, the barley-ricks, the wheat-ricks and hay-ricks, the enormous barns, some over 250 feet in length, the vast 400-acre fields, the flocks with 4000 sheep and lambs in them, and the overwhelming abundance of straw: 'Cattle and horses are bedded up to their eyes. The yards are put close under the shelter of a hill, or are protected by lofty and thick-set trees. Every animal seems comfortably situated; and in the dreariest days of winter these are, perhaps, the happiest scenes in the world.'

They might have been, but they weren't, because amid this astonishing fecundity and richness – it was a painting by Constable made flesh – were scenes of such devastating poverty that Cobbett came away sickened and ashamed. The predictions of Richard Baxter had come true. The men and women who lived and worked in these Arcadian valleys were 'tormented by an accursed system that takes the food from those that raise it, and gives it to those that do nothing that is useful to man.' These valleys would be the most delicious places on earth

> if those, whose labour makes it all, trees, corn, sheep and everything, had but *their fair share* of the produce of that labour. What share they really have of it one cannot exactly say; but I should suppose that every labouring *man* in this valley raises as much food as would suffice for fifty or a hundred persons, fed like himself!
>
> In taking my leave of this beautiful vale, I have to express my deep shame, as an Englishman, at beholding the general *extreme poverty* of those who cause this vale to produce such quantities of food and raiment. This is, I verily believe it, the *worst used labouring people upon the face of the earth.* Dogs and hogs and horses are treated with more civility; and as to food and lodging, how gladly would the labourers change with them! This state of things never can continue many years! By *some means or other* there must be an end to it; and my firm belief is that that end will be dreadful. In the meanwhile I see,

and I see it with pleasure, that the common people know that they are ill used; and that they cordially, most cordially, hate those who ill-treat them.

Cobbett turned to the Bible, using the voice of Amos the prophet to excoriate the landlords who had destroyed the communities which had once occupied these valleys:

> Hear this, O ye that swallow up the needy, even to make the poor of the land to fail . . . that we may buy the poor for silver, and the needy for a pair of shoes . . . Shall not the land tremble for this; and every one mourn that dwelleth therein? . . . saith the Lord God . . . I will turn your feasts into mourning, and all your songs into lamentation.

Norden's idea that community should be based on love had simply disappeared. The parliamentary enclosure movement of the previous century had eroded and in some places removed the last rights of the copyholders to keep their animals on what had been the common grazings. The whole idea of communality evaporated. The great landowners, the Pembrokes included, re-acquired the commons and gradually removed the customary rights on them. The families that had been copyholders became landless farm-workers, dependent on the cash wages paid for their labour. What looked like an equality and even liberty in the market was in fact a form of rightlessness.

The wars with France which persisted throughout the long eighteenth century until 1815 created a falsely inflated market, delaying the recognition of what had happened. After Waterloo, at the end of the Napoleonic wars, the catastrophe struck. Prices fell, rents shrank, poverty became usual, the old families of the chalkland valleys failed and new men entered in their place. Banks called in their loans and landlords their rents. Bankruptcies, seizures, arrests and imprisonments for debt coloured the lives of these villages. Men came to be hired for as little as a week at a time. Many farmers lost everything and even applied for the hand-outs from a social welfare system that had been devised in the sixteenth century and could not cope with anything resembling this. Any suggestion of continuity, of the custom of the manor, of practices observed 'time out of mind' would have been laughed to oblivion. This was the world, for which Arcadia was nothing but a prettiness seen from a drawing-room window, which made Cobbett feel ashamed.

The presence of the free market in labour and land was nothing new. Many deeds from the thirteenth and early fourteenth centuries have survived describing the deals conducted by small landowners in and around Wilton. But the growing sense that the market was king – whether in land or labour – became the crucial transformation in early modern England. In the first earl's survey made in 1566 there were twenty-one copyholders in Wilton itself. By the time of the survey done for Philip Pembroke in 1631–2 there were only five copyholders and twenty-two tenants 'by indenture', holding what were effectively modern leases. By 1831 there were two hugely rich farmers in Wilton, both tenants of the earl. Neither did any farm work himself – too grand – and they relied for their riches on employed labourers. There was not a single man who worked his own land. That tradition and that connection had gone. Instead, Wilton had a population of 113 adult male agricultural labourers, the men whom Richard Baxter had called 'the poor enslaved husbandmen of England', and Cobbett saw as the *worst used labouring people upon the face of the earth.* Almost 500 of such men, rioting in the 1830s against the tithes paid to the Church and the introduction of mechanical threshing machines, against the pauperisation of their lives, were transported to Tasmania, with men from Wylye, Bishopstone, Bower Chalke and Ramsbury among them. Fifteen others were hanged. In those figures, and in that conclusion, one can see the death of a communal idea.

Bibliography

Manuscript Sources

SWINDON AND WILTSHIRE RECORD OFFICE

A1/110 Great Rolls of Wiltshire Quarter Sessions (1631E/151 for the libel sung by Jane Norrice of Stoke Verdon; 1642H/158 and 1646T/179 for marks of the illiterate villagers)

G23/1/40 A list of losses by the citizens of Salisbury December 1644

P2/L/268 William Locke's Inventory 1660

P5/1626/11 Probate inventory re-used to record costs of Parliamentarian soldiers quartered in Fisherton Anger 1645

212B/7181 Final agreement on marriage of Charles Lord Herbert and Lady Mary Villiers 1635

784/1 Parish Register of Odstock, Wilts, 1541–1745

1553/25 1563 Survey of 'Terrae Pembrochianae'

2057/A1/2 Pembroke estate surveys and Wilton domestic accounts, 1630s

2057/F1/2 George Owen, A Catalogue of all the Earls of Pembroke, c.1625

2057/F1/14 Sermon delivered at the funeral of William 3rd earl of Pembroke, 1630

2057/F2/1 Catalogue of the nobilitie of England, 1628

2057/F2/36 Garter Statutes drawn up for 3rd Earl of Pembroke

2057/H1/1a Inigo Jones/John Webb drawings

2057/H5/1 Wilton House Inventory and valuation 1683

2057/P1/49 Plan to accompany sale particulars of Pembroke estates at Bower Chalke, Broad Chalke, Stoke Farthing and Bishopstone, 1919

2292/2 A transcript of a letter about the capture of Marlborough during the Civil War, mid-19th century

SHEFFIELD ARCHIVES

EM1351–1362

Elmhirst Muniments: Executorship and Financial Papers of Sir Robert Pye

Articles of Agrement between the La. Dutchess of Buckingham and the
Earl of Pembroke and Montgomery 1635

HOUSE OF LORDS JOURNAL OFFICE
Main papers
10/14/7/3527 Pembroke dispute with Mowbray July 1641
10/1/23 Summons to York from King Charles to E of Pembroke
May 1642
Note x.B.B. 108 Pembroke's Draft apology July 1641
10/14/9/3616 Assessment of estates Feb 1643
10/1/130 Appointment as Ld Lieutenant Monmouth July 1642
10/1/139 Letter re demands for money Dec 1642
10/1/142 Servants to Oxford Jan 1643
10/1/156 Cutting down trees and killing deer in Hyde Park August 1643

PUBLIC RECORD OFFICE, KEW
SP 14 State papers domestic, James I
SP 16 State papers domestic, Charles I
SP 18 State papers domestic, interregnum
SP 25 Council of State papers

HATFIELD HOUSE
Accounts, general, 12/19
Bills, 247, 670

BRITISH LIBRARY
Sloane MS 4014 Thomas Moffet (or Muffet) illustrated manuscript
volume of spiders and insects
Add MSS 40630 f 234 Wiltshire Committee for Sequestrations
Add MSS 30305 f 76 Letter to Sir Thomas Fairfax re Clubmen
Add MSS 34195 Pembroke's row with Maltravers

PRINTED SOURCES
John Adamson, 'The Baronial Context of the English Civil War',
Transactions of the Royal Historical Society, 5th series, 40 (1990),
93–120
——, 'Parliamentary Management, Men of Business, and the House of

Lords, 1640–49' in Clive Jones, ed., *A Pillar of the Constitution* (London, 1989), 21–50

——, 'Politics and the Nobility in Civil-War England', *Historical Journal*, 34 (1991), 231–55

——, *The Noble Revolt: The Overthrow of Charles I*, Weidenfeld & Nicolson, 2007

Paul Alpers, *What is Pastoral?*, University of Chicago Press, 1996

John Aubrey, *The Natural History of Wiltshire*, Wiltshire Topographical Society, 1847

G.E. Aylmer, *The Struggle for the Constitution*, Blandford Press, 1975

Susan J. Barnes, Nora de Poorter, Oliver Millar and Horst Vey, *Van Dyck: A Complete Catalogue of the Paintings*, Yale UP, 2004

Mavis Batey, *Alexander Pope: The Poet and the Landscape*, Barn Elms Publishing, 1999

Mary Beal, *A Study of Richard Symonds: His Italian Notebooks*, Garland, 1984

Edward Berry, *Shakespeare and the Hunt*, Cambridge UP 2001

Joseph Bettey, *Wiltshire Farming in the Seventeenth Century*, Wiltshire Record Society, 2005

John Bold with John Reeves, *Wilton House & English Palladianism*, HMSO, 1988

John Buchanan-Brown, editor, *John Aubrey: Brief Lives*, Penguin, 2000

Jan Bremmer & Herman Roodenburg, *A Cultural History of Gesture*, Polity Press, 1991

Susan Brigden, *New Worlds, Lost Worlds: The Rule of the Tudors 1485–1603*, Penguin, 2000

Christopher Brown, *Van Dyck*, Phaidon, 1982

Glenn Burgess, *The Politics of the Ancient Constitution: An Introduction to English Political Thought 1603–1642*, Macmillan, 1992

——, *Absolute Monarchy and The Stuart Constitution*, Yale UP, 1996

Mildred Campbell, *The English Yeoman*, Yale UP, 1942

Charles Carlton, *Going to the Wars: The Experience of the British Civil Wars 1638–1651*, Routledge, 1992

Thomas Chaffinge, *The Iust Mans Memoriall*, Nathaniel Baxter, 1630

John Chandler, 'The Country Parson's Flock: Bemerton in 1632', *Sarum Chronicle*, 6, 2006

Edward, earl of Clarendon, *The History of the Rebellion and Civil Wars in England*, in six volumes, edited W. Dunn Macray, Clarendon Press, 1888

——, *His maiesties answer to the propositions presented to him at Hampton Court . . . by the Earle of Pembroke and others*, 1647, (WSRO 2057/F6/4)

D.J.H. Clifford, *The Diaries of Lady Anne Clifford*, Alan Sutton, 1990

M.M. Colvin, 'The South Front of Wilton House', *Architectural Journal*, cxi, 1954

Hadrian Cook and Tom Williamson, editors, *Water Meadows: History, Ecology and Conservation*, Windgather Press, 2007

Julian Cornwall, *Revolt of the Peasantry 1549*, Routledge Kegan Paul, 1977

David Cressy, *England on Edge: Crisis and Revolution 1640–1642*, Oxford UP, 2006

B. H. Cunnington, editor, *Records of the County of Wiltshire, being Extracts from the Quarter Sessions Great Rolls of the Seventeenth Century*, George Simpson, 1932

Richard Cust, *Charles I: A Political Life*, Pearson Longman, 2005

H.E. Davidson, *The Sword in Anglo-Saxon England*, Boydell Press, 1994

Isaac de Caus, *Wilton Garden*, 1650

Katherine Duncan-Jones, *Sir Philip Sidney: Courtier Poet*, Hamish Hamilton, 1991

——, editor, *Shakespeare's Sonnets*, Arden Shakespeare, 1997

——, editor, *The Countess of Pembroke's Arcadia (The Old Arcadia)*, Oxford World's Classics, 1999

Eilert Ekwall, *Concise Oxford Dictionary of English Place-Names*, Clarendon Press, 1960

Amy Louise Erickson, *Women & Property in Early Modern England*, Routledge, 1993

C.H. Firth, *The House of Lords during the Civil War*, Methuen, 1974

Anthony Fletcher, *The Outbreak of the English Civil War*, Edward Arnold, 1981

Susan Foister, *Holbein in England*, Tate Publishing, 2006

Mark Girouard, *Robert Smythson & The Elizabethan Country House*, Yale UP, 1983

——, *The Return to Camelot: Chivalry and the English Gentleman*, Yale UP, 1981

Emilie E.S. Gordenker, *Anthony Van Dyck and the Representation of Dress in Seventeenth-Century Portraiture*, Brepols, 2001

Lieutenant Hammond, 'Relation of a short survey of the Western Counties', *Camden Miscellany*, xvi, Camden 3rd Series, lii, 1936

Margaret P. Hannay, *Philip's Phoenix: Mary Sidney, Countess of Pembroke*, Oxford UP, 1990

Margaret P. Hannay, Noel J. Kinnamon and Michael Brennan, *Domestic Politics and Family Absence*, Ashgate, 2005

John Harris, 'Variable Geometry', *Country Life*, September 15, 1988

Paula Henderson, *The Tudor House and Garden*, Yale UP, 2005

William Herbert & Sir Benjamin Rudyerd, *Poems*, (1660), 2nd edition, London 1817

John Harris, Stephen Orgel and Roy Strong, *The King's Arcadia: Inigo Jones and the Stuart Court*, Arts Council, 1973

Cynthia B. Herrup, *A House in Gross Disorder: Sex, Law and the 2nd earl of Castlehaven*, Oxford UP, 1999

Christopher Hill, *The Century of Revolution 1603–1714*, Thomas Nelson, 1961

Historical Manuscripts Commission, *Reports and Calendars*, several dates

Houses of Parliament, *Petition of parliament to the King, delivered by Lord Pembroke and others; with the King's answer*, 1642, (WSRO 2057/F6/2)

Maurice Howard, *The Early Tudor Country House: Architecture and Politics 1490–1550*, George Philip, 1987

Michael Hunter, *John Aubrey and the Realm of Learning*, Science History Publications, 1975

Ronald Hutton, *Debates in Stuart History*, Palgrave Macmillan, 2004

Susan E. James, *Kateryn Parr: The Making of a Queen*, Ashgate, 1999

W.K. Jordan, *Edward VI: the Young King*, Allen & Unwin, 1968

Eric Kerridge, editor, *Surveys of the Manors of Philip, earl of Pembroke and Montgomery 1631–2*, Wiltshire Archaeological and Natural History Society, 1953

——, 'The Movement of Rent 1540–1640', *Economic History Review*, 2nd Series, VI, 1953

Lisa M. Klein, 'Lady Anne Clifford as Mother and Matriarch', *Journal of Family History*, Vol. 26, No 1, Jan 2001, 18–38

James F. Larkin and Paul L. Hughes, *Stuart Royal Proclamations. Vol. i, Royal Proclamations of King James I 1603–1625*, Clarendon Press, 1973

James F. Larkin, *Stuart Royal Proclamations, Vol ii: Royal Proclamations of King Charles I, 1625–1646*, Clarendon Press, 1983

Agnes Latham, editor, *William Shakespeare: As You Like It*, Methuen, 1975

Anne Laurence, *Women in England 1500–1760: A Social History*, Weidenfeld and Nicolson, 1994

James Lees-Milne, *The Age of Inigo Jones*, Batsford, 1953

Tresham Lever, *The Herberts of Wilton*, John Murray, 1967

C.G. Lewin, 'Housekeeping in Salisbury, 1640', *Sarum Chronicle*, 5, 2005, pp 14–25

Roger Lockyer, *Buckingham*, Longman, 1981

——, *James VI & I*, Longman, 1998

C.E. Long, editor, *Richard Symonds's Diary of the Marches of the Royal Army*, Cambridge UP, 1997

Tony Maclachlan, *The Civil War in Wiltshire*, Rowan Books, 1997

Elizabeth Mazzola, *Favorite Sons: The Politics and Poetics of the Sidney Family*, Palgrave Macmillan, 2003

Oliver Millar, *The Age of Charles I: painting in England 1620–1649*, Tate Gallery, 1972

——, *Van Dyck in England*, National Portrait Gallery, 1982

Walter Montagu, *The Shepherds' Paradise*, The Malone Society, 1997

John Morrill, *Tudor & Stuart Britain*, Oxford UP, 1996

Christopher Morris, editor, *The Journeys of Celia Fiennes*, Cresset Press, 1947

John Nichols, *The Progresses of Queen Elizabeth I*, John Nichols, 1823

J.E. Nightingale, *Memorials of Wilton*, George Simpson, 1906

John Norden, *The Surveiors Dialogue*, 1610

David Norbrook, *Writing the English Republic: Poetry, Rhetoric and Politics, 1627–1660*, Cambridge UP, 1999

——, editor, *The Penguin Book of Renaissance Verse*, Penguin, 1992

——, *Poetry and Politics in the English Renaissance*, Oxford UP, 2002

Michelle O'Callaghan, *The 'shepheards nation': Jacobean Spenserians and Early Stuart Political Culture 1612–1625*, Oxford UP, 2000

Richard Ollard, *Clarendon and his Friends*, Hamish Hamilton, 1987

Stephen Orgel and Roy Strong, *Inigo Jones: The Theatre of the Stuart Court*, 2 vols, University of California Press, 1973

Erwin Panofsky, 'Et in Arcadia ego: Poussin and the Elegaic Tradition', in *Meaning in the Visual Arts*, Doubleday 1955

George Parfitt, *Ben Jonson: The Complete Poems*, Penguin, 1996

Ann Pasternak Slater, editor, *George Herbert: The Complete English Works*, Everyman, 1995

Sidney, earl of Pembroke, *A Catalogue of the Paintings & Drawings in the Collection at Wilton House*, Phaidon, 1968

Anthony Powell, *John Aubrey and his Friends*, Hogarth Press, 1988

J.M. Powell, *Mirrors of the New World: Images and Image-Makers in the Settlement Process*, Dawson, 1977

Michael Powis et al., editors, *Broad Chalke: A History of a South Wiltshire Village its Land and People*, Broad Chalke Millennium Book, 1999

R.E. Pritchard, *Mary and Philip Sidney: The Sidney Psalms*, Carcanet, 1992

R.B. Pugh and Elizabeth Crittall, editors, *Victoria County History, Wiltshire*, Oxford UP, 1956–1965

Oliver Rackham, *The History of the Countryside*, Dent, 1986

——, *Trees & Woodland in the British Landscape*, Dent, 1993

——, *Woodlands*, HarperCollins, 2006

Barbara Ravelhofer, *The Early Stuart Masque: Dance, Costume and Music*, Oxford UP, 2006

Violet A. Rowe, 'The Influence of the Earls of Pembroke on Parliamentary Elections, 1625–1641', *The English Historical Review*, Vol. 50, No. 198, 242–256. Apr. 1935

Conrad Russell, *The Causes of the English Civil War*, Oxford UP, 1990

——, *Parliaments and English Politics 1621–1629*, Oxford UP, 1979

Kevin Sharpe, *The Personal Rule of Charles I*, Yale UP, 1992

Kevin Sharpe and Peter Lake, editors, *Culture and Politics in Early Stuart England*, Macmillan, 1994

Kevin Sharpe, *Remapping Early Modern England: The Culture of Seventeenth-Century Politics*, Cambridge UP, 2000

Geoffrey Shepherd, editor, *Sir Philip Sidney: An Apology for Poetry*, Manchester UP, 1973

Narasingha P. Sil, *William Lord Herbert of Pembroke 1507–1570, Politique and Patriot*, Edwin Mellen Press, 1992

Quentin Skinner, *Liberty before Liberalism*, Cambridge UP, 1998

Paul Slack, editor, *Poverty in Early-Stuart Salisbury*, Wiltshire Record Society, 1975

Kim Sloan, *A New World: England's First View of America*, British Museum Press, 2007

David L. Smith, *Constitutional Royalism and the Search for Settlement, c.1640–1649*, Cambridge UP, 1994

James Smith, *Wilton and its Associations*, Salisbury, 1851

R. Malcolm Smuts, *Culture and Power in England 1585–1685*, Macmillan, 1999

David Starkey, editor, *The English Court from the Wars of the Roses to the Civil War*, Longman, 1987

Lawrence Stone, *The Crisis of the Aristocracy 1558–1641*, Oxford UP, 1967

——, *The Family Sex and Marriage in England 1500–1800*, Weidenfeld and Nicolson, 1977

Roy Strong, *The Elizabethan Image: painting in England 1540–1620*, Tate publications, 1970

——, *The Renaissance Garden in England*, Thames & Hudson, 1998

——, *Henry, Prince of Wales and England's Lost Renaissance*, Thames & Hudson, 1986

Charles R. Straton, editor, *Survey of the Lands of William First Earl of Pembroke*, 2 vols, Roxburghe Club, 1909

Keith Thomas, *Man and the Natural World: Changing attitudes in England 1500–1800*, Allen Lane 1983

Joan Thirsk, *Alternative Agriculture: a history from the Black Death to the present day*, Oxford UP, 1997

Joan Thirsk and J.P. Cooper, *17th-century Economic Documents*, Oxford UP , 1972

Elizabeth McClure Thompson, *The Chamberlain Letters*, John Murray, 1966

Sophie Tomlinson, *Women on Stage in Stuart Drama*, Cambridge UP, 2005

Richard Tuck, *Philosophy and Government 1572–1651*, Cambridge UP, 1993

David Underdown, *Revel, Riot and Rebellion: Popular Politics and Culture in England 1603–1660*, Oxford UP 1985

John Webb, *The Most Notable Antiquity of Great Britain Vulgarly Called Stonehenge*, 1655

N.J. Williams, editor, *Tradesmen in Early-Stuart Wiltshire: A Miscellany*, Wiltshire Archaeological and Natural History Society, 1960

Raymond Williams, *The Country and the City*, Chatto & Windus 1973

George C. Williamson, *Lady Anne Clifford, Countess of Dorset, Pembroke and Montgomery 1590–1676: Her Life Letters and Work*, (1922) S.R. Publishers, 1967

Tom Williamson, *Shaping Medieval Landscapes: Settlement, Society and Environment*, Windgather Press, 2003

Virginia Woolf, 'The Countess of Pembroke's Arcadia' in *The Second Common Reader*, Hogarth Press, 1932

Blair Worden, *The Sound of Virtue: Philip Sidney's* Arcadia *and Elizabethan Politics*, Yale UP, 1996

Giles Worsley, *Classical Architecture in Britain: the Heroic Age*, Yale UP, 1995

——, *Inigo Jones and the European Classicist Tradition*, Yale UP, 2007

Henry Wotton, *Elements of Architecture*, London, 1624

John Wroughton, *An Unhappy Civil War: The Experiences of Ordinary People in Gloucestershire, Somerset and Wiltshire 1642–1646*, Lansdown Press, 1999

Index

Abbot, George, Archbishop of Canterbury, 192, 199

Adelwold, Saint, Bishop of Lindisfarne, 46

Alexander, Sir William, 190

Alfred the Great, King of the West Saxons, 46

Anglesey, Christopher Villiers, 1st Earl of, 193

Anne Boleyn, Queen of Henry VIII, 49

Anne of Denmark, Queen of James I, 111, 210

Antrim, Randal MacDonnell, 1st Earl of, 222

Arcadia: and social order, 1–2; and classical ideals, 3–5; in America, 5–7; as English ideology, 5, 7–9, 17, 101; and conservatism, 27, 36, 177; and lives of the poor, 29; and clearances, 68–9; and customary rights and obligations, 97, 178; Mary Pembroke' commitment to, 100–1; depicted by Philip Sidney, 116–18; and sovereignty of desire, 116–17; and ruling authority, 119–20; death and mortality in, 137; and Shakespeare's *As You Like It*, 145–9, 212; and modernity, 154, 177; and personal freedom, 156, 177; tournaments and masques, 186–9; opposition to James I's court life, 191; poetry, 195; and court, 212; Milton on, 265; destroyed by Civil War, 268; and hierarchy and mutuality, 269–70

aristocracy: role under Elizabeth, 108; relations with Crown, 118–19; and state authority, 120

Arundel, Thomas Howard, 14th Earl of, 182

Ascham, Roger, 55, 106

Astill, Thomas, 249

Athelstan, King of the English, 47

Aubrey, John: on Wiltshire landscape, 10, 89; on Philip Sidney, 11; on Wilton, 12; at Broad Chalke, 15, 48, 86, 88; on Gawen home, 23; describes William Pembroke, 50; on William Pembroke's flight after murder, 53; on William Pembroke's acquisition of Wilton, 58; on Stourton's challenging William Pembroke, 77; on Bishop of Winchester's visit to William Pembroke, 80–1; records stories from great-uncle Anthony Browne, 93; on rural life, 98; on Henry Pembroke's marriage to Mary Sidney, 99; on Henry Pembroke's interest in heraldry, 104; on Clarendon Park, 109; on Philip Pembroke's Wilton, 213; on fire at Wilton, 217

Aubrey, Richard, 15

Bacon, Francis, 190

Bacon, Sir Nicholas, 84

bakers: rules and regulations, 165

Ballard, Anthony, 253

Barford St Martin, Wiltshire, 38–9, 171, 173

Baxter, Richard, 271–2, 274, 276

Baynard's Castle, London, 58, 74, 79, 105, 192, 209, 242

beating the bounds, 43–4

Bedford, Francis Russell, 4th Earl of, 223

beggars *see* vagrants and beggars

Bemerton, Wiltshire, 241, 254

Bennett, Thomas, 258

Bevin, John, 174

Bible, Holy: English version, 125

Bishopstone (manor), Wiltshire, 81

Black Death (1348–9): effects, 33–4

Blome, Richard: *Gentleman's Recreation*, 69

Bodenham, Cecily, 49–50

Boneman, William, 202

Bower Chalke, Wiltshire, 48

Bowlton, William, 160

Breton, Nicholas, 128–9

Bridgewater, John Egerton, 1st Earl of, 201

The Earls of Pembroke in
the Sixteenth and Seventeenth Centuries

Figures in the van Dyck painting of the family at Wilton
are in CAPITALS

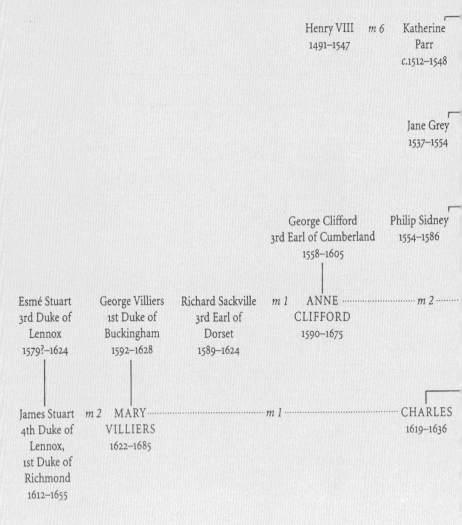

Henry VIII   *m 6*   Katherine
1491–1547   Parr
                  *c.*1512–1548

Jane Grey
1537–1554

George Clifford   Philip Sidney
3rd Earl of Cumberland   1554–1586
1558–1605

Esmé Stuart   George Villiers   Richard Sackville   *m 1*   ANNE ·········· *m 2* ········
3rd Duke of   1st Duke of   3rd Earl of   CLIFFORD
Lennox   Buckingham   Dorset   1590–1675
1579?–1624   1592–1628   1589–1624

James Stuart   *m 2*   MARY ·· *m 1* ································· CHARLES
4th Duke of   VILLIERS   1619–1636
Lennox,   1622–1685
1st Duke of
Richmond
1612–1655